The Obligation Mosaic

Chicago Studies in American Politics

A series edited by Susan Herbst, Lawrence R. Jacobs, Adam J. Berinsky, and Frances Lee; Benjamin I. Page, editor emeritus

Also in the series:

The Obligation Mosaic

Race and Social Norms
in US Political Participation

ALLISON P. ANOLL

THE UNIVERSITY OF CHICAGO PRESS CHICAGO AND LONDON

The University of Chicago Press, Chicago 60637
The University of Chicago Press, Ltd., London
© 2022 by The University of Chicago
Published 2022
Printed in the United States of America

31 30 29 28 27 26 25 24 23 22   1 2 3 4 5

ISBN-13: 978-0-226-81226-7 (cloth)
ISBN-13: 978-0-226-81257-1 (paper)
ISBN-13: 978-0-226-81243-4 (e-book)
DOI: https://doi.org/10.7208/chicago/9780226812434.001.0001

Library of Congress Cataloging-in-Publication Data

Names: Anoll, Allison P., author.
Title: The obligation mosaic : race and social norms in US political participation /
    Allison P. Anoll.
Other titles: Race and social norms in US political participation | Chicago studies in
    American politics.
Description: Chicago ; London : The University of Chicago Press, 2022. | Series:
    Chicago studies in American politics | Includes bibliographical references and index.
Identifiers: LCCN 2021031996 | ISBN 9780226812267 (cloth) | ISBN 9780226812571
    (paperback) | ISBN 9780226812434 (ebook)
Subjects: LCSH: Political participation—United States. | Minorities—Political
    activity—United States. | Social norms—Political aspects—United States. |
    Political participation—Social aspects—United States.
Classification: LCC JK1764 .A527 2022 | DDC 323/.04208900973—dc23
LC record available at https://lccn.loc.gov/2021031996

pates consistently lower political participation among Black Americans and Latinos who, on average, lack resources and higher political involvement among White and Asian Americans who are resource rich.

Yet, across a spectrum of participatory behaviors, this is decidedly not the case. Black Americans regularly overcome barriers to participation, turning out at rates close to or exceeding those of White Americans, while Latinos and Asian Americans often trail behind. The 2012 presidential election of Barack Obama to his second term provides a case in point. The election marked a historic year for Black turnout, with proportionally more of the Black community showing up at the polls than any other racial group in the United States.[1] Two-thirds—or 66%—of Black Americans turned out to elect the next president of the United States, compared to 64% of White Americans, 48% of Latinos, and 47% of Asian Americans (File, 2013). The result was a nearly twenty-point gap between Black and Asian Americans' turnout, the two groups most different from each other in average socioeconomic resources. But rather than the high-resourced group dominating the polls, it was the low-resourced group that showed up, helping usher President Barack Obama into his second term.

An analysis of turnout over time controlling for both socioeconomic resources and naturalization hammers home this point: resources alone do not explain participation levels across racial groups in America.[2] Rather, resources are a consistently weaker predictor of political participation among minority Americans than they are for Whites (Abrajano and Alvarez, 2010; Tam Cho, 1999; Lien et al., 2001; Wong et al., 2011). Figure 1.1 shows predicted turnout in presidential elections between 2000 and 2008 using Current Population Survey data for each racial group and holding constant naturalization status, education, and income.[3] The data demonstrate that regardless of election year, predicted turnout is consistently higher among White and Black Americans than among Latinos and Asian Americans. Furthermore, Black Americans regularly outperform the other groups, while Asian Americans are often the least likely to vote. The result is a gap between these two most different groups that is quite large, ranging from 23% to 28% depending on the year.[4]

Why is it that seemingly underresourced groups sometimes manage to overcome the odds of structural disadvantage to engage in politics, while others, even those with plenty of resources, remain inactive? More specifically, why is it that, for decades, Black Americans have partici-

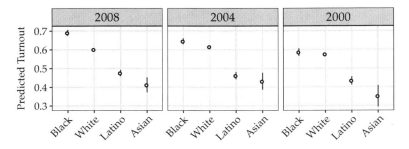

FIGURE 1.1 Predicted likelihood of turning out, controlling for resources

Notes: Turnout estimated for each group separately, controlling for income, education, and nativity status. Plotted point estimates represent predicted probabilities with education set at a high school degree, family income held at $40,000–49,999 a year, and nativity status set at US born. Ninety-five percent confidence intervals are plotted with vertical lines, but because of the large sample, many points are very precisely estimated, and confidence intervals are not visible.

pated in politics at rates far exceeding their resource levels, while Asian Americans have consistently remained the least active racial group despite rapidly rising resources?

Social norms, or the unspoken rules and habits of a group, provide a possible answer. A relatively new literature suggests that norms are a central part of the participatory story (e.g., Gerber, Green, and Larimer, 2008; McClendon, 2014; McKenzie, 2004; Sinclair, 2012). Humans look to each other for cues about how to act—even in the political world—and they seek social rewards from members of their community (Cialdini and Trost, 1998; Tankard and Paluck, 2015). When individuals are embedded in networks that are politically active, they become more involved as well (McKenzie, 2004; Sinclair, 2012), and messages that leverage norms can change political outcomes (Gerber and Rogers, 2009; McClendon, 2014; White, Laird, and Allen, 2014). Across the array of traditional and contentious forms of political behavior, scholars have shown that social information and observation can increase participation, presenting an alternative theory of involvement compared to the resource model.

And yet the current canon on social norms has remained agnostic about how these mechanisms might produce across-group differences in political involvement. Selecting a single group or network and using lab or field experiments to examine the effect of norms-based interventions on individual participatory choices, this scholarship focuses on the *micro mechanisms* of social pressure. This approach reflects the broader psychological tradition that this work takes its inspiration from and where the concepts were first tested experimentally (Asch, 1955; Cialdini and Trost, 1998; Sherif, 1936). But it remains unclear from its findings if social norms can help explain broader group-based variation in political participation like the trends in voting we observe across race.

Can social norms, so central to shaping the participation of individuals, also explain group-level differences in turnout and other forms of political activism? This is the question that brought me to a picnic bench on a community college campus nestled in the hills of the San Francisco Bay Area in spring 2014. I was there talking with Aisha, a first-generation Asian American living in San Francisco, who had agreed to chat with me before her 9:00 a.m. class.[5] Aisha and her family had immigrated to the United States twenty years earlier and settled in California. I asked Aisha how she would describe herself to someone who does not know her—my opening question in many interviews—and she told me a story about her grandfather:

> My grandfather—he's a musician. . . . He plays classical, south Indian music. . . . And he's been trained from his father, so my great-grandfather. It's been in our family for four or five generations. . . . I started learning from [my grandfather], continued here [in the United States] with a couple other teachers and, even when he was in India, my sister and I, we both started learning from him again through the phone. . . . I'm very honored to be part of that, just, you know, live up to my tradition and keep up the tradition in my family.

As I sat for a few hours the next day coding each passage of this interview, I did not think much of Aisha's opening comments. At the time, her discussion of tradition, ancestral lineage, and pride in continuing a family custom seemed to my naive ear devoid of politics, irrelevant in my search for the variables that shaped engagement in the political sphere. But four months later, I interviewed Martin, a man of similar age and education to Aisha who lived across the country in the suburbs of Washington, DC. Martin, who is Black, also talked about the influence of a grandparent on his life and the way it shaped his perspective of the world.

> [My grandmother] is ninety-six years old, so she grew up in an era where she experienced so much hate. . . . She actually was involved in the [civil rights] movement. Actively involved. . . . She marched on Washington, and she did things locally in her community. . . . My grandmother, you know, she was

my light. When I was at the lowest parts of my life I could call my grandmother. . . . I thought about the struggles that she had to go through. And
then I was almost like, how dare me even complain? You know, look what she
had to endure. Could I have made it if I had to endure the things that she did?
I don't know.

I went on to ask Martin whether his grandmother votes, and he responded, "Absolutely. That's not even a question. Absolutely. She votes.
. . . Because there was a time where she couldn't."

Slowly, from these interviews, I began to build a grounded theory of
norm divergence in the United States. Martin, like Aisha, extolled the
virtues of honoring the sacrifices and traditions of those in the past but
the two Americans, embedded in different racial groups and histories,
connected different behaviors to their acts of honoring. Aisha empha-
sized her cultural heritage through music, honoring the past through
continuing to learn and perform traditional South Asian songs; Martin coupled political participation with honoring, giving me a synopsis of
Oprah Winfrey's headline-catching speech on the franchise four years
before the celebrity took the stage with Stacey Abrams. I discovered that
while many Americans told me that honoring their forebears, continuing tradition, and looking to the past were core tenets of their identities and centrally defined their sense of obligation, the behaviors that
followed from these expectations diverged remarkably by race and reflected each group's unique composition, history, and experiences.

In this book, I advance a novel theory of norm divergence in the
United States. I argue that two norms—the honoring ancestors and helping hands norms—appear in cultures across the world and traverse the
boundaries of race in America. However, how one honors the past or
helps those in need is highly context dependent. Experiences in the past
and status in the present shape the content of group-based social norms,
producing variation in the behavioral expressions of compliance. When
these norms are coupled with political participation, as Martin and Winfrey model, they become potent forces of mobilization, helping some
groups overcome resource constraints to engage politically, while others
remain inactive even with resources.

I call this theory of political participation the racialized norms model
(RNM). In a nutshell: social norms about the value and meaning of political participation vary by race due to both racial segregation and distinct group histories. These norms, I find, have enormous consequence

on the landscape of political participation in the present moment, deciding who participates in politics, who stays home, and which groups are able to overcome the inherent costs and barriers of political participation. But the honoring ancestors and helping hands norms also generate pathways for change, providing opportunities to mobilize traditionally marginalized Americans. I show that strong participatory norms in Black communities help members of this group confront an array of barriers in the political arena. If Asian American and Latino elites or community members are similarly able to couple these two norms, already widespread but apolitical in these communities, to political involvement, the rewards would likely be immense.

Defining Key Concepts

Over the course of this book, I engage with three big concepts: *social norms*, *race*, and *political participation*. As a first-order concern, I will determine if social norms related to political participation exist in the United States; then, test whether they diverge by race; and finally, determine if their existence and divergence affects involvement in politics at the individual and group levels. Because of the enormity of these concepts, it is worth spending some time up front establishing what I mean by each, especially given the abundance of scholarship developed over many years on the three topics individually.

What Are Social Norms?

The power of social norms features prominently in a diverse body of literatures ranging from behavioral economics to normative theory (e.g., Durkheim, 2014; Elster, 1989; Foucault, 2012). I gather my insight primarily from social psychology, a subdiscipline that has spent the better part of the past half century defining and studying the influence of norms (Asch, 1955; Cialdini and Trost, 1998). Borrowing from Tankard and Paluck (2015), I define social norms as the unwritten rules and standards that describe typical or desirable behavior within a context or group. Norms are not formalized rules or institutional law; rather, they more closely mirror habits and customs that are consciously or subconsciously adopted. In simpler terms, social norms define—without formally defining—what is typical, acceptable, desirable.

Social psychologists delineate three types of norms, each distinct in the pathway through which they influence action (see Cialdini and Trost 1998 for a review). Social norms that affect individuals by providing information about what others do, devoid of any moral or prescriptive claims, are called *descriptive norms*. These norms motivate behavior simply by providing individuals with information about possible routes of effective or common action (e.g., Goldstein, Cialdini, and Griskevicius, 2008; Perkins, Craig, and Perkins, 2011). *Injunctive norms*, on the other hand, prescribe behavior. They define what is good and moral within the boundaries of a group and influence human action through the promise of social rewards for compliance or sanctions for deviance (e.g., Gerber, Green, and Larimer, 2008; Panagopoulos, 2010). Over time, external injunctive norms are integrated into one's sense of identity and morality. These *personal norms* motivate action by evoking concepts of obligation and eliciting cognitive or affective considerations like guilt, self-esteem, and values (Schwartz, 1977; Thøgersen, 2006).

Reams of evidence demonstrate that collectively, social information, pressure, and self-esteem powerfully shape human behavior. Norms can make people conform to illogical standards (Asch, 1955), engage in behavior they blatantly oppose (Westphal and Bednar, 2005), and even encourage life-threatening choices (Crandall, 1988). But social norms also motivate important prosocial behavior, helping to lubricate social relations and address collective action problems (Cialdini and Trost, 1998; Paluck and Green, 2009). These social needs are nowhere more abundant than in the world of politics, where recent scholarship confirms that norms influence everything from policy positions to political participation (e.g., Chong, 1994; Gerber, Green, and Larimer, 2008; Janus, 2010; McClendon, 2018; White and Laird, 2020). To name just a few persuasive examples, the randomized presentation of descriptive information about turnout changes commitment to voting (Gerber and Rogers, 2009) and the application of social observation can alter the direction and magnitude of campaign giving (Sinclair, 2012; White, Laird, and Allen, 2014).

This robust literature confirms that social norms matter in the political arena, but we can push this literature forward by considering how *groups* undergird the content and enforcement of participatory social norms. Groups are the backdrop of social behavior, the compost in which norms are cultivated (Hogg, 2003; Ellemers, Spears, and Doosje, 2002). Groups delineate the boundaries between people and, in doing so, influence the social information one receives (Larson and Lewis,

2017). They determine the extent to which an individual cares about the acceptance and admiration of those around them (Huddy, 2013). And the cohesiveness of a group shapes levels of observation and the ability to sanction (Oliver, 2010). Groups, then, influence whether an individual will ever confront a particular social norm and whether the stakes will be high enough to induce compliance when they do. My interest is in one particular category of groups that reigns supreme in many American contexts: race.

What Is Race?

Race is arguably the oldest and most consistent cleavage in the American political landscape. Its influence appears in the anatomy of the US Constitution, which identified enslaved Africans as only three-fifths human and denied them representation of any kind. Race is the spark that ignited the nation's only civil war, killing more than half a million Americans but freeing eight times that number. And still today, the government's role in solving issues of racial income inequality, police brutality, and immigration figures prominently in both local and national elections.

Political scientists have long acknowledged this "centrality of race in the study of American politics" (Hutchings and Valentino, 2004, 383), generating decades worth of research on the subject. Much of this scholarship has focused on the racial attitudes of White Americans and the political behaviors that follow. White racial animus is historically quite high in the United States—although it has changed in its expression over time—and affects a wide range of political outcomes (Kinder and Sanders, 1996; Tesler, 2013). Racism has influenced the structure of cities and redistributive policy (Gilens, 2009; Trounstine, 2018), influences candidate choice (Mendelberg, 2001), and continues to be primed on the campaign trail (Banks and Hicks, 2018). The internalization and activation of racial animus among White Americans remain, arguably, the determining factor in presidential politics (Sides, Tesler, and Vavreck, 2018).

But the study of *racism* is distinct from the study of *race*. The former seeks to define, measure, and determine the causes or effects of prejudice against an out-group; the latter seeks to investigate the meaning and origin of racial categories and ascertain the implications of categorization on in-group behavior and attitudes. This conceptual distinction often leads to differences with respect to the populations under study.

Research on racism tends to evaluate the attitudes and behaviors of the dominant, majority group, focusing on White attitudes toward "the other" in the context of the United States. In contrast, scholarship on race has worked to develop across-group theories of attitudes and behavior or focused on the within-group attitudes of racial minorities (e.g., Dawson, 1994; Masuoka and Junn, 2013; Mora, 2014; Smith, 2014a).[6]

Our focus in this book is primarily race, not racism. I am interested in examining how macro forces divide and define social space based on race and infuse group identity with meaning. By race, I refer to a set of phenotypical characteristics that vary across people, have robust historical meaning, and are infused with social consequence within a specific context (Omi and Winant, 2014). In the United States, racial categories reflect a complicated amalgam of historical forces that have divided and defined people with long-lasting consequences on dialect, diet, skin color, status, religion, and resources, to name a few (Sen and Wasow, 2016). These categories are not a product of some natural, stable order but, rather, reflect political power and contestation over time (Haney Lopez, 2006; Prewitt, 2013; Omi and Winant, 2014).

My focus is on the four largest racial groups in the United States: Asian, Black, Latino, and White Americans. In my studies, the race of an individual is based on his or her self-selection into a category, the choice likely reflecting widespread beliefs about the ancestral, phenotypical, and experiential components that comprise race in the United States (Hochschild and Sen, 2018; Omi and Winant, 2014; Prewitt, 2013). This measure of race should be thought of as capturing *group membership*, or inclusion in a group based on arguably objective characteristics (Huddy, 2013), but in the world of race, determining "objective characteristics" is anything but straightforward (Mora, 2014; Prewitt, 2013). The US Census, for instance, currently defines Hispanic/Latino as an ethnicity rather than a race, but mounting evidence suggests members of this group increasingly view the label as a racial category, and statistical analyses almost always mirror this thinking (e.g., Gonzalez-Barrera and Lopez, 2015; Reist, 2013; Rodriguez, 2000; Prewitt, 2013). In my own analyses of survey data, I define four racial categories: single-race non-Hispanic Whites, single-race non-Hispanic Blacks, single-race non-Hispanic Asian Americans, and Latinos who may additionally identify as White, Black, or Asian.[7]

My focus on single-race individuals and the analytical bounding of racial categories for the purposes of statistical tests should not be taken as evidence that race is in fact easily defined, measured, or even truly categorical in nature. Rather, it is of critical importance to note that the boundaries of race are fluid, constantly constructed and redrawn within the context of a society (Omi and Winant, 2014; Davenport, 2020; Prewitt, 2013; Saperstein and Penner, 2012). In the United States, racial categories have changed over time and are regularly contested (Davenport, 2018; Haney Lopez, 2006; Mora, 2014). And widespread consensus suggests that rather than something natural or essential, race is a *social construction*, meaningless outside a specific time and context (Hirschman, 2004; Omi and Winant, 2014; Prewitt, 2013).

In addition to *racial group membership*, I engage with a few other conceptualizations of race throughout this book. The first is racial group identity, or the degree to which an individual has integrated the importance of that group into their sense of self and need for belonging (Huddy, 2013; McClain et al., 2009). An individual may self-select into a group based on his or her understanding of the objective characteristics undergirding that category but not feel closely connected to others in the group or consider that group's expectations very often (McClain et al., 2009; Wong, 2010). This is one element of *racial group embeddedness* that likely affects conformity to norms: if an individual cares deeply about inclusion in a specific group, social information and social rewards will weigh more heavily in their decisions (Hogg, Terry, and White, 1995). I'll call this sense of closeness to other group members *psychological embeddedness.*

In addition to psychological embeddedness, *geographic embeddedness* and *social embeddedness* in one's racial group may affect the absorption and enactment of group-based norms. By geographic embeddedness, I refer to the racial composition of one's immediate physical space—namely, one's neighborhood (Oliver, 2010; Velez and Wong, 2017; Wong, 2010). By social embeddedness, I mean the degree to which an individual's close social ties are primarily coracial (Marsden, 1987; McPherson, Smith-Lovin, and Brashears, 2006). These two concepts of racial group embeddedness capture not what is going on inside an individual's head but rather the broader racial context in which they function. The physical and social arrangement of peoples has been shown to affect perceptions of group cohesion (Enos, 2017), the flow of information (Larson and Lewis, 2017; DeSante and Perry, 2016), and levels of trust and interaction (Oliver, 2010). Together, these factors may contribute to social norms by affecting the clarity of signal one receives about group-based norms as well as the levels of observation and enforcement one faces.

Non-White Americans have been a meaningful component of the nation for as long as it has existed (Takaki, 2008), but understanding their political behaviors and attitudes has arguably never been more important. In 2012, the number of babies born to racial minorities in the United States outnumbered those born to only-White families, reflecting surging immigration, differences in birthrates, and multiracial unions—a first in the nation's history (Tavernise, 2012). This newly minted cohort of non-White Americans is one of many indicators contributing to the projection that the United States will be a majority-minority nation by midcentury, with no single racial group comprising the bulk of the country's population (US Census Bureau, 2012). Some, touting "demography as destiny," cite the growing numbers of non-Whites as inherently leading to increases in political power for traditionally marginalized groups. Almost by definition, comprising a larger part of the population in a majoritarian government should lead to more representation and responsiveness. Yet the political power of American citizens relies importantly on political involvement (Michelson and Monforti, 2018; Ramírez, 2013). To understand whether minority Americans in the coming years will exert increasing power over the political infrastructure requires a look at the determinants of participation for these groups.

What Is Political Participation?

This book will focus on identifying the causes of political participation and sources of its variation, but this endeavor is only worthwhile if participation itself matters for outcomes we care about. If political involvement among citizens has no effect on political representation, policy outcomes, or the production of a peaceful and prosperous society, then understanding why some people participate but not others is of little consequence. Similarly, if inequalities in political participation across politically relevant groups produce no practical difference in the political world compared to the counterfactual of equal participation, then, again, identifying sources of variation is a pursuit of little value. Defining what exactly political participation is, discussing its theoretical connection to democracy, and analyzing the empirical evidence to date about if and when it matters can help determine whether studying it is a worthy undertaking.

In classic theories of democracy, political participation is revered. It is believed to be the bedrock of a representative government, the mechanism through which the people select their rulers and set the agenda. Actions as diverse as rioting, attending parent-teacher association meetings, voting in presidential elections, and boycotting have all managed to find a home under the umbrella term *political participation* in past treatises (e.g., Conway, 2000; Enos, Kaufman, and Sands, 2017; Verba, Schlozman, and Brady, 1995). These behaviors are united under a common banner when they have "the intent or effect of influencing government action" (Verba, Schlozman, and Brady, 1995, 38). While political participation is not always successful at achieving its goals, it does, at its inception, have the ambition of affecting the legal distribution of rights and resources in society (Wolfinger and Rosenstone, 1980). This focus on policy separates political participation from other forms of civic volunteerism or neighborhood involvement.

How exactly does political participation influence government action? The answer depends on the type of political participation under study. Voting influences policy outcomes through the selection of like-minded individuals and by providing reelection incentives that hold officials accountable, in theory (Dahl, 2005; Griffin and Newman, 2005; Mayhew, 1974). But voting alone is not particularly communicative. While policy issues are many and multidimensional, the choice between candidates is often circumscribed. As a result, elected officials must use other means to identify the issues important to their constituents. Nonelectoral political participation provides one dimension of information, communicating top concerns and educating elected officials about policy possibilities (Dahl, 2005; Gillion, 2013; Kingdon, 1984; Verba and Nie, 1987).

In theory, then, political participation is the link between the preferences of the ruled and the policies of the rulers, but many modern social scientists have questioned whether this link works as theorized. Noting the multitude of examples where majority positions do not become the law of the land, the massive influence of the wealthy few, and the instability of citizen policy preferences, some have suggested that the "folk theory of democracy" is rotten at its core (Achen and Bartels, 2017). Most individuals do not have fixed or reliable preferences, this line of scholarship argues (Achen and Bartels, 2017; Converse, 1964; Lenz, 2013), and even when they do, elected officials often do not enact those preferences into law (Bartels, 2016; Gilens, 2005). In this account, inequalities in political participation exist, and the structural mechanisms of responsiveness are built on faulty assumptions: democracy is unresponsive not just to the inactive few but to the majority of citizens who may or may not know what they want anyway.

One response to critics regarding the value of participation is that involvement in political life and self-governance are important for reasons unrelated to policy outcomes. Political participation in and of itself may create better, happier citizens. Early theorists including John Stewart Mill and Jean-Jacques Rousseau argued that democratic political participation can have positive psychological and social consequences, increasing the quality of citizen character, fostering a sense of belonging, and generating regime stability (for reviews, see Delli Carpini and Keeter, 1996; Pateman, 1970). Modern empirical work suggests there is basis in these claims, showing that participating in system-affirming acts like voting and campaigning creates higher levels of external efficacy and feelings of governmental legitimacy (Finkel, 1985, 1987). Furthermore, institutional opportunities for direct and deliberative democracy that engage citizens also change them, increasing political knowledge and cooperation (Delli Carpini, Cook, and Jacobs, 2004; Tolbert and Smith, 2005).

These positive externalities, though, are likely beside the point for the majority of citizens, who look to their government for the fair arbitration of resources, production of high-quality public education, stimulation of economic opportunities, enforcement of justice in the courts, and furbishment of safe neighborhoods. These individuals and the many formal organizations that work to lobby the government, mobilize the public, and organize neighborhoods each year are interested in real outcomes as a result of their efforts. Democratic government demands more than that individuals *feel* like the system is responsive; it demands substantive representation and actual responsiveness.

So when does political participation produce positive, measurable increases in substantive representation, if ever? With respect to voting, a convincing body of work suggests that turnout levels, per se, are not very important. Rather, it is the relative turnout across groups that influences policy outcomes, at least at the state level. Work on redistributive spending and the implementation of welfare policies like Aid to Families with Dependent Children, Temporary Assistance for Needy Families, and the State Children's Health Insurance Program show persuasively that relative turnout between the rich and the poor in the preceding election affected stringency in state-level adoptions of these federal policies

(Avery and Peffley, 2005; Fellowes and Rowe, 2004; Franko, 2013; Hill and Leighley, 1992). Furthermore, class bias in turnout at the state level has lasting effects on income inequality, potentially because an upper-class bias in turnout leads to fewer restrictions on predatory lending and a lower minimum wage (Avery, 2015; Franko, 2013). Hajnal and Trounstine (2005) find that localities with more equitable turnout among racial groups have higher-quality representation for racial minorities. When Latinos and Asian Americans turn out at rates commensurate with their size in urban metropolitan areas, they are more likely to be represented by mayors of their choosing and coracial city council members.[8]

At the federal level, evidence on whether turnout influences representation is more mixed and requires nuance to interpret. Scholars have argued that full voter turnout would likely have only marginal effects on the partisan composition of Congress (Highton and Wolfinger, 2001b; Sides, Schickler, and Citrin, 2008), but within party, elected representatives would likely be more liberal in their platforms and show less ideological alignment with White Americans (Griffin and Newman, 2005, 2007; but see Ellis, Ura, and Ashley-Robinson, 2006). Simulations suggest the incorporation of otherwise disenfranchised individuals, like those with felony convictions, would alter only a few close federal elections, but these alternative outcomes would have multiplicative downstream consequences due to the staying power of incumbency advantage (Manza and Uggen, 2002). Political participation and turnout equality does seem to matter for policy outcomes and substantive representation at the federal level, although imperfectly so.

Setting voting aside, evidence suggests nonelectoral political participation that is either contentious or information-rich influences substantive representation. Examining both the scope and salience of minority political protests, Gillion (2013) shows that activism during the civil rights era affected the voting record of congressional representatives in locations where protests took place, shaped the content of executive orders, and had agenda-setting effects on the Supreme Court. Enos, Kaufman, and Sands (2017) show that the 1992 riots in Los Angeles led to more support for redistributive spending on education. Griffin and Newman (2005) find that individuals who contact senators are more likely to see their ideological preferences reflected in policy outcomes. And Kalla and Broockman (2016) show that campaign contributions increase the likelihood of securing meetings with congresspeople and their senior staff.

Even under conditions of full electoral involvement, policy outcomes would likely still be skewed in the direction of the extremely wealthy and organized lobbies, though (Gilens, 2005; Grossmann, 2012). As a result, some have suggested the only way forward is through systematic revisions to government with respect to campaign finance and distribution of economic resources, actions that begin with the powerful rather than reform initiated by everyday people (Achen and Bartels, 2017; Gilens, 2005; Page and Gilens, 2017). History suggests, though, that power and resources such as these are never freely given; they must be demanded, fought for, and taken.[9] Political participation is a power resource (Avery, 2015; Korpi, 2006; Stephens, 1979), an arrow in the quiver of those historically boxed out of self-governance, and a pathway for change, however imperfect. Studying political participation and examining when and how people overcome the inherent costs of involvement are important for understanding how broader systematic reform might be achieved.

Plan of the Book

My intention for this book is to explain why and show how norms about political participation vary by racial group in the United States today. I begin this task in chapter 2, building a theoretical framework that draws insight from across social science disciplines. Social norms shape the incentive structure for political participation, I argue, but divergent histories and continued racial segregation create variation in the form and strength of these norms. Americans of different racial groups have for centuries experienced their government in distinctly different ways. From citizenship to the franchise, property rights to incarceration, Asian, Black, Latino, and White Americans have engaged with, and continue to experience, remarkably different institutional constraints (Dawson, 1994; Jiménez, 2010; Lerman and Weaver, 2014; Masuoka and Junn, 2013; Takaki, 2008). These separate historical narratives combine with the systematic separation of groups through persistent and widespread racial segregation to form contexts ripe for norm variation (Larson and Lewis, 2017; Lawler, Ridgeway, and Markovsky, 1993; Logan and Stults, 2011; McPherson, Smith-Lovin, and Cook, 2001; White, Laird, and Allen, 2014). I combine these insights to create the RNM, which concludes that norms about the value and meaning of political participation likely vary across racial groups in the United States in ways that matter significantly for engagement.

The RNM has a number of observable implications. If the theory is correct, we should, one, find racial variation—by group membership and embeddedness—in the form and strength of social norms related to political participation. Two, strong participatory social norms should predict political involvement and explain at least some of the observed differences in turnout across groups. Three, social rewards for political participation should vary across racial groups and levels of embeddedness, reflecting the prescriptive rather than purely personal nature of norms. Four, messages that evoke norms should increase participatory commitments among groups familiar with the norms' political connection.

As these implications detail, the RNM anticipates that participatory social norms will vary across racial groups in the United States. But the model does not in itself identify which norms, specifically, are of consequence. I use original qualitative interviews and the method of grounded theory development in chapter 3 to identify norms related to political participation. I focus my inquiry on two groups who share minority status in the US but exhibit remarkably different political behavior: Black and Asian Americans.

Analyzing twenty-three original interviews, I show that two norms—the honoring ancestors and the helping hands norms—relate to political participation. References to these norms emerge ubiquitously across interviews and shape individuals' orientations toward self, their group, and the world. But the behavioral expectations that follow from these norms vary by racial group membership. For many Black Americans, honoring ancestors means claiming political rights once unavailable to the group, and helping those in need includes correcting injustices of racial discrimination and poverty through political action. For Asian Americans, compliance with these same norms is often expressed in apolitical ways. Members of this group are more likely to report that they honor their ancestors through continuing cultural traditions, and helping those in need must be balanced with obligations to family and financial stability. From these observations, I build a generalizable expectation about participatory norms in the United States: Americans of different races share core commitments to help those in need and honor the past, but group-based histories influence the behavioral expression of these norms and their possible connection to politics.

Having identified specific norms that might vary across groups, I turn to designing and validating measures of these norms in representative samples of the nation's four largest racial groups. For this work, I draw extensively from the Participatory Social Norms Survey (PSNS), an original online study I conducted in March 2018. The survey was administered using the platform GfK, which draws respondents from a preconstructed probability sample. The survey was administered to American citizens who were at least eighteen years of age, was fielded in both English and Spanish, and lasted roughly twelve minutes.[10]

The PSNS is a unique data set in three respects. First, the study includes a sizable number of respondents from each of the four largest racial groups in the United States. One thousand White, 1,000 Latino, 1,003 Black, and 1,020 Asian respondents are included. This unique multiracial data set allows for detailed within-group explorations and precise across-group comparisons with respect to the strength and effect of participatory social norms.[11]

Second, the PSNS includes unique batteries of questions designed to measure social norms and racial social context. Using a combination of census block indicators, name-generator questions, and psychological batteries, I develop and deploy three kinds of racial embeddedness measures throughout my analyses. I study the moderating effect of the racial composition of geographic census block, the racial composition of a respondent's close social network, and the strength of racial identity with respect to group closeness. When combined with my unique measures of social norms, these measures provide a novel account of norm variation in the United States within groups, across groups, and at varying levels of racial embeddedness.

Finally, the PSNS includes multiple measures of political participation. It has self-reported voting history in national elections and validated voter history for multiple years. It gauges frequency of participation in local politics and engagement in contentious political activities, including protests. I use these measures to go beyond explaining political participation in salient national elections—the focus of the vast majority of scholarship on political participation to date—to explore how norms shape involvement in higher-cost forms of engagement including political rally attendance and local politics.

In chapter 4, I turn to testing empirically the observable implications of the RNM using the PSNS. I begin with an examination of the honoring ancestors norm. I find that a commitment to honor the sacrifices and struggles of those in the past is widely endorsed in the United States, but the behavioral interpretations of this norm—that is, how one goes about honoring the past—vary systematically by racial community. Expressions of the norm, I argue, are tied to the timing and nature of ancestral arrival in America and the group's location on the racial hierarchy with respect to perceived foreignness. I introduce and validate a novel norms measure that captures the degree to which an individual believes that honoring the past requires political involvement. I show that this measure is distinct from other known political variables including racial linked fate, political interest, and partisanship, and its strength varies not just with racial group membership but also with geographic, social, and psychological group embeddedness. Racial community in the United States shapes the expression of the honoring ancestors norm and its relationship to politics.

In chapter 5, I undertake a parallel investigation but for the helping hands norm, defined as a prescriptive commitment to help those most in need. Again turning to the PSNS, I show that the helping hands norm is widespread in the United States but takes on a variety of behavioral forms including religious, charitable, and political activities. Like honoring ancestors, a politicized interpretation of the helping hands norm varies in its propensity and strength across both racial group membership and embeddedness, but this divergence is muted compared to the previous norm. I develop and validate an index measure that captures the degree to which an individual believes helping those most in need requires political involvement.

In chapters 6 and 7, I shift my attention from examining political attitudes to their effect on political behaviors—namely, involvement in politics. The first behavior under study: turnout in high-salience federal elections like those for Congress or the presidency. Using my novel norms measures, I find that a politicized version of the honoring ancestors norm is strongly related to validated turnout in federal elections. The effect size, which ranges from 17% to 35% depending on the group, outpaces traditional explanations like education, income, racial linked fate, political recruitment, and even political interest. Furthermore, accounting for both the prevalence and predictive capacity of these norms explains the participatory overperformance of Black Americans compared to other racial minorities.

Next, I use two novel survey experiments to demonstrate variation in peer-level social rewards for voting and responsiveness to elite-level priming. In the first experiment, I show that Black Americans evaluate potential neighbors who are regular voters more positively than do either White Americans or Latinos, a finding that is strongest among Black respondents who live in primarily Black neighborhoods. In the second, I show that attempts by elites to prime the honoring ancestors norm—like the comments of Oprah Winfrey in Marietta, Georgia—effectively increase the perceived importance of voting, but only among groups that already connect the norm to politics. Namely, comments like Winfrey's are most likely to increase a commitment to voting among low-propensity Black voters.

Voting in federal elections may be the most common form of political participation in the United States, but as I have discussed, it is not necessarily the most important. Rather, higher-cost forms of participation like involvement in local elections, protesting, and contacting government officials are both more communicative and likely more effective in changing policy outcomes. This is especially true for racial minorities who have less electoral influence in national elections due to both their minority status and de jure and de facto disenfranchisement. In chapter 7, I turn to examining the relationship between participatory social norms and forms of political involvement other than turnout in federal elections. I find that both the honoring ancestors norm and the helping hands norm shape participation in local elections and other, nonvoting forms of involvement. In these contexts, the helping hands norm is often a stronger predictor of political involvement than the honoring ancestors norm, suggesting its unique connection to high-cost participatory acts.

Experimental evidence further shows that social rewards for nonvoting activities like political rally attendance diverge by racial group membership and embeddedness. Minority Americans are more likely than Whites to reward individuals involved in these high-cost, system-challenging behaviors. Further, elite-level priming of participatory norms proves a fruitful avenue for increasing willingness to engage in local political organizations for even traditionally inactive groups.

Surveying my findings, some may be disposed to conclude that "weak norms" cause Asian Americans and Latinos to participate in politics at relatively low rates; this interpretation is incorrect. Participatory social norms are a resource communities can wield to overcome the inherent costs and barriers of engagement, both of which are significantly higher and more prevalent for racial minorities in the United States regardless of income and education levels (Fraga, 2018; Philpot and Walton, 2014; Ramírez, Solano, and Wilcox-Archuleta, 2018). My findings show that in the absence of personal, participatory norms, all minority groups—including Black Americans—would be severely disadvantaged compared to White Americans when it comes to turnout. But exceptionally strong participatory norms in many Black communities that reward engagement allow this group to overcome disadvantage and turn out at a rate roughly equal to that of Whites.

Understanding this distinction—that norms are not a source of minority deficiency but rather a powerful resource that can confront otherwise entrenched inequalities—generates unique insight about how norms might be leveraged to change patterns of political participation in the United States. Policy changes that lower the cost of engagement or attempt to level the resource playing field likely influence turnout rates but are also the product of hard-fought battles that require political participation and mobilization. This catch-22 begs us to consider whether there are alternative methods that organizers and activists can pursue to build their base and confront participatory inequalities.

In chapter 8, I propose that organizers should adopt an asset-based approach that utilizes norms to mobilize racial minorities in the United States. This idea draws on the principles of asset-based community development, which evaluates the resources and skills that communities *do have* to build capacity and power rather than focusing on what communities lack. To date, the vast majority of research on inequalities in political participation focuses on the latter rather than the former, outlining what is missing or identifying barriers to participation in communities of color. In contrast, I suggest that the helping hands norm and the honoring ancestors norm are two resources widely shared in the United States and are especially potent in minority communities. Identifying these latent norms as assets to be activated, organizers should work to explicitly couple these concepts with political participation. Doing so may prove an especially successful tactic for groups traditionally left behind by political elites.

In 1976, President Jimmy Carter famously remarked that the United States is "not a melting pot, but a beautiful mosaic," full of people with "different beliefs, different yearnings, different hopes, different dreams." This book reveals that the nation's mosaic extends also to its participatory social norms. Most Americans share a deep commitment to honor the past and assist those in need, regardless of their race. But whether these obligations translate into political participation depends fundamentally on racial context. Understanding the connection between social norms and race, and the macro forces that influence both, allows us to explain political participation across individuals and groups in new and unexpected ways. It also reveals how the obligations Americans feel to honor the past and care for those in need can be harnessed in the movement for more equitable political participation and representation in America.

CHAPTER TWO

The Racialized Norms Model

W hy do some people participate in politics, while others stay home? What produces group-level trends in participation if not resources alone? I introduce the racialized norms model, a novel theory of political participation that links the micro mechanisms of participation with the macro forces of America's racialized society. The RNM anticipates that social norms matter for involvement in politics but the content and enforcement of these norms varies across racial groups due to both historical social context and present-day racial segregation. The framework allows us to anticipate when and where divergence in norms will emerge and produces a set of testable implications I outline at the conclusion of this chapter and engage with over the remainder of the book.

Calculating Costs and Benefits

A framework developed over fifty years ago provides a starting point for our exploration of why some people participate in politics while others do not. Presented first by Anthony Downs (1957) and Mancur Olson (1965), this framework argues that three variables are central for understanding participatory choices: the costs associated with participating, the possible benefits from involvement, and the (perceived) likelihood one's engagement will affect the outcome (Blais, 2000; Downs, 1957; Olson, 1965; Riker and Ordeshook, 1968). Each of these considerations alone has spurred entire traditions of research (e.g., Blais, 2000; Fraga, 2018; Gomez, Hansford, and Krause, 2007; Haspel and Knotts, 2005; Soss, 2002; Verba, Schlozman, and Brady, 1995), but together, the three

variables produce a puzzle for social scientists studying political participation that they have tried to solve since its inception.

Let's start by considering costs. Engaging in politics takes time and
money, among other resources, all of which disincentivize engagement
in the democratic process. Even voting, a relatively simple and straightforward act, requires large amounts of resolve and planning. An eligible citizen must be properly registered, needs to know an election is taking place, must collect information about the candidates, has to find time
and transportation to travel to the polls, needs to provide a valid photo
identification with a matching address in some states, and often, must
wait in line during a workday to cast a ballot. These resources and information costs add up, especially for busy, distracted Americans with families, jobs, health challenges, and a wealth of alternative leisure activities
on which to spend their time.

But the substantive benefits of political participation—our second bin
of considerations—surely outweigh the costs, an advocate of the democratic process might say. After all, think of everything at stake if one can
influence how the government levies its power: access to clean water, a
qualified police force, public high schools, and the assurance that everything from airplanes to swing sets meet certain standards of safety, just
to name a few. Policy outcomes on these issues, along with the thousands
of others considered by government officials each year, have the ability to dramatically improve—or undermine—the quality of individuals'
lives. Surely, these expansive and impactful potential benefits outweigh
the rather trivial costs of participating, right?

Not so fast, scholars embedded in this framework would say. Instrumental benefits that people wish to achieve when they engage in politics
have a number of properties that mitigate their centrality in the decision
process. First, the achievement of them is uncertain. Competing interests in the public sphere mean that political participation comes with relatively little assurance of return on investment. Even large-scale social
movements that persist over time and involve many organized interests
are usually only partially successful in implementing their goals (Gillion, 2013; Hogan, 2007). Uncertainty about the outcome and the low
likelihood that any individual's unique contribution will be the deciding factor reduces the power of substantive benefits to motivate action
(Downs, 1957; Olson, 1965; Riker and Ordeshook, 1968).

Second, most political goods are *collective* in nature. They require
many people working together to achieve but, once enacted, are widely

THE RACIALIZED NORMS MODEL

shared (Olson, 1965; Salisbury, 1969). The collective nature of the final good means that an individual could, theoretically, achieve all the benefits of government without lifting a finger. If others coordinate, endure the costs of participation, and are successful, even an individual who stays at home watching television while a revolution wages on will still receive the benefits. The collective nature of the final goods, along with uncertainty about outcomes, incentivizes *free riding*: individuals reason that they can achieve all the benefits without any of the costs by letting others do the work.

Together, the element of uncertainty, the low likelihood that one's actions will be decisive, and the collective nature of the final good comprise our third bin of participatory considerations in classic models: the perception that one's political participation will matter. Formalized in scholarship by rational-choice theorists in the mid-twentieth century, this *logic of collective action* and the *calculus of voting* lead to a rather dismal conclusion: political participation is almost always irrational, with the costs outweighing the benefits, and even under the best of circumstances, likely will not occur (Downs, 1957; Olson, 1965; Riker and Ordeshook, 1968).[1] These foundational texts have gone on to become a standard part of the political behavior canon, included in syllabi across the country and incorporated into multiple disciplines. Their proliferation reflects their persuasiveness; the arguments are compelling and logical and challenge social scientists of all stripes to think through the various components of the participatory process instead of just assuming involvement is natural or inevitable as some of the earliest theorists did (de Tocqueville, [1835–40] 2000; Madison, [1787] 2004).

And yet, to optimists—like me[2]—and to practitioners who come to this puzzle with decades of organizing work behind them, the logic of collective action, its assumptions, and the resulting conclusion may seem intuitively incorrect. Or at least incomplete. After all, history is full of moments when activists like James Lawson, Ella Baker, and Delores Huerta joined with countless others to seek a new distribution of power and resources in American society (Hogan, 2007; Keyssar, 2009; McAdam, 1988; Takaki, 2008). These individuals were willing to absorb even huge costs in pursuit of uncertain, collective goods—facing violence, prison time, and financial distress. But these pioneers of justice are not alone. Other Americans, too, regularly absorb smaller costs to engage in collective action. For instance, between 3 and 6 million Americans turned out to participate in the 2017 Women's March (Chenoweth and Pressman, 2017), nearly half the eligible population showed up at the polls in the 2018 midterm election (McDonald, 2018), and 14% of Americans reported donating to a political campaign in 2017 (*The Public, the Political System and American Democracy*, 2018). The logic of collective action suggests that people should never participate in politics—and yet, sometimes, they do.

So what's missing from this classic formulation of political participation? What other factors might encourage people to engage in politics? One answer to these questions is that not all the benefits of political participation come from political outcomes (Chong, 1991; Riker and Ordeshook, 1968; Uhlaner, 1986; Uhlaner, Cain, and Kiewiet, 1989). Rather, a number of benefits can come from engaging in the process itself and may encourage individuals to participate. These benefits do not face the same constraints of uncertainty and collectivism that the instrumental benefits do. Rather than being collective, they are *selective*: individuals get them if and only if they show up (Chong, 1991; Riker and Ordeshook, 1968; Salisbury, 1969). As a result, selective benefits are not weighted against the likelihood that a political goal is achieved and so can more fully offset inherent costs.

I often explain selective versus instrumental benefits to my students like this. In the classic framework, an individual goes to a political rally to achieve a collective good—say, universal health care. This outcome suffers from all the problems we've discussed: it is uncertain, hinges on the participation of many people, is costly, and encourages free riding. But there are other reasons to go to a political rally, above and beyond the instrumental purpose of the event. An individual might want the free T-shirt that is being handed out by the organizers (a material benefit). Or she might go to find new, like-minded friends who are also attending the event (a social benefit). Or the person might attend the rally just to feel good about herself and the democratic process afterward (a psychological benefit). Each of these benefits exists apart from the actual outcome of the rally—that is, whether it is effective at achieving universal health care—and as a result, does not suffer from the free-rider problem.

Accounting for these selective benefits—both intrinsic and extrinsic—fundamentally changes the calculus of engagement. Instrumental, outcome-based benefits begin to matter only so far as they opt people into a pool of possible participants. After that, who shows up depends on the trade-off between inherent costs and selective rewards. When the benefits—social, psychological, material—outweigh the costs, people engage in politics.

The selective benefits approach to solving the collective action problem, as well as the collective action problem itself, fit squarely within a *rational-choice framework*. As part of this theoretical umbrella, people are believed to act as human calculators, identifying their goals, weighing the costs and benefits of each action, and enacting the most effective solution.[3] But there's another way to think about selective benefits that comes from a rich literature in social psychology, not economics. This literature centers on groups, norms, and social processes in explaining the seemingly irrational behavior of human beings. And in doing so, it comes to many of the same conclusions.

The Centrality of the Social

While economists, political scientists, and sociologists in the mid-twentieth century worked to solve the collective action problem, psychologists just across campus were interested in a different—but it turns out, fundamentally related—question: Why do people sometimes do seemingly irrational things, especially when surrounded by peers? In a discipline-changing set of early studies, Solomon Asch (1955) and Leon Festinger (1957), among others, demonstrated that social information and expectations powerfully shape human cognition and behavior. Information from peers can make everyday people ignore clear indications of danger and provide incorrect answers to questions with straightforward solutions (Asch, 1955; Latane and Darley, 1968). Further, this social information is only selectively absorbed: individuals are more likely to model their behaviors on those similar to them in salient ways rather than unlike them (Festinger, 1954). Far from a rational calculator, this scholarship suggested that the human brain is easily—overwhelmingly—influenced by the *need to belong*. Attitudes and behaviors that subsequently follow are founded on this social information, even if false or inefficient.

Much like early studies on the irrationality of collective action established a cottage industry of political behavior scholarship, these foundational works changed the trajectory of psychology. In centering the group in human cognition rather than the individual, a new subdiscipline—

social psychology—was born, and from it, sixty years of scholarship have proliferated (Ross, Lepper, and Ward, 2010). Now, a rich literature across disciplines shows that groups serve as a fundamental organizing principle for the human mind (e.g., Enos, 2017; Hogg, 2003; Kinder and Kam, 2010; Tajfel and Turner, 1986). Even arbitrary and momentary groups can orient behavior and attitudes, but socially salient groups— ones that exist across contexts and over time—are even more central, developing into an individual's sense of self and identity (Ellemers, Spears, and Doosje, 2002; Hogg, 2003; Tajfel and Turner, 1986).

Central to the process of translating the psychology of groups to the behavior of individuals are social norms, or the unwritten rules and habits of a group. These social norms communicate both average and aspirational group behavior. They tell individuals—often subconsciously—how to fit in, act effectively, garner respect, and be good (Cialdini and Trost, 1998; Tankard and Paluck, 2015). In doing so, groups and their social norms solve a more fundamental human cognition problem. The world is wildly complicated with endless sources of information. Using social categories and the norms associated with them can help focus the information that is relevant and useful and, in doing so, render an incredibly complex world more manageable (Dawson, 1994; Hogg, 2003).

Social psychologists generally sort norms into three categories, based on their purposive usefulness to human beings and how they affect behavior (Cialdini and Trost, 1998). First, social norms can provide information about effective action. In a world of uncertainty, people must quickly consume information from their environment and make choices about how to behave. Through observing the behavior of others, people obtain "social proof" regarding effective actions for achieving certain goals and mimic that behavior. These *descriptive norms* capture the average behavior of a group or environment (Aarts and Dijksterhuis, 2003; Cialdini, Reno, and Kallgren, 1990; Gerber and Rogers, 2009). They work as a heuristic for how to behave, especially in situations that are novel, uncertain, or ambiguous (Cialdini and Trost, 1998).

Second, social norms help actors build and maintain relationships. While Maslow's 1943 hierarchy of needs places food and shelter on the bottom two tiers, decades of social psychological research have confirmed the importance (and sheer force) of the desire to belong, a need that often trumps more fundamental resources (Crandall, 1988; Uhlaner, 1986). *Injunctive norms*, the second type of norm, serve to capture this dynamic, illustrating the valued social behaviors of a group. Injunctive norms speak not necessarily to what behaviors *are* practiced, as descriptive norms do, but rather what behaviors *should be* practiced. While descriptive norms function largely off a need to gather information and act upon it, the force of injunctive norms is motivated by the promise of social rewards and sanctions (Cialdini and Trost, 1998). Thus, while actors following descriptive norms will migrate toward the mean behavior of a group, actors adopting injunctive norms migrate toward the behavior of prototypes, or individuals identified as normatively good who represent the group ideal (Morrison and Miller, 2008).

Finally, social norms serve a central role in building and managing self-concept. Norms that are wholly external originally can become *personal norms*, internalized through the development of either morality or identity (Morris et al., 2015; Schwartz, 1977; Thøgersen, 2006). Identities, derived largely from external feedback regarding worth and social categorization, help individuals to both understand their relevant categories of comparison and anticipate the actions and reactions of others (Tajfel and Turner, 1986). Once an identity is established, people engage in actions and embrace attitudes that conform to that identity in an attempt to decrease self-concept distress (Hogg, 2003; Tajfel and Turner, 1986). Thus actions that were once guided by external norms—and the promise of either social rewards or sanctions—become internally motivated. These personal norms function as a kind of internalized panopticon, guided by the desire to avoid cognitive dissonance and guilt or affirm one's sense of self. Scholars have shown that these personal norms are powerful predictors of other-regarding behaviors (Thøgersen, 2006).

The influence of all three types of social norms on human behavior has been demonstrated in contexts as varied as amusement parks, elementary schools, hotel rooms, libraries, and sororities, to name a few (Aarts and Dijksterhuis, 2003; Cialdini, Reno, and Kallgren, 1990; Crandall, 1988; Goldstein, Cialdini, and Griskevicius, 2008; Westphal and Bednar, 2005). Within these contexts, researchers have shown how behaviors spread through social networks and that norms-based interventions can change behavior in prosocial directions (Crandall, 1988; Larson and Lewis, 2017; Paluck and Green, 2009; Perkins, Craig, and Perkins, 2011). Messages aimed at updating information about average behavior, changing prototypical references, or adding social observation are all proven methods for influencing outcomes (Tankard and Paluck, 2015).

This influence also extends to political outcomes. In recent years, a persuasive set of studies has shown that social information and social pressure alter a wide range of political behaviors. This includes turnout, vote choice, and even more costly forms of political involvement (e.g., Bond et al., 2012; McClendon, 2014; McKenzie, 2004; Sinclair, 2012; White, Laird, and Allen, 2014; White and Laird, 2020). Through novel field and lab experiments as well as observational work, we have learned that messages threatening neighborly observation increase turnout significantly more than alternatives (Gerber, Green, and Larimer, 2008), that political giving to campaigns and candidates is a function of peer networks (Sinclair, 2012), and that providing opportunities to publicize participation increases involvement in even contentious political activities (McClendon, 2014). In each of these situations, individuals face costs for participating—sometimes even relatively high costs—but expanding the opportunities for social rewards or levying the threat of social sanctions changes the calculus of political involvement and can increase participation.

Here is where the literature on social psychology connects—I think quite beautifully—with a rational-choice framework of political behavior. The collective action problem and its proposed solutions suggest that selective incentives encourage engagement in politics; work from social psychology tells us the need to belong powerfully shapes behavior. Together, these two literatures teach us that social and psychological benefits in particular may be a potent part of the participatory process. Yes, political participation is costly, and yes, governmental outcomes are often uncertain, but the anticipation of social and psychological rewards in the form of acceptance, respect, or self-concept management that come through the process of participating may overwhelm these costs and uncertainties. Social information, standards, and expectations are central parts of human behavior and must be considered when evaluating why people do anything, including participate in politics.

Building a Theory of Groups

This is usually where the story ends. Benefits from participating that exist outside the actual substantive outcome of politics help to motivate political action, solving the participatory paradoxes put forward by Downs and Olson. Social benefits—or the promise of social sanctions—prove especially powerful for this. Scholars have demonstrated time and again that the application of social pressure and observation can increase engagement in politics. We have from these two traditions a strong understanding of why *individuals* engage in politics.

But what about *groups*? How do we explain variation across politically relevant cleavages in American society—like the ones we observe with respect to race—using this framework? So far, we can't. Reflecting the psychological tradition it pulls from, work on social norms and political participation has focused primarily on testing the *micro mechanisms* of political participation. That is, scholars concentrate on a specific group and setting where they assume political participation is socially valued and then use a lab or field experiment to isolate how pressure, information, or observation change what individuals do politically within that setting.

If we want to explain across-group variation, though, we will need more than this. We need to determine whether the participatory factors we have identified as so influential for political participation vary in their presence, effect, or form across types of people. We need a theory of groups that goes beyond assuming people seek acceptance from them to one that anticipates how macro forces might systematically shape the content and enforcement of participatory social norms across them.

For this, we turn to two new literatures, one in sociology on racial segregation and a second on the history of race in America, that show how institutional constraints and experiences vary by racial group. Both of these literatures identify characteristics of American society that divide and define peoples. Racial segregation creates geographic, social, and psychological space between members of different groups, allowing for norms to develop and be enforced dissimilarly. Distinct histories infuse membership with meaning, producing divergence in the content of group-based social norms. In joining these two literatures with that we already know about the micro mechanisms of social pressure, we are able to build a theory of norm divergence in the United States that explains both individual and group-based patterns.

Racial Segregation

For most of the nation's history, and still today, individuals of different racial groups occupy remarkably separate social spaces (Jargowsky, 1996; Logan, 2011; Massey and Denton, 1993). Racial groups in the United States, on average, live in separate neighborhoods, attend different schools, consume different media, and form close ties with those who primarily share their own race (Dougherty, 2003; Logan and Stults, 2011; McPherson, Smith-Lovin, and Cook, 2001; Reardon, Yun, and McNulty Eitle, 2000). Despite the work of activists over decades to deconstruct the legacies of residential and institutional segregation, these patterns persist. Empirical work has shown that racial minorities and White Americans typically live in neighborhoods that are disproportionately coracial and attend schools that are even more segregated (Logan, Stowell, and Oakley, 2002; Reardon and Owens, 2017). Recent influxes in immigration among Latinos and Asian Americans have led to a resurgence in ethnic enclaves. And White Americans make up even smaller proportions of minority neighborhoods than they did just twenty years ago (Logan, 2011; Logan and Stults, 2011).

This segregation in American macrostructures—defined as the physical and institutional arenas that exist over multiple iterations of people (Lawler, Ridgeway, and Markovsky, 1993)—fosters social separation between individuals of different races. Macrostructures often provide the reasons for individuals to interact, giving them opportunities to come into contact with one another and form relationships (Lawler, Ridgeway, and Markovsky, 1993). If schools, neighborhoods, houses of worship, and other macrostructural institutions are disproportionately coracial, then so too will be the smaller, more intimate set of social ties that develop within them. For instance, Americans continue to have friends who are primarily the same race as themselves and are married to individuals who share their race (Lofquist et al., 2012; Marsden, 1987; McPherson, Smith-Lovin, and Cook, 2001). Even with increases in interracial marriage and interracial childbearing (Davenport, 2018; Tavernise, 2012; US Census Bureau, 2012), roughly 90% of Americans are married to same-race partners (Lofquist et al., 2012).

This racial segregation that exists, on average, in the United States today is not an inevitable arrangement of peoples but a reflection of political forces. Hundreds of years of American policy making have created racial categories as we understand them today. Through laws governing the flow of human bodies into the nation and restrictions on intermarriage, miscegenation, and citizenship, economic, legal, and social policy have produced macrostructures in the United States that sort and constrain individuals on otherwise apolitical traits (Katznelson, 2006; Haney Lopez, 2006; Massey and Denton, 1993; Omi and Winant, 2014; Trounstine, 2018). In a hypothetical world with a different political past, the social and geographic arrangement of peoples would be remarkably different.

But in the nation as it exists today, Americans are sorted by racial group, and many people experience relatively high levels of embeddedness into these groups. This reality has implications for the development and enforcement of social norms. Others have shown that when social or geographic space is dense with in-group members, information is more accessible, trust tends to be higher, and observation is easier (DeSante and Perry, 2016; Larson and Lewis, 2017; Oliver, 2010). These are factors that collectively increase norm signals and the ability to dole out social rewards and sanctions for behavior (White and Laird, 2020). Segregation, too, magnifies the perception of differences between in- and out-group members and may increase the perceived impermeability of group boundaries (Enos, 2017; Tajfel and Turner, 1986). Under these circumstances, the stakes for acceptance by the group and the need to coordinate with other members increases precipitously. High levels of racial segregation, then, likely lead to increased norm-enforcement and compliance.

But segregation may also affect the *content* of group-based social norms, not just their strength and enforcement. Segregation, by definition, denotes that physical and/or social space exists between individuals of different groups. This space provides the opportunity for unique norms to emerge. Social norms develop in response to repeated interactions between individuals (Bicchieri, 2016; Meeussen, Delvaux, and Phalet, 2014), and these interactions are patterned by macrostructural forces (Lawler, Ridgeway, and Markovsky, 1993). By separating individuals of different groups, the encounters that lead to norms are also divided and will, over time, produce norm divergence.

Social separation, then, is a prerequisite for unique group-based norms to develop, but it is in and of itself an insufficient condition. Rather, for norms to develop differently across groups, incentives, constraints, and experiences *must also* diverge. These aspects of a group shape the content of norms, defining both what is normal and what is prescribed. Segregation provides the space for norms to develop and be enforced differently, but distinctiveness in group histories defines what exactly the norms are that form in this space.

Distinct Group Histories

To even a naive observer of American history, it should be obvious that individuals of different races have faced distinct historical constraints and opportunities. From means of arrival to access to resources to share of political power, race has served as a fundamental dividing line in not just American politics but in American life (Dawson, 1994; Hutchings and Valentino, 2004; Takaki, 2008). To name just a few examples: American wealth—distributed with extreme inequalities—was built through the exploitation of non-White Americans over the course of centuries (Takaki, 2008). Exclusion from New Deal policies that created a middle-class (White) America meant Black Americans were denied the ability to unionize, buy homes, and attend universities (Katznelson, 2006). Drug policies designed in the 1970s and 1980s continue to have far-reaching implications for Black and Brown communities (Alexander, 2012; Burch, 2013). And restrictive immigration laws that denied entry to almost all people living in Asian countries for more than a century have meant that the majority of Asian Americans in the United States today are relative newcomers (Masuoka and Junn, 2013).

Life in America is shaped profoundly by racial group membership, but possibly nowhere is this truer than in groups' relationship to their government. Government has been a primary force in deciding which groups get what and controlling the boundaries between peoples (Lopez, Passel, and Rohal, 2015; Trounstine, 2018). Government has withheld fundamental democratic rights from certain groups, provided clear economic advantages to others, and applied punitive powers unequally (Alexander, 2012; Katznelson, 2006; Keyssar, 2009; Lerman and Weaver, 2014; Takaki, 2008; Waters and Kasinitz, 2015). But a group's relationship to government is not only about what its members are denied; it is also about what they receive, from whom they receive it, and how policy outcomes are achieved (Bobo and Gilliam, 1990; Dawson, 1994; Gillion, 2013; Griffin and Keane, 2006). On each of these dimensions, racial groups also vary. Due to group size, resources, and unrestricted access to the franchise, some are able to achieve policy outcomes simply by engaging in the electoral process; others must turn to contentious political action in the form of protest to achieve social change (Fraga, 2018; Gilens, 2005). Furthermore, some racial groups have long and storied histories with political parties and organizations, while others are systematically overlooked in traditional mobilizing efforts (Dawson, 1994; Ramírez, Solano, and Wilcox-Archuleta, 2018; White, Laird, and Allen, 2014; Wong, 2008).

These patterns of lived experience, shaped by legal constraints and animated by people's responses, make up the historical context of a group. It is this context that infuses membership with meaning. An individual's identity—the central building block of self in relationship to others (Tajfel and Turner, 1986)—is given content through the habits and values of a group that are built over time in response to environmental constraints and opportunities. Across the globe, all humans wear clothing, but what is fashionable depends on the group's climate and culture. Everyone eats, but cuisine varies widely by region. While segregation may provide the possibility for group norms to develop differently, groups must face unique opportunities and constraints, defined by their history, to observe norm variation.

An Inclusive Theory of Political Participation

We can join together what we've learned about the many elements of political participation—both the micro and macro—to generate a new theory and set of expectations about how social norms may affect the behavior not just of individuals but also of groups. The inherent costs involved in the participatory process inhibit engagement in politics, but selective rewards in the form of social and psychological incentives can counter these costs. The amount of social and psychological incentives available to individuals is shaped by the normative expectations of their groups. If groups are both socially separated from each other and have experienced distinct constraints and opportunities historically, then the content of social norms related to political participation is likely to vary. As a result, so too is the distribution of social and psychological rewards available for political participation, creating group-based patterns in engagement above and beyond those produced by costs alone.

Let us return momentarily to the four big participatory factors laid out by previous research we have discussed so far. The *benefits* available to groups who are able to influence the political process are widespread, but we know that Americans of different racial groups face variation in the *costs* they must overcome to engage in politics (Verba, Schlozman, and Brady, 1995). This includes the structural costs imposed or alleviated by political elites (Philpot and Walton, 2014; Ramírez, Solano, and Wilcox-Archuleta, 2018; Rosenstone and Hansen, 1993). We also know groups experience variation in the *probability that their engagement will matter* and their perception of this estimate (Bobo and Gilliam, 1990; Butler and Broockman, 2011; Fraga, 2018). Experiences with government can decrease political efficacy among certain groups (Lerman and Weaver, 2014; Soss, 2002) and their minority status means non-White Americans in many places are inherently at a disadvantage in the policy-making process (Fraga, 2018). We have also learned that social and psychological *selective incentives* that flow from social norms can help individuals overcome the inherent costs and uncertainty of the participatory process (Gerber, Green, and Larimer, 2008; McClendon, 2014; Salisbury, 1969).

To this robust literature, we now add a final piece: racial segregation and distinct group histories that constrain and create opportunity likely produce variation in the social and psychological incentives members of different groups face to participate. As a result, not only should costs and the perception that engagement matters shape outcomes across groups but so too should variation in participatory social norms and their enforcement. I call this theory of political participation the racialized norms model. It joins insight on the micro foundations of human behavior with the macrostructural components of American society to understand the forces that shape American political participation. Figure 2.1 presents its core elements visually.

Beginning from the left of the figure, we see that two macrostructural forces are at work. The first, historical group context, infuses membership with meaning and as we have learned, diverges based on racial group membership in ways likely relevant to participatory social norms. Distinct norms that may develop because of divergent histories are further reified by continued racial segregation—our second macrostructural consideration. Segregation by racial group provides space for norms to develop differently, increases the importance of group acceptance, and affects the ability of group members to sanction each other. As a result,

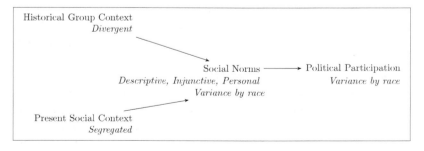

FIGURE 2.1 The racialized norms model

geographic, social, or psychological embeddedness in a group—rather than just group membership—will shape the degree to which an individual confronts and adopts group-based norms.

This brings us to the second stage of the model. Macro forces of segregation and distinct group histories should affect all three types of social norms: descriptive, injunctive, and personal. In shaping the general habits and behaviors of a group, historical social context influences descriptive norms about the prevalence of participation within one's community. Racial embeddedness at the level of neighborhood, intimate social ties, or psychological group closeness should affect how easily individuals observe these behaviors and use them as cues for effective action. Historical context will also shape the normative prototypes of a group and the corresponding valued behaviors. Living in segregated social environments aids in the spread and enforcement of these injunctive norms, driven primarily by the threat of group-based social rewards and sanctions. Finally, over time external norms are internalized into personal norms—the core moral values that guide behavior and attitudes (Thøgersen, 2006). These norms affect individuals through the desire to avoid self-concept distress and are stronger when developed in a context with clear injunctive norms about what is morally right, good, and expected (Cialdini and Trost, 1998).

In the first and second stages of our model, segregated and divergent macrostructures lead to variation in norms about political participation. These norms should be thought of as encompassing the attitudes of individuals about the value and meaning of political participation and their willingness to sanction or reward others for engagement. In the third stage, we see how these norms affect participatory outcomes—namely, the choice to engage in politics. Individuals with strong personal norms about political participation should be most likely to engage. These personal norms—along with injunctive and descriptive norms—are expected to vary in their propensity across racial groups. Rather than just observing individual-level variation in participation, we should also observe group-level variation. And because racial segregation increases the intensity of these signals, we would expect these effects to be the strongest among individuals who are surrounded by coracial group members at the geographic and social levels or have a close psychological connection with their group.

This broad theoretical framework produces a number of testable implications. First, historical differences in lived experiences should produce variation in the form and/or strength of social norms related to political participation. That is, groups should exhibit variation in both the norms they connect to political participation and the relative strength of those norms. These norms should vary both by racial group membership and by racial group embeddedness.

Second, political participation should be most likely to occur among those individuals who have internalized norms valuing political participation. Extant work shows that these integrated social norms are often the strongest predictors of behavior in prosocial settings (Thøgersen, 2006), but the propensity to internalize these norms should vary by group. Because of this variation in the strength of personal norms, and because of their importance in predicting political behavior, accounting for norms in models of political participation should reduce variation in involvement across groups.

The RNM further anticipates racial variation in the social and psychological pressures individuals confront to participate. But the ability of these pressures to influence observed behavior depends critically on other elements of the equation as well—namely, costs. Structural barriers to participating in the form of resource constraints and inequities in mobilization also vary systematically by group (Philpot and Walton, 2014; Ramírez, Solano, and Wilcox-Archuleta, 2018; Verba, Schlozman, and Brady, 1995). To have a positive outcome, the selective benefits of participating—those social and psychological rewards for involvement in the process itself that we care so much about—must surmount the inherent costs. Because costs vary by group, the level of social benefits required to encourage participation among members is also variable. Groups with lower costs and smaller structural barriers require fewer selective benefits to reach a participatory outcome. In contrast, groups for whom participation is more costly—due to either lower resources or higher structural barriers—will require more selective benefits to reach the same outcome.

Third, group-based interpretations of the value and meaning of political participation will affect not just personal norms but also injunctive norms. This should be observable in the level of social rewards and sanctions groups dole out to those engaged in politics. Because we expect norms to vary by both racial group membership and racial embeddedness, we can expect to observe variation in the social rewards for political participation at the group level and by community context.

Finally, social norms about the value and meaning of political participation should be able to be primed in ways that affect participatory attitudes and behaviors. Exposure to a cue that brings the social expectations of one's community to the fore should influence the degree to which an individual says participation is important, plans to engage, and commits to involvement. However, the effect of these priming cues should also be variable. Priming a norm that is not prevalent in one's community should produce little to no attitude and behavior changes. Furthermore, priming a norm among those who have already internalized their community's norms should have little effect on intention to engage. Rather, priming social norms about the value and meaning of political participation will be most likely to affect individuals who both occupy communities where the norm is prevalent and have not internalized the norm themselves. In these cases, external considerations, like cues from elites, rather than internal ones, can drive behavior.

Combining the macrostructures of American life with the micro mechanisms of human behavior leads us to anticipate variation in social norms with respect to participation by racial group membership and racial group embeddedness with far-reaching consequences for who shows up in the political sphere. But what exactly are these norms that matter for political participation? And how do they vary across racial groups in the United States? We turn to answering these questions next.

Which Norms?

The combination of divergent group histories and continued racial segregation suggests that norms about political participation likely vary across racial groups in the United States. This is the first testable implication of the racialized norms model, one on which the remaining claims hinge. Still for us to determine, though, is *which* social norms matter for political participation and how we expect them to vary.

How should we go about identifying these norms? One option is to look at previous scholarship, but there, surprisingly, we find a void. Extant work on the social norms of political participation has focused on *civic duty*, or a sense of obligation to the state (e.g., Blais, 2000). This appears first in a piece by Riker and Ordeshook (1968), who introduce the *D term* into the calculus of voting. This variable captures the psychological incentives to participate ranging from "the satisfaction from compliance with the ethic of voting" to "affirming one's allegiance to the political system" (8). Work inspired from this original instantiation has continued to imagine participatory social norms as primarily encompassing a sense of duty to the political system (Blais, 2000; Blais and Achen, 2019) or has simply asserted the existence of a civic duty norm when leveraging social sanctions (e.g., Gerber, Green, and Larimer, 2008). As a result, the existing taxonomy of social norms related to political participation is quite limited.

But we face another challenge in relying on extant scholarship: it is based almost entirely on White people. Much like the political behavior canon more broadly (García Bedolla, 2019), this work asserts generalizable conclusions based on mostly White samples that either control for or drop racial minorities out of the analyses entirely (Masuoka and Junn, 2013). If we base our hypotheses about which norms matter for participation on this work, we build in the assumption that the same things that matter to White people matter to all people. The components of the racialized norms model—along with other work in race, ethnicity, and politics—suggest this is at best a false assumption and at worst a dangerous one (Barreto and Segura, 2009; García Bedolla, 2019; Masuoka and Junn, 2013).

And so if extant literature provides little guidance on which social norms matter for political participation or intuition about how they vary across groups, where might we look instead?

I turn to the thoughts and insights of everyday people. A rich literature in sociology, race, ethnicity, politics, and political theory has, for some time, argued that centering the voice of nonacademics can generate new theory that is grounded in a lived reality rather than the ivory tower (Ackerly et al., 2018; Glaser and Strauss, 1967; Harris-Lacewell, 2010; Walsh, 2008). This approach to theory development is inductive in nature—it builds generalizations by examining specific cases rather than testing assertions in gathered data (Charmaz, 2014). As a result, grounded theory development is ideal for our purposes, letting us skirt a number of extant issues. We can investigate norms among non-White groups and generate new theory about how these norms vary without being limited to the concept of civic duty previously dominating the field. Following this inductive approach, we can later return to deductive scholarship, testing whether our generalizations materialize in large-scale empirical data.

To build a grounded theory of participatory social norms, I use original interviews with twenty-three Black and Asian Americans living in metropolitan areas across the United States. My interviews were designed to unearth—rather than to test for—social norms related to political participation. I asked respondents to tell me about the guiding principles of their lives, their role models, the impetus for their choices in career and leisure activities, and their relationship to their communities. Through these interviews, I generate ideas about the norms perceived to shape Americans' lives and when, if ever, these norms connect to political participation. I then use a two-step coding process to analyze these interviews, looking for patterns and insights that might generalize (Charmaz, 2014).

My results suggest that two social norms in particular shape attitudes about the value and meaning of political participation across racial groups in the United States. The first, the *honoring ancestors norm*, captures a prescriptive commitment to honor the sacrifices, struggles, stories, and traditions of those in the past, especially ancestral community members who paved the way for opportunities in the present. The second, the *helping hands norm*, embodies the notion that people should take care of others who are most in need. These two norms centrally orient the life choices and beliefs of Black and Asian Americans alike but vary in their connection to political participation. Reflecting group histories and resource realities, Black Americans often tie these norms to political involvement, suggesting that the way one honors the past is through claiming the political rights once denied to the group and that the best way to help people in need includes grassroots political change. Asian Americans, in contrast, argue for the fulfillment of these norms through continuing cultural traditions, seeking economic stability, and helping others around them through direct service. Neither group's behavioral interpretations of core social values are normatively better or worse, but they are different. And if the implications of the racialized norms model are correct, these differences may have far-reaching implications not just for political attitudes but also for political behavior.

The Method of Grounded Theory

Although encompassing a rich history in other fields, grounded theory development is relatively uncommon in political behavior research. This is likely due to a number of factors: the causal revolution in the social sciences, the spread of survey sampling techniques, and an epistemological emphasis on generalizability (Coleman, 1986; García Bedolla, 2019; Mahoney, 2006). But grounded theory is a rigorous methodology with the ability to produce novel insights in previously understudied areas (Charmaz, 2014). As a result, some of the most influential books in the social sciences—books that have gone on to produce cottage industries of empirical work—are based in qualitative methodologies (e.g., Bonilla-Silva, 2017; Cramer, 2016; Waters, 1990).

Because of its rarity, however, the method of grounded theory may require some introduction. Grounded theory involves taking an inductive, iterative approach to knowledge development based on qualitative interviews or ethnographic data (Charmaz, 2014). The value of grounded theory lies in its reliance on the voice of everyday people to generate ideas about how the world works (Michener, 2018). During the process of collecting data, the researcher uses a method of coding to apply analytical categories to each segment of text. Over the course of the data collection process, the analyst refines these categories and pulls generalizable concepts from the data set that can then either stand alone or be used as hypotheses for further empirical work. Because the data collection and analyses are done concurrently in grounded theory development, interview protocols are flexible, with questions posed in later interviews responding to earlier data collection findings (Charmaz, 2014).

I apply this methodology to twenty-three original interviews conducted between May 2014 and December 2017. My interview subjects are US citizens at least eighteen years of age who identify as either Black or Asian American and speak fluent English. My choice to interview members of these two racial groups is based in both theoretical and practical reasons. Practically, qualitative interviewing is time intensive,[1] and from the start of the project, I knew my research would involve not just qualitative interviews but large-N empirical data as well. Excellent examples of fully qualitative treatises abound (e.g., Bonilla-Silva, 2017; Jiménez, 2010; Waters, 1990), but my interest in understanding how norm variation connects to national turnout trends and patterns of political participation meant that eventually my work would return to survey data.

Furthermore, my focus for the qualitative portion of the project was to identify norms that might matter for political participation in the United States and vary across groups. This meant that over the course of my interviews, I had to be able to observe norm differences that I could later use to develop survey measures and experiments. Small differences, even if present, might be difficult to identify with the relatively few interviews I planned to complete. So I selected the two groups for which I expected to observe the largest degree of variation: Black and Asian Americans. Examining these two groups holds constant the minority status of the population but exploits a dimension of difference I care deeply about: the propensity to engage. Previous scholarship has shown repeatedly that Black Americans often participate at relatively high rates both in the aggregate and when controlling for socioeconomic resources, while Asian American turnout is significantly lower despite the group's on-average high level of resources (File and Crissey, 2012; Fraga, 2018; Uhlaner, Cain, and Kiewiet, 1989). Examining these two groups, I hoped, would help me identify norms that varied across American racial groups more generally.

My search for research participants took place in three areas of the country: the San Francisco Bay Area; the Washington, DC, metropolitan area; and Nashville, Tennessee. I recruited participants through a combination of referrals and direct requests. About half the interviews were generated by asking people in my network to refer me to people they knew—whom I did not—who fit the criteria. This included my acquaintances' colleagues, friends, classmates, and fraternity brothers, all of whom were at least two degrees of social separation away from me. The other half came from leveraging random interactions with strangers in my daily life. I recruited one participant from a recreational boxing class, another after a Craigslist exchange, and a third from the post office. My selection of locations was again based on both practical and theoretical reasons. In designing my protocol, I worried that completing interviews in regions where I could only be for short periods of time would mean I had to target elites or contact individuals through preexisting community organizations. By interviewing in regions where I lived, worked, or had family, my recruitment of participants could meander, leveraging random interactions or snowballing through contacts.

At the end of the process, I had completed fifteen interviews with Black Americans and eight with Asian Americans. The vast majority of these took place in person in public libraries, individuals' workplaces, conference rooms, and coffee shops, but three were conducted over the phone. At first glance, these numbers may seem relatively small and difficult to generalize from. Indeed, if I were writing a full-length book on simply these cases, careful scholars of qualitative methodology would likely be concerned. The methodological standard of the field is to interview to the point of "saturation," or where the same principles are repeated over and over across interviews. For some of the best qualitative books in the social sciences, this often involves between fifty and one hundred interviews (see Bonilla-Silva, 2017; Jiménez, 2010; Waters, 1990), but research suggests the actual saturation points are actually much lower, estimated at around thirteen interviews (Guest, Bunce, and Johnson, 2006). Furthermore, scholarship like mine that uses qualitative interviews simply to generate hypotheses—rather than as the end of the line of inquiry—often settles on much fewer cases (e.g., Carter, 2019).

My small number of interviews, though, means this exploration should not be thought of as a statistical sample in any sense of the concept. In fact, my respondents are generally better educated but younger than the average American, likely reflecting the social spaces where they were recruited.[2] What these interviews do give us, though, is depth. People are complicated, wonderfully so, and talking with them can reveal a lot about the cross-pressures they face on a daily basis, how they experience the world, and the knotted mixtures of motivations that drive behavior. Having sorted through all these complexities, we can turn to generating novel theories, ideas, and hypotheses for testing in nationally representative samples. So have patience, young grasshopper; we'll get to tests of generalizability and statistical significance in chapters 4–7.

Grounded theory is based on inductive principles—one begins with observations and draws generalizable principles from there rather than the other way around—but as the previous chapter suggests, I was already working within a theoretical framework. I knew I cared about norms and I had read quite a lot by the start of these interviews about how they develop and are enforced, measured, and observed. And I expected these norms to vary across groups. My interview protocol and subsequent analyses were informed, then, by these social psychological principles and hypotheses. But induction still played a role in my theorizing. I entered the study without extant hypotheses about *which* norms mattered, *how* they varied, or *what* the social contexts were that shaped their divergence.

My initial protocol was designed to ask questions about people, feelings, and beliefs that likely influenced behavior either through social rewards (injunctive norms) or by invoking cognitive dissonance (personal norms). I began each interview with questions that were explicitly apolitical, asking respondents about sources of pride, concepts of success, characteristics of role models, and requirements of group membership. My hope was that these questions would reveal information about the social expectations of groups and whether any of these expectations was tied to political participation. Importantly, I did not want to begin with questions about political participation and see how people defended their choice to be active or not but rather to examine core normative concepts and see whether any of these brought respondents *to* politics. I was interested in both what was connected to political participation and what was not, with absence being as telling as presence. My protocol was flexible and changed over time. Responses to early interviews shaped the questions I asked in later interviews as patterns emerged pointing to the types of norms I should be paying attention to.[3]

After my first few interviews—three in a row with young Asian American women in the Bay Area—I thought I was not getting anything. These women's lives were fascinating, and our conversations revealed rich insights about gender roles, parental expectations, immigration, and work ethics, but there was no talk of political participation. It was not usually until the end of the interviews when I finally—desperately—prompted them, that I got some basic information of their political histories and views. At the time, I could not figure out what to do with this information, and I started to doubt the process. Were my questions too vague? I wondered. Was my approach of focusing on apolitical topics in hopes of uncovering, rather than leading to, participatory social norms the wrong one? The initial set of seventy-four codes, derived by hand-categorizing these three interviews passage by passage, included everything from "sons vs. daughters" to "home country" to "hobbies."

It was not until I began coupling these interviews with responses from Black Americans that the clear parallels and political ramifications started to emerge. Respondents across racial groups cared fundamentally about the same things: they loved their families, respected the sacrifices of those in the past, sought economic security, wished to help others, and desired a life of meaning. However, when placed in the context of bigger, structural features that shaped these groups' histories, opportunities, and experiences, the behaviors attached to these motivations were often distinct. How one honored the past depended, fundamentally, on what had happened in the past; helping those in need was shaped greatly by who was imagined as needy.

From the total eighty-two codes I applied in the full coding of early interviews, an emergent theory developed: groups shared a number of core, fundamental norms, but their interpretation—the behavioral ramifications—varied. With this central concept in mind, both I and a graduate research assistant returned to the data, independently coding the transcripts again, now with a radically reduced seventeen codes in use. Through this process, I identified two social norms with broad ramifications for political participation in the United States: the *honoring ancestors* and *helping hands* norms. Both Black and Asian Americans discussed the importance—socially and personally—of honoring the past and helping others, but only Black Americans connected these concepts to political participation. Work in psychology and anthropology suggests values like these may be universal, transcending place and peoples (Graham et al., 2013; Hefner, 1991; Schwartz, 1992; Steadman, Palmer, and Tilley, 1996), but I find that the interpretations, social expectations, and behavioral habits that derive from these beliefs—that is, the social norms of groups—are heavily dependent on context. Specifically, honoring the past and helping others have group-specific schemas that matter for who shows up and turns out in the political sphere.

The Honoring Ancestors Norm

The importance of honoring the past came up repeatedly in my conversations with Black and Asian Americans, but who ancestors were and what was required in the process of honoring them varied significantly. I found that a basic, widely shared value to recognize and respect the stories, struggles, and traditions of those in the past took on group-specific meaning, responding to history and group membership. Black Americans often saw honoring the past as requiring the claiming of civil and political rights their ancestors had fought for over the course of generations. Asian Americans, on the other hand, were more likely to connect the honoring ancestors norm to cultural activities and financial success, grounded in ancestors of other nations and those who had immigrated seeking the American dream. Despite both groups showing strong normative commitments to honoring the past—naming this value continually as a guiding principle in their lives—the meaning of "honor your ancestors" was heavily community dependent; who ancestors are matters for how groups honor them.

Ancestors and the importance of honoring the past seemed to be an ever-present topic on the minds of individuals I talked with. Asked about how they spent their leisure time, respondents mentioned ancestors; asked about how they got their name, respondents mentioned ancestors; asked about their careers, respondents mentioned ancestors. Black and Asian Americans alike talked about "being mindful of where your people come from," feeling a duty "to a whole heritage," "living up to my traditions," and feeling "a connection to the land" of their ancestors. References to the past and to ancestors came in two forms: familial and imagined (Anderson, 2006). Mentions of "my grandmother" were as common as "my people," sewn together into a single concept of those in the past who sacrificed, paved the way, and built traditions.

However, each group's historical context shaped how Black and Asian Americans envisioned their ancestors and the corresponding behaviors that were required for the process of honoring. As a result, a single, shared value about "honoring the past" took on group-specific interpretations, informed by the group's historical experiences and narrative of the past. Specifically, Black Americans, a group with roots connecting back to the very founding of the nation, often argued that honoring the past required claiming the rights—political, educational, and economic—their ancestors had fought for over the course of centuries. Asian Americans, on the other hand, a group for whom the majority of members are either first- or second-generation immigrants, were more likely to connect the honoring ancestors norm to cultural activities and financial success, drawing from the traditions of other nations and the hopes of their immigrant forebears.

Honoring Ancestors among Black Americans

Black Americans almost always located their ancestors in the United States and discussed the legacy of mass disenfranchisement and oppression of their group. Today, the vast majority of Black Americans in the United States have family ties reaching back to the era of slavery and Jim Crow.[4] These periods of harsh oppression subjected most group members to violence, poverty, and second-class citizenship. Reflecting this history, respondents discussed the "segregated South" their parents and grandparents grew up in and the "bias that goes back four hundred years that we are always gonna be deemed second class or not even citizens." Regularly, Black respondents explicitly connected their ancestors to those "from the middle passage and slavery," explaining, "We were never, ever meant or intended to be citizens."

But the Black people I talked with also discussed how their ancestors—familial and imagined—fought for incorporation into democratic citizenship. Black Americans saw their ancestors as struggling against mass oppression over the course of centuries in search of the franchise and other civil and political rights. Mentions of this history came up in topics as varied as career choices, fashion, the origin of respondents' names, holiday dinner table stories, and the memory of grandparents. Black respondents regularly mentioned specific civil rights leaders when explaining their own behaviors and choices ("The other pair are Malcolm X glasses. . . . I get a lot of compliments on them";[5] "Why the law? . . . I remember Martin Luther King") and reified those who were involved in the civil rights struggle. For instance, Martin talked extensively about his grandmother, whom he calls "his light." A thirty-two-year-old police officer who moonlights as a Methodist minister, Martin explains, "[My grandmother] had the courage to stand up against injustice . . . in a time where you could have lost your life."[6] DeMarkus elaborates, "You have a people here who, their whole purpose for the whole time has been fighting just to be recognized as humans. Before that we weren't even three-fifths human."

This concept of ancestors as people who struggled for political and civil rights influenced group norms about the appropriate ways to honor the past. Referencing both their own intrinsic motivations and the social expectations of their peers, Black Americans talked about political participation, specifically voting, and taking advantage of educational opportunities as central ways to honor their ancestors' stories and sacrifices. Three remarkably similar statements about voting made by Black Americans living in different parts of the country exemplify this:

> But I get out and vote because it's the thing to do. Because I had people who fought for me to be able to vote, and I'm gonna exercise my rights.—Alexus, Nashville, TN

> It disheartens me when I hear that people say, "Oh, I just didn't have time to go out and vote." I'm like, what do you mean? We went through so much just to get that right. Why would you not exercise it?—Martin, Washington, DC, metropolitan area

> I think also, especially for me, being a Black woman, I think [voting] is so important, and I think it's important in many groups, like women and people of color who have been denied voting rights in the past. . . . There's so many people who have fought for this right and who actually, at some point, didn't have this right.—Tisha, San Francisco Bay Area

Alexus, Martin, and Tisha all cite historical group exclusion and the struggle for enfranchisement as their primary impetus for voting. For many Black Americans, the duty they felt to vote was deeply connected with a concept of honoring the past. Their predecessors, both familial and in the broader sense of the group, had fought and died for the franchise. To not vote would be to disrespect the efforts of those brave men and women whose sacrifices expanded the franchise; it would be to show irreverence to a history of oppression and struggle.

Both psychological orientations (personal norms) and social expectations (injunctive norms) motivated Black respondents to vote as a way to honor the past. Martin, for instance, discusses his decision to vote in

2008 for Barak Obama as motivated by his grandmother, a woman who had actively participated in the civil rights movement: "I can honestly say I thought that I owed it to my grandmother to have her see her dream before she died." Martin goes on to explain, "You better not dare say anything to any older person that's over fifty years old and say I'm not voting. . . . You would get thrown out. You might get beat down. [Laughs.] Because so many people were moved that night when they announced that [Barack Obama] had won. It was seeing the outcome of things that had been prophesied in the Bible. It was the Negro spiritual songs that were sung many years, 'We Shall Overcome.'" In his comments, Martin highlights the social consequences of not appropriately honoring the legacy of the civil rights struggle as a Black American. He says that any person alive before the passage of the 1965 Voting Rights Act would "[get you] thrown out" for not voting.

Social norms theory suggests that external expectations like these are, over time, incorporated into a person's sense of morality (Cialdini and Trost, 1998; Hogg, 2003; Mori, Chaiken, and Pliner, 1987). Socialization over a lifetime, including repeated exposure to group concepts of what is good and right, become personal norms (Thøgersen, 2006). Unlike injunctive norms that are motivated by the expectation of external, social benefits, these personal norms motivate behavior through a desire to avoid self-concept distress. Monica provides an example of how personal norms can shape behavior as she tells me about the one time she was unable to vote—the result of a bureaucratic snafu rather than a lack of effort: "I remember one year I didn't vote. I had moved, and I guess I didn't change my address [in time]. . . . I was literally close to tears when they said I couldn't vote because, I mean . . . I always [vote]."

Monica is not just a regular voter; she is a committed, passionate voter. She goes on to explain that her commitment to voting—her sense of "civic duty"—is based on the fact that voting is a right that many have lived without. She cites South African apartheid, saying, "I always think about after apartheid fell, and you would see those photographs, pictures of the lines of people in South Africa who, for the first time, could vote."

Both Monica and Martin identify value intrinsic to the process of voting as their reason for turning out. They vote not because they wish to influence the outcome of an election but rather because the act of voting honors a community of the past. Many Black Americans I talked with were suspicious of the American political system and felt voting was unlikely to produce high-quality representation for their community. The instrumental benefits at stake in any given election was not what brought them to the polls. Rather, they voted because they wished to honor the sacrifices and struggles of their ancestors. Tisha, for instance, explains, "I'm a pessimist by nature, so there was a part of me that was like, oh, voting doesn't change anything," but she votes because "people of color . . . have been denied voting rights in the past" and "there's so many people who have fought for this right." Alexus similarly tells me, "Everybody knows politics is not voting. It's already predesigned, prepicked," but also, "I get out and vote because . . . I had people who fought for me to be able to vote." Despite concerns about the effectiveness of voting and the responsiveness of the political system, the intrinsic value of honoring ancestral struggles propelled some Black Americans to the polls.

In addition to voting, Black Americans often connected educational opportunities to the honoring ancestors norm. Those in the past had been excluded from and fought for not just political rights but also access to a broader array of civic opportunities including the right to an education. As a result, honoring the past through fully embracing the rights and opportunities withheld from predecessors sometimes included a discussion of education. Black respondents often mentioned being the first member in their family to graduate from high school or college and discussed pursing education and economic opportunities as part of the way to honor their ancestors' struggles. One respondent told me, "There was a time where black people could be killed for reading." Another revealed the following: "I think back upon the many lives that were lost for people, African Americans who tried to go and read and write, and were killed, were lynched just because they tried to get an education. And how dare me not think about that, take that into consideration. And now I have the opportunities that someone died for. . . . So I have a duty. Not just to me, but to a whole heritage, a whole race of people."

Thus, for Black Americans, the honoring ancestors norm took on a very specific flavor. Informed by the group's history, Black Americans often saw honoring the past as requiring the claiming of political rights through voting and civil rights by seeking out educational opportunities. These acts were prescriptively valued and socially rewarded. A duty to the state did not guide engagement in politics, nor did the possibility of instrumental rewards in the form of electoral outcomes. Rather, the value of voting for many was tied tightly to the goal of honoring the past and remembering the sacrifices and struggles of ancestors. To vote was to make good on a community-based social norm.

Honoring Ancestors among Asian Americans

Asian Americans were just as likely to talk about their ancestors in interviews, but their stories about the past and what they meant for their lives were different from those of Black Americans. Asian Americans have a history in the United States that dates back centuries; they helped build the transcontinental railroads, participated in the California gold rush, and were quarantined during the Second World War (Takaki, 2008). However, the vast majority of Asian Americans I talked with were either first- or second-generation citizens. Their nativity reflects demographic realities key to understanding the Asian American population in the United States today. The passage of the 1965 Immigration and Nationality Act served to dramatically revitalize and increase the number of Asian immigrants to the United States (Masuoka and Junn, 2013; Zong and Batalova, 2016). As a result, nearly 90% of Asian adults in the United States are either first- or second-generation citizens (see appendix C, table C.2).

The parents and grandparents of the Asian Americans I talked with had immigrated to the United States from nations as diverse as China, India, the Philippines, and Japan, sometimes with intermediary stops in other nations.[7] However, respondents were nearly unified in their discussions of immigration as a key defining feature in their lives. One respondent told me, "A story about myself is inevitably a story about my parents because I am a child of immigrants"; another said, "Immigration made my life possible. . . . To my parents I do owe a debt of gratitude, and I just really try to honor them in every way that I can."

With shorter histories in the United States, Asian Americans often looked to their families' ethnic country of origin when explaining their ancestors' stories and discussed the sacrifices their parents and grandparents had made to give them opportunities available in the United States. As a result, Asian Americans often spoke of honoring the past by continuing cultural activities including learning musical instruments, serving certain foods around holidays, and observing marital practices tied to their ancestors' home country. Samaira explains that learning classical South Asian music was a way "to have a much deeper connection to our home country." In continuing this heritage, she sees herself carrying on a "really rich musical tradition." Other respondents similarly discussed participating in ethnicity-based pageants as a way to remember their ancestors' legacy and the importance of language. Jonathan describes relearning Chinese in college after having lost much of the language as a child. "It was an act of reclamation," he says.

Aisha may best demonstrate the important personal and injunctive components of the honoring ancestors norm as tied to cultural practices and traditions. A twenty-five-year-old college graduate whose family immigrated to the Bay Area from India, Aisha chose to participate in an arranged marriage, which she believed was an important way to honor the traditions and culture of her family. She tells me, "I went through the whole arranged marriage process and that's a huge deal in our community. Arranged marriages have been in India for generations. . . . I'm not trying to brag or anything—but I've heard people say . . . 'People are so proud of what you did—going with what your parent said, going with the arranged marriage.'" Here, Aisha cites the very social nature of her choice—honoring her family's heritage of arranged marriages—brings her respect and social rewards in her community. Aisha compares this with a friend of hers who went against the wishes of her family to pursue a partnership outside the tradition of arranged marriages: "She ended up marrying a guy she fell in love with. Her parents were not very happy— you know, her mom is definitely not happy. . . . [Marrying someone outside the caste] messes up your community circle. . . . I'm sure she's happy and all, but you know there's some things that she can't participate in."

Aisha highlights the social exclusion that can come from choosing a path outside of the cultural traditions of her community. Like many Asian Americans I talked with, Aisha highlights the way she altered the tradition slightly by asking her parents to delay the process until she finished college. Asian Americans often balanced the cultural demands of honoring their ancestors with their desire for autonomy and American identity. But even with this balancing act, the importance of honoring ancestors through continuing cultural practices featured prominently.

Asian Americans also linked the honoring ancestors norm to financial success, citing their parents' and grandparents' sacrifices to immigrate to a country with economic and educational opportunities. Jonathan, an Ivy League graduate pursuing a medical degree, tells me, "[My parents] were top of their class back in China, and they came here for more opportunities, at least economic opportunities." Samaira's parents immigrated from India. She similarly explains, "The majority of South Asians immigrated to the US after the Immigration Act of 1965, in which period Americans really needed skilled labor. . . . And in order to be one of the really successful doctors for whom the gates to this country were thrown open, you had to be the very best. . . . Every single one of us had valedictorian parents. . . . And every single one of us is trying to live up to them." This concept of economic success as tied to honoring the sacrifices of ancestors came up repeatedly in discussions of goals and sources of pride. "Being successful," one respondent told me, "means being able to earn an income to support yourself and your family."

Unlike Black respondents, though, Asian Americans did not connect the honoring ancestors norm to political participation. For Black Americans, politics often came up organically with references to the struggle for the franchise, a common theme across interviews. For Asian Americans, this connection was almost never made. Despite the fact that Asian Americans have a rich history of both labor and political struggles in the United States (Takaki, 2008), most Asian respondents did not feel connected to this community or narrative. At the end of one of my final interviews, I asked an Asian American woman explicitly about this. She had spent much of the interview talking about the honoring ancestors norm, among other things. I asked her if she thought honoring her ancestors could ever require involvement in politics. She replied, "I don't think that my ancestors, particularly my grandparents and parents, would have thought of me being a very politically active person as something that they wanted for me. Only because I think that they think of political activism as a response to struggle. And so I think that they would think that my political activism means that I have something to be politically active about, which means that I've struggled against something, which means that they haven't done their job."

The interview data suggest that group-specific interpretations of honoring ancestors may matter greatly for variation in political participation across groups. Shaped seemingly by the historical factors of immigration and integration into the American narrative, the honoring ancestors norm may require different actions for compliance based on group membership. Both Black and Asian Americans I talked with cared deeply about honoring the sacrifices and struggles of those who came before them, but how they went about doing so was shaped by the constraints and narratives of their groups.

TABLE 3.1 **Behaviors tied to honoring ancestors**

	Black Americans	Asian Americans
Economic	✓	✓
Political	✓	
Cultural		✓

Table 3.1 summarizes variation in the behaviors tied to the honoring ancestors norm for each group. On average, Black and Asian Americans both tied educational and economic opportunities to the honoring ancestors norm. Both groups saw their predecessors as making sacrifices on these dimensions, providing present-day group members with these opportunities through their efforts. Whether one's community of the past was made up of recent immigrants from other nations or people fighting for equal rights in a country opposed to them, the sacrifices of ancestors often brought respondents to a prescriptive commitment to excel and care for their families economically. Systematically, I saw that both Asian and Black Americans were likely to cite the honoring ancestors norm as demanding that they pursue economic stability for their families, often through educational attainment.

Black and Asian Americans diverged, however, in connecting cultural and political behaviors to the norm. For Black Americans, honoring the past required claiming the political rights, especially the franchise, that the group's ancestors fought for. For Asian Americans, honoring the past required continuing the cultural traditions of their ancestors.[8] In both cases, respondents felt both psychological and social pressures to conform to these norms. But only in the case of Black Americans did the honoring ancestors norm lead to valuing, rewarding, and engaging in political participation.

The Helping Hands Norm

The second concept that appeared repeatedly in interviews but diverged in form and strength between the two groups was the helping hands norm. The helping hands norm encompasses the prescriptive commitment to help others, especially those in need. Black and Asian Americans alike discussed helping others as a central component of good citizenship and community membership, but the behaviors each group attached to the norm, and the norm's relative strength or priority, were different. Specifically, Black Americans were more likely to believe that helping those in need required coordinated political action and policy change. Asian Americans, on the other hand, were more likely to cite direct service and charitable activity. Furthermore, while Black Americans often located the helping hands norm as a central part of their sense of self and community, Asian Americans are more likely to restrain the helping norm, sometimes seeing it in conflict with components of the honoring ancestors norm. Speculating from the interview data, I argue this divergence may be the product of group orientations toward upward mobility and the extent of structural barriers to economic stability.

What does it mean to be a good citizen? Be a good community member? Black and Asian Americans alike almost always discussed the importance of taking care of people in need and helping around the community when asked such questions. A good citizen and community member looks outward, is conscious of his or her surroundings, and works to improve them. A good citizen lends a helping hand to those who need one. Referencing the helping hands norm, respondents told me about the value of "helping others who are less fortunate than you," choosing their careers because it was "a way to somehow get involved in improving life for people" and because treating others well was "the one rule I try to follow the most." Wrapping this concept in normative principles, they often told me that helping others was a deep source of pride for themselves and their families, and they saw success as tied to their ability to give back to their community.

However, the interpretation of the norm—and also, in this case, its relative strength—was dependent on group membership. In particular, Black Americans were more likely to couple political involvement and grassroots policy change with the helping hands norm, while Asian Americans more regularly discussed direct service. These differences appeared to be grounded in the groups' own experiences with economic struggles, discrimination, and perceptions about what was required to live a flourishing life. Furthermore, Black Americans often elevated the helping hands norm to a priority, even entangling it with the honoring ancestors norm. Asian Americans, on the other hand, sometimes saw the helping hands norm in conflict with the more important honoring ancestors norm and, as a result, placed caveats on its implementation.

Helping the Needy among Black Americans

The Black Americans I talked with often discussed taking care of those in need as a way to attain respect from others as well as a core organizing principle for their choices. When asked what it means to be successful, a number of Black respondents told me success includes "making a difference," "giving back to my community and where I came from," and "what you do for people." Helping others, especially those in need, was often what respondents were most proud of about themselves and what they believed others valued about them. For instance, Tisha explained, "I think [my parents] are really proud that I stuck to what I was passionate about, which is serving others."

When asked how exactly they take care of others or what the best ways to help people in need are, Black Americans regularly turned to community-based participation and policy change. Drawing from their own experiences and concerns over the group's struggles, Black Americans believed that helping others required engaging in the political sphere, especially at the local level. Doreen, Monica, and Tisha, three Black women I interviewed, provide examples:

> My life has been about service. I've worked for the state, I've worked for a youth organization that helped kids whose parents were incarcerated, I've served Hurricane Katrina evacuees. . . . I've seen that direct service level piece. . . . And we still have the same problems. So not to take anything away from those endeavors and people in the community who have nonprofits that do those things, but I'm realizing more and more that in order to impact change, it needs to happen on the policy level. And if it's gonna happen on the policy level, I need to have a seat at the table to change it. . . . I want to have a say. I want to speak for those people, 'cause I've lived it.—Doreen, Nashville, TN

> I want to change policy. . . . I can fight on the ground level all day, and I'm fine with doing that. I'm fine with helping everyday people. But then I also recognize how important actually changing the policies and the legislation in this country is. And so I think right now that's kind of where I'm leaning, is into going into policy and advocacy.—Tisha, San Francisco Bay Area

> I think to be a good citizen, we want you to be gainfully employed so that you can pay taxes. Which is how we take care of people who don't have. . . . I

realize so much more clearly now that [paying taxes] is the way that we care
for not just those who are in need, but that's how we have roads, and that's
why we have bridges, and we have all the things that we need. . . . I just
thank God that I can pay taxes, because that's how we take care of [people].
—Monica, Washington, DC, metropolitan area

These three women, spread across the country, connected the helping
hands norm not necessarily to voting but to more costly activism, including running for office, working on campaigns, and paying taxes. These
respondents, among others, often commented on the value of not just
governmental reform but also community-based reform. Many Black respondents stated that governmental intervention is problematic when its
solutions are not rooted in the community or designed by people with
relevant experience. They advocated for more grassroots approaches to
policy change that "start at home."

When explaining why helping others requires political participation, respondents often reached for both their own experiences and their
group's experiences with structural disadvantage and discrimination.
Tisha, for instance, talks about her family's and friends' negative interactions with the legal system when she was young and her own time in
foster care. Pointing to these experiences, and explaining how a combination of race and class seemed to undermine fair outcomes, Tisha explains, "As I got older . . . I started participating in a lot of advocacy for
foster youth and just learning that kids do have rights, and you're actually supposed to meet with your attorney . . . and just feeling like wow, I
got [cheated], so how many other kids are out here getting [cheated] with
crappy lawyers? And it's like, this isn't right."

Tisha's comments reflect important empirical and historical realities
about Black Americans' experiences in the United States. While the Voting Rights Act and the Civil Rights Act opened a world of economic and
political opportunity once prohibited to Black Americans, they did nothing to compensate those same citizens for centuries of barriers to economic prosperity. Many have argued that, as a result, barriers to home
ownership and exclusion from welfare opportunities that preceded these
monumental pieces of legislation continue to haunt the economic stability of Black Americans today (e.g., Katznelson, 2006). Furthermore,
Black Americans continue to face systematic barriers to employment and
are disproportionately affected by punitive carceral state policies (Alexander, 2012; Pager, 2003; Pager and Shepherd, 2008; Western, 2006).[9]

In the face of these challenges, many Black respondents took a multi-dimensional approach to helping people in need, citing not just political participation but also charitable and religious action. For instance, Royce discusses a mission trip he took and how "doing physical labor . . . felt like I was actually changing people's lives." Martin regularly cites the Bible when discussing helping others. "We need to get away from feeling like we're the victims of something," he tells me, and "by going back to the church, through teaching and preaching, I think that we can do that. We can change the mindset of a people."[10] As a result, there may be more diversity in the Black public's approach to the helping hands norm than there is in the honoring ancestors norm.

Helping the Needy among Asian Americans

Asian Americans also talked about helping others as a core component of community membership, but in a prioritized list of how they should spend their time, Asian Americans sometimes limited the reach of the helping hands norm and saw it as competing with other obligations. For instance, many Asian Americans told me it was important to "be realistic" about how they allocate their time and sometimes identified certain components of the honoring ancestors norm as in competition with the helping hands norm for their resources. With only so much time and energy available in a day, obligations to family and school or work came first. For instance, Amber explains that her parents were "more worried about me focusing on school" than community engagement but that if she did not "shirk [her] other duties," they might support activities like helping others if she "felt strongly enough about it." Lisa similarly tells me that "[my parents] want to make sure I keep myself realistic. . . . Be sure you can take care of yourself, and take care of your pets, whatever is in your care, and you're free to pursue those things."

When Asian Americans I talked with did elaborate on how they might take care of others in need, they spoke of individual acts of kindness or charity rather than political participation. These behaviors included opening doors for the elderly, providing food to the homeless, and being kind to strangers. Sometimes Asian Americans told me about how these individual-based actions could make larger, society-wide change through the "domino effect." In discussing ways society can take care of people in need, Aisha describes the plot of an Indian movie she once watched: "I do something for you and you say, 'Hey, thanks for . . .'

and I say, 'No, I don't want a thanks, I want you to go help three other people.' . . . So I think it just kinda ends up spreading out, it's one of those—the domino effect, you know. One person tells three people, and then these three people tell three other people. It's kinda multiplying like that. And that's a very powerful message." Similarly, Tala chronicles a YouTube video she saw just a few weeks prior to our interview: "It's kinda like that domino effect—if you help someone, then in the future someone else would help you. This question kinda reminds me of this video I watched. [Describes video.] That was really inspiring—that video." Both Aisha and Tala suggest that small acts of kindness rather than political participation can solve systemic social ills. When thinking of how to care for others in need, they identify primarily forms of direct service.

Some Asian Americans I talked with did identify political participation and policy change as the best way to help others, but they described these opinions as in conflict with the broader expectations of their community. Both Jonathan and Samaira, for instance, talked about "generational poverty" and "community advocacy" as defining their orientations toward helping others. But their communities, they explained, admired a different set of behaviors that they often saw themselves fighting against or being in conflict with. Jonathan tells me that in his experience, the Asian American community has "given into that perverse logic of the model minority myth, where you don't need rights or don't need civic engagement because the underhanded deal of the market or of society has treated you quite well."

In this comment, Jonathan alludes to how immigration policy in particular has aided in the structural advancement of Asian Americans. Samaira, too, brings up this point in her interviews, discussing in detail the 1965 Immigration and Nationality Act. Known as the Hart-Celler Act, this monumental piece of legislation moved the nation's immigration policy away from racially based quotas toward a system that gave priority to both family reunification and skilled labor (Masuoka and Junn, 2013). Since the policy change, the Asian American population has grown in the United States from 1.3 million to 18 million citizens, with an estimated 16 million able to immigrate as a direct result of this immigration reform (Lopez, Passel, and Rohal, 2015). Selection on skill and the growing number of visas tied to economic sponsorship have served to bring a particularly well-educated, well-resourced group of Asian Americans to the United States. In 2013, an estimated 57% of these newly arrived

TABLE 3.2 **Behaviors tied to helping the needy**

	Black Americans (stronger)	Asian Americans (weaker)
Direct service	✓	✓
Political	✓	
Religious	✓	

Asian immigrants had completed at least a bachelor's degree, compared to only 30% of US-born adults (Lopez, Passel, and Rohal, 2015). In 2016, the median income for Asian American families was $83,183, $40,000 more than the national average for Black Americans and $15,000 more than for White Americans (Fontenot, Semega, and Kollar, 2018).[11] Asian Americans and their families generally arrive in the United States equipped with a set of skills that allows them to engage successfully with the American labor market.

These differences in exposure to structural discrimination seem to orient respondents toward the helping hands norm. Grievances about inequity in the American legal, financial, and political systems lead Black Americans to translate the highly valued helping hands norm into political behaviors and practices, especially high-cost, local political activism. In contrast, the generally well-resourced and highly educated Asian Americans I talked with were less likely to see a connection between helping others and political participation. Rather, when discussing how to care for those in need, Asian Americans more often mentioned direct service to those around them. Further, the tenets of the helping hands norm seemed to conflict for some Asian Americans with the demands of the honoring ancestors norm. Helping others, especially outside the home, was perceived as a barrier to the financial and educational goals tied to honoring the sacrifices of those in the past. Drawing together these insights, table 3.2 presents the various behaviors groups connect to the helping hands norm and how they might vary in their connection across groups.

Norms Broadly Held but Uniquely Construed

A grounded theory approach to identifying participatory social norms brings to the fore two norms with possible implications for political participation: the honoring ancestors and helping hands norms. My analyses suggest that these norms are widely endorsed in the United States, cross-ing racial and ethnic boundaries but that they vary in their behavioral interpretations. A group's history, narratives, constraints, and opportu-nities breathe life into these simple prescriptive concepts, giving them meaning. The resulting group-based content of the honoring ancestors and helping hands norms is a set of beliefs about how best to honor the past and take care of those in need, which also provide signals to others about compliance.

Sometimes these norms seem to demand political participation from group members. Rather than duty to the state or even the search for in-strumental benefits, duty to one's community of the past and to those most in need may animate the choice to engage in politics. These com-mitments appear to serve as guiding principles in a wide array of life choices, defined and reinforced by one's social space, but are only some-times coupled with political participation. Macro forces in the form of immigration law, integration into the American political system and nar-ratives, and exposure to structural deprivation and discrimination ap-pear to shape this coupling. As suggested by the RNM, the distinct di-rectives and demands of one's community are reflective of its history. We turn next to testing these concepts empirically and expanding our anal-yses to include not just Asian and Black Americans but each of the four largest racial groups in the United States.

CHAPTER FOUR

Finding Purpose in the Past

For as long as America, the nation, has existed, racial group has mattered for orientations toward politics. The degree of attachment to one's racial group shapes everything from vote choice to attitudes on immigration, redistribution, crime, and partisanship (Dawson, 1994; Hutchings and Valentino, 2004; Kinder and Kam, 2010; Masuoka, 2008). In this chapter, I show that the importance of this relationship to the group is not tied simply to the present but also extends into the past. Who our ancestors are, what we believe they sacrificed for us, and how we interpret their traditions and struggles all influence how we honor them. In the United States, where ancestry is tied to race and where racial group experience diverges, the stories and realities of these ancestors are remarkably different by racial group membership.

I use data from the Participatory Social Norms Survey to empirically test a number of suppositions derived from racialized norms model and from my in-depth interviews, discussed in the previous two chapters. My focus in this chapter is on the honoring ancestors norm, defined as the prescriptive commitment to honor the stories, struggles, and sacrifices of those in the past. I find that most Americans, regardless of race, think it is important to honor the past and those who paved the way for them. However, how one honors the past is much less universal; rather, individuals of different races disagree, on average, about the best ways to honor their ancestors. Some groups systematically tie the honoring ancestors norm to political participation, infusing involvement in politics with normative force. For these individuals, the way one honors his or her ancestral predecessors is through claiming the civil and political rights those in the past fought so hard for them to have. Individuals in other groups are systematically more likely to tie the honoring ancestors norm to cultural activities and economic stability. These content differences in the honoring ancestors norm vary not only by group membership but also by geographic, social, and psychological group embeddedness, providing evidence of their contextual nature.

Throughout this chapter, I present and validate new survey measures, showing they converge, diverge, and predict just as they should. These measures become of great importance later in the book when I move from outlining the content of norms to examining whether they predict political behavior in the public sphere. Before turning to this analytical work, though, let's explore what exactly the ancestors norm encompasses and delineate expectations about variation for each racial group.

Conceptualizing Ancestors

In the previous chapter, I examined interview data drawn from my conversations with twenty-three Black and Asian Americans in metropolitan areas across the country. These interviews helped me identify the honoring ancestors norm as a concept with relevance for political participation in the United States; they also suggested that this norm might vary in its construction across racial groups. Part of the value of grounded theory like this—work that centers on the voices of everyday people—is that it can generate new insight separate and apart from scholarly cannons. Now, having identified this norm inductively, I circle back to extant scholarship to determine what we might already know about honoring ancestors as a concept in the social science literature and beyond.

Traces of the honoring ancestors norm—both as a concept and with respect to its prevalence—appear in research that crosses social science disciplines. Scholars in anthropology and psychology argue that the importance of honoring the past appears in cultures and countries around the world: ancestral worship is ubiquitous in human religions (Sheils, 1975; Steadman, Palmer, and Tilley, 1996), respect for tradition and honoring elders appears in studies of universal values (Schwartz, 1992), and moral foundations theory connects the foundations of sanctity and authority to ancestral honoring (Haidt, 2012; Graham et al., 2013).

The prevalence of a normative commitment to honor the past likely derives from its positive contribution to human survival and reproduction. Because values like fairness, benevolence, and ancestral honoring are seen in nearly every human civilization, they are thought to have instrumental purpose (Buss and Kenrick, 1998; Graham et al., 2013; Kirkpatrick, 1999; Hefner, 1991). Adhering to the wisdom of ancestors may serve as a heuristic for effective action, thriving under the gauntlet of natural selection (Baum et al., 2004). That is, doing what kept people alive yesterday will likely keep one alive today. And because the propensity to honor the past may aid in maturation and thus, mating, the trait proliferates in the population.

But what kept people alive yesterday is not the same for those living in the desert as for those nestled in the mountains, near the sea, or in a city. Rather, the behaviors that get bound to the process of ancestral honoring are highly variable and dependent on context. Much like how the phenotypes we observe in people are affected by the interplay of genotype and environment, the honoring ancestors trait expresses itself differently based on history. Who ancestors are, the legacies attached to them, and the behaviors demanded in the process of honoring one's predecessors are contextually derived (Scheffler et al., 1966). A commitment to honor the past may be universal, but what the past prescribes is highly variable.

I argue that it is through this process of trait to behavioral expression that group norms form. A broad array of factors can shape this behavioral expression—physical location, access to resources, experiences with violence, and constraints on opportunity, to name a few—but collectively, they infuse an evolutionarily selected trait like the desire to honor the past with meaning. It is here that the relevance of the racialized influence model becomes clear and can be applied specifically to honoring ancestors: because of divergent historical contexts and continued segregation, what it means to honor the past likely diverges across racial groups in the United States.

The link between ancestral honoring and racial group norms may be especially prevalent given the perceived heredity of race in the United States. Despite mounting evidence regarding the fluidity of race (see Davenport, 2020, for a review), Americans still largely perceive race as stable, inherited at birth, and largely genetic (Hochschild and Sen, 2018; Waters, 1990). This belief produces a descent construct that ties together the familial and the racial: race is inherited through one's family, and because of this, individuals of the same race share a common, imagined set of ancestors (Chandra, 2006; Scheffler et al., 1966). Parents, grandparents, and other family members serve as ancestral prototypes, but so do members of the broader racial community.

This ancestral construct as featuring both familial lineage and connections to a broader people was evident in my interviews. Respondents often toggled back and forth between discussing their familial ancestors—parents or grandparents who almost always shared the respondents' race—and their racial or ethnic communities of the past. Take, for instance, a statement from DeMarkus, a Tennessee native living in the Nashville area, as he talks about how the civil rights movement set a national precedent for movements of inclusion: "As a Black man, I'm so prideful of . . . my ancestors and people. My grandmother would tell me [about] being in Nashville and going into those lunch counters. I'm talking about Miss Sally, she would tell me about that. I'm so proud that they was a part of that." Here we see the unconscious movement between mentions of ancestors, my people, grandmothers, and iconic moments in the group's history—specifically, the disruptive movement tactics used to integrate Nashville's lunch counters. Asian Americans too often lumped their familial ancestors—parents and grandparents—with their ethnic and communal ancestors, discussing the religion and cultural practices of their ancestral country of origin.

The fluidity between familial ancestors and racial ancestors in the United States is well exhibited in the comic-based blockbuster movie *Black Panther*. Ancestors are a prevalent theme in this movie with T'Challa and Erik Killmonger, the leading protagonist and antagonist respectively, both visiting the "ancestral plane" as part of their transcendence into power. When they do so, the lead characters meet with family members. In these instances, "ancestors" refers to genealogical predecessors—specifically, fathers.

But at other points in the film, "ancestors" encapsulates a broader, imagined community of racial forebears. Near the conclusion of the film, Killmonger faces his death and requests, "Just bury me in the ocean with my ancestors that jumped from the ships 'cause they knew death was better than bondage." Here Killmonger refers to a community of ancestors, drawing on collective memory in his reference to the millions of enslaved Africans transported to the Americas between 1525 and 1866. Reflecting both the objective and subjective elements of racial identity, then, group members in the United States likely forge ancestral constructs based on familial and racial group membership, with elements both real and imagined (Anderson, 2006; Carter, 2019; Chandra, 2006).

Black and Asian Ancestors, a Rejoinder

My interviews suggested that Black and Asian Americans diverge with respect to normative behaviors bundled into ancestral honoring. Specifically, Black Americans commonly motivated their choices to participate politically by discussing the sacrifices and struggles of those in the past. Asian Americans discussed the sacrifices of their ancestors, too, but these stories often led to a cultural expressions of the norm. Asian Americans honored their ancestors by continuing traditions around food, family, marriage, holidays, and dress. In addition, both groups connected the honoring ancestors norm to economic and educational success.

I suggested that nuances in people's perceptions about their ancestors yields differences in the behaviors that are bundled into the honoring ancestors norm. When Black Americans referenced their ancestors, they called upon their American forebears, who were subjects of slavery, violence, segregation, and exclusionary citizenship. These ancestors were victims of horrible atrocities, yes, but they were also warriors, resilient in their fight for human dignity and democratic voice. Because of their sacrifices, Black Americans in the United States today have de jure access to education, economic mobility, and the right to vote. Often Black Americans I talked with remained cynical about the efficacy of the American political system or its commitment to helping Black people flourish; regardless of these hesitations, voting and engaging in political life were important because they were a way to honor the stories and sacrifices of ancestors.

Previous scholarship on Black ideology and identity hint at the prominence of this narrative in structuring life for Black people in the United States. In his empirical work on Black political ideology, Dawson (2003) argues that *disillusioned liberalism* is potentially the most common system of political thought among Black Americans (see also Harris-Lacewell, 2010). This ideology, built over the course of generations and in direct conversation with American liberalism more generally, highlights the value of democratic self-governance and egalitarianism while critically analyzing the nation's historical record of exclusion.

Asian Americans regularly discussed the sacrifices and traditions of their familial and cultural ancestors too, but whereas Black Americans' ancestors were firmly rooted in the United States, Asian Americans regularly discussed their family's immigration stories and the culture or traditions from their country of origin. Although not all Asian Americans in the United States are recent immigrants, many are. As of 2018, 48% of Asian American citizens were born in another country; another 42% are the children of immigrants, with at least one parent born in another nation (see appendix C, table C.2). This modal category of Asian Americans as first- or second-generation immigrants and as individuals who choose to leave their home country often for economic opportunities in the United States likely shapes the group's perceptions of their ancestors. Although Asian Americans are multiethnic from diverse countries of origin (Wong et al., 2011), group members largely share in an experience of immigration and perceived foreignness from their (White) American peers (Kibria, 2002; Lee, 2005; Tuan, 1998).

These findings suggest that both demographic and perceived foreignness may drive variation in ancestral norm formation across racial groups in the United States. In their work on racial hierarchy, Zou and Cheryan (2017) identify two theoretical dimensions contributing to group experiences and stereotypes in America (see also Lee, 2005). The first, *perceived inferiority*, closely reflects a multitude of works on racial hierarchy in the United States that locate Black Americans and other racial minorities below the dominant, White group in terms of perceived intellectual, cultural, and economic prestige (e.g., Hochschild, Weaver, and Burch, 2012; Masuoka and Junn, 2013; Sidanius and Pratto, 1999). The second—*perceived cultural foreignness*—captures the degree to which a group is thought to deviate from prototypes of American cultural integration. The authors find evidence that Latino and Asian Americans are more likely to experience discrimination on this dimension than Black and White Americans and that out-groups identify Black and White Americans as more stereotypically American (see also Kibria, 2002; Tuan, 1998; Wong, 2010).

With respect to the honoring ancestors norm, I argue that it is this second dimension rather than the first that undergirds normative variation across racial groups in the United States. Black Americans, by and large, locate their ancestors in the United States and are perceived as more American than other racial minority groups. Black Americans are well integrated into US narratives about the struggle for freedom and democratic rights, and they draw from these narratives, as well as the experiences of their US-based familial ancestors, when constructing the behavioral elements of the honoring ancestors norm. Furthermore, the institution of slavery served to obscure, if not obliterate, known ethnic origins for most Black Americans.[1] And cultural and political elites, who themselves perceive Black Americans as less foreign than other minorities, reify narratives about Black Americans' struggle and fight for democratic inclusion.

In contrast, Asian Americans on average have more recent immigration experiences and are perceived as more foreign by American outgroups, regardless of immigration timing. As a result, group members are less fully integrated into American myth and narratives about struggles for democratic representation, despite the historic existence of these experiences (Takaki, 2008). Both the demographic realities of the group and the near absence of entrepreneurial efforts to build alternatives means that Asian Americans may look to their families' immigration experiences and nation-of-origin cultural distinguishers to determine the behaviors appropriate for honoring the past.

This theoretical frame produces clear expectations regarding across-group variation. Black and Asian Americans will likely both exhibit a strong commitment to the honoring ancestors norm, but Black Americans will be more likely than Asians to connect this norm to political participation. Furthermore, individuals who are more contextually embedded in their respective groups will receive clearer signals about their groups' norm and as a result exhibit even stronger variation with respect to its political content.

The framework also alludes to possible dimensions of within-group difference. Nativity status among Black Americans, for instance, may temper a commitment to honoring ancestors through participatory avenues. With alternative ancestral traditions to draw from like narratives based in country of origin, recent Black immigrants may be more likely to connect the honoring ancestors norm to alternative behaviors like cultural activities or seeking economic stability. Scholars like Candis Watts Smith (2014a) and Mary Waters (2009) have argued that Black immigrants are integrated rather quickly into the American racial hierarchy, but their status as recent immigrants can produce a more varied understanding of their racial category, especially in relationship to ethnicity. As a result, Black immigrants and their children—a relatively small but growing group (Smith, 2014a)—may be less likely to imagine their ancestors through the traditional racial lens of their native-born counterparts and instead rely on their ethnicity.

In contrast, Asian Americans who harbor strong panethnic identities may internalize an expression of the honoring ancestors norm that more closely resembles average Black attitudes. That is, ancestors may shift from country-of-origin immigrants—a perception that demands continuing cultural traditions—to seeing their ancestors more fully through the lens of American history and American narratives about democratic struggle and sacrifice. Through this lens, Asian Americans, much like Black Americans, have faced hundreds of years of legal exclusion from citizenship, property rights, and labor protections and have through court cases, strikes, and social movements fought for full integration into the American demos (Takaki, 2008). As a result, embeddedness in geographic or social ethnic enclaves may reduce the norm's perceived connection to politics, but psychological embeddedness in the Asian American community writ large might increase a political interpretation.

White and Latino Ancestors, an Extension

The combination of qualitative interviews and insight from previous scholarship suggests that two components of foreignness may shape group beliefs about how to honor ancestors: group demographic composition with regard to immigration timing and precipitated cause and the group's perceived foreignness, regardless of an individual's immigration status. My qualitative work focused on only Black and Asian Americans, but my goal is to build a unified theory of social norm divergence in the United States that extends to each of the four largest racial groups. Now, with these theoretical dimensions in hand, we are tasked with developing a set of expectations for whether and how the honoring ancestors norm will manifest for the remaining two groups: Latinos and White Americans.

Let's start with Whites. Like the vast majority of Black people in the United States, White Americans are primarily individuals with distant arrival histories. The postcolonial period of American history was marked by White immigration from primarily English-speaking nations, while the late nineteenth and early twentieth centuries saw a surge of White immigrants from nations like Germany, Italy, and Poland. In recent decades, however, immigration of new White people to the United States has waned to a mere trickle. With more than one hundred years having passed since the last large wave of White immigrants, today's census figures suggest that 92% of White people in the United States are at least third-generation Americans (see appendix C, table C.2).

The spanning generational distance from initial arrival means that for most White Americans, ancestral immigrants are embodied mostly in stories, and potentially once meaningful ethnicities are now largely symbolic. White Americans may draw from their (imagined) ethnic ancestors when discussing their last names, personality traits, or marked holidays but for the most part are able to put on and take off their ethnicity like a hat: they draw from it when it is enjoyable and useful but otherwise cast it aside (Gans, 1979; Waters, 1990).

Still, qualitative work suggests that stories of ethnic ancestors seem to inform many Whites' worldview. In her qualitative classic, Mary Waters (1990) shows how multigenerational White Americans often imagine their ancestors as (legal) immigrants seeking and achieving the American dream of a middle-class life. White Americans may see honoring their ancestors, then, through an economic and educational lens: honoring ancestors requires working hard to support one's family economically and taking advantage of educational opportunities.

But additional research suggests that White Americans also, on average, perceive themselves and each other as uniquely American. Zou and Cheryan (2017) show that White Americans were significantly less likely than Asian Americans and Latinos to report experiencing foreignness-based prejudice and are perceived as more American by in-group and out-group members alike. Many political scientists have similarly demonstrated both an implicit and explicit connection between Whiteness and Americanness, more so than for other racial groups (Devos and Banaji, 2005; Masuoka and Junn, 2013; Pérez, Deichert, and Engelhardt, 2019; Theiss-Morse, 2009; Wong, 2010).

Strong American identities among White people are often infused with commitments to democratic procedures and ideals—despite the equally racially restrictive tendencies—along with norms of patriotism and individualism (Theiss-Morse, 2009; Wong, 2010). The content of this identity reflects widespread narratives of America as a democratic and capitalist nation, often with at least undertones of White supremacy. The celebrated "Founding Fathers" are all White (many were also slaveholders); soldiers in wars ranging from the American Civil War to World War II are often depicted as entirely White (despite the presence of non-White participants); and the "titans" of American industry are

White (their stories often told without discussion of the ways most of the nation's wealth was amassed using Black and Brown bodies). White Americans may imagine their ancestors as uniquely fighting for freedom at home and abroad, building revolutionary democratic systems and pulling themselves up by their bootstraps to seek economic prosperity. Ancestors perceived in this way should lead White people to believe that honoring the past requires both economic expressions and political participation.

This conception of ancestors as fighting for civil and political rights mirrors a narrative prevalent among Black Americans, but with important ironies. While White Americans may perceive their ancestors as bearers of freedom, equality, and democratic principles of self-governance, Black Americans talked about their ancestors fighting against these same White ancestors for democratic inclusion. Both narratives involve ancestors fighting for democratic rights, but who ancestral group members struggled *against* is very different depending on racial group membership. This distinction may appear in commitments to traditional democratic participation (i.e., voting) versus more contentious forms of political behavior (i.e., protesting) that challenge status quo systems and have been used by racial minorities excluded from the franchise to seek integration into full citizenship (Gillion, 2013; Theiss-Morse, 2009).

What about Latinos? Again, we can consider the demographic composition of the group and perceptions of foreignness when hypothesizing about practices used to express ancestral honoring. Census figures estimate that more than half of Latinos in the United States are recent immigrants (see appendix C, table C.2). The earliest Latinos did not immigrate but, rather, were incorporated into the citizenry through war. Throughout the 1800s, the American government acquired the lands currently known as Texas, California, and Puerto Rico—among other southwestern territories—and along with it, the peoples who lived there (García Bedolla, 2015; Jiménez, 2010; Takaki, 2008). Since these foundational moments, the flow of immigrants from countries in South and Central America to the United States has continued largely unabated and even increased in the past half century ("America's Foreign Born in the Last 50 Years," 2019; Grieco et al., 2012; Jiménez, 2010). Today, nearly 17% of Latino citizens in the United States are first-generation Americans; they were born in another nation and undertook the process of naturalization to become American citizens.[2] Another 40% are second-generation citizens; their parents immigrated and then they, these children of immigrants, were born into full citizenship rights (see appendix C, table C.2). Demographically, then, Latinos as a group fall somewhere between Asian Americans—the vast majority of whom are first- or second-generation immigrants—and Black and White Americans, most of whom are at least third-generation citizens.

The ongoing stream of immigrants from Central and South America into the United States may also shape perceptions of foreignness for all group members, regardless of immigration status. Zou and Cheryan (2017) find that much like Asian Americans, Latinos are often stereotyped as less American and face foreignness-based prejudice (see also Lee, 2005). Tomás Jiménez (2010) argues that the continued nature of immigration to the United States serves to remind even multigenerational Latinos of their ethnicity and replenish it with cultural traditions from nations of origin. Examining Mexican Americans, in particular, Jiménez (2010) explains, "Although later generations of Mexican Americans display a remarkable degree of social and economic integration into U.S. society, ongoing Mexican immigration, or immigrant replenishment, sustains both the cultural content of ethnic identity and the ethnic boundaries that distinguish groups . . . replenishment provides the means by which Mexican Americans come to feel positively attached to their ethnic roots. But it also provokes a predominating view of Mexicans as foreigners, making Mexican Americans seem less like a part of the U.S. mainstream than their social and economic integration and later-generation status might suggest" (5). Mexican Americans make up the majority of the Latino population in the United States today, but the recent influx of immigrants from South America suggests the same logic may extend to other ethnic groups as well.

Ethnic replenishment may be even more pronounced considering the declining centrality of political parties in incorporating new immigrants into politics. Janelle Wong (2008) argues that advances in targeted mobilization and the usages of voter rolls have led political parties to focus increasingly less on organizing new voters and more on perceived likely voters (see also Hersh, 2015). In contrast to previous periods when (primarily White) immigrants were a focus of mobilization efforts (Dahl, 2005; Erie, 1990), more recent Latino and Asian Americans immigrants confront fewer appeals from candidates, campaigns, and elites. As a result, newer immigrants likely confront fewer cohesive messages targeted at their groups—for instance, messages about how ancestors fought for the franchise—and fewer requests to mobilize than in previous generations and when compared to current White and Black Americans (Ramírez, Solano, and Wilcox-Archuleta, 2018).

These realities of immigration, joined with the perception of foreignness from other citizens (Lee, 2005; Masuoka and Junn, 2013), suggest that many Latinos may feel closely connected to ancestors located in other nations and draw upon ethnic cultural practices and traditions when expressing ancestral honoring. Furthermore, ethnographic research suggests that many Latino immigrants come to the United States with great optimism about economic and educational opportunities (Portes and Rumbaut, 2001, 2006). Much like the nearly 50 million Asian Americans who have crossed an ocean seeking prosperity in the past forty years (Zong and Batalova, 2016), many Latinos cross the border seeking the American dream. We might expect then that most Latinos will also couple ancestral honoring with activities that seek economic or educational success.

A Set of Expectations

The qualitative grounded theory combined with extant historical and empirical scholarship leads to clear expectations about how the honoring ancestors norm likely operates across racial groups in the United States. First, the importance of honoring ancestors, the past, and the struggles of those who came before will likely appear with universal prevalence across the four groups as research from anthropology and psychology suggests. However, groups made up largely of recent immigrants and who are perceived as more foreign both by in- and out-group members should be more likely to connect economic and cultural practices to the honoring ancestors norm. In contrast, racial groups composed mostly of multigeneration Americans who are perceived as primarily American by in- and out-group members will be more likely to connect economic and political practices to honoring ancestors.

Figure 4.1 arranges the four groups in the United States along this continuum of perceived foreignness and demographic composition with respect to timing of arrival in the United States. Overlaid on this continuum are my expectations regarding the propensity of group members to connect the honoring ancestors norm to political participation.

To the far right of the continuum lie Black and White Americans. These two groups are composed largely of citizens whose ancestors

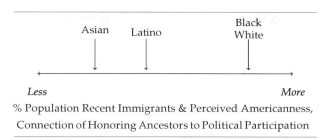

FIGURE 4.1 Expected group variability in the political ancestors norm

arrived in the United States at least three generations ago. Aided by cultural and political elites, these groups are well integrated into American narratives regarding the sacrifices and struggles for democracy and perceive themselves as distinctly American. As a result, most Black and White people in the United States may look to their American ancestors when imagining what has been sacrificed for them and what is required in respecting the past. Drawing from stories of these ancestors, real and imagined, members of these two groups may link the honoring ancestors norm to political participation, reflecting widespread narratives about the nation's (anti)democratic history.

To the far left of the spectrum are Asian Americans. As a group composed largely of recent immigrants and whose members are perceived as more foreign regardless of immigration status, Asian Americans will be less likely to couple the honoring ancestors norm with political participation. I expect most Asian Americans will look to ethnic cultural practices and traditions as well as the economic dreams of immigrant ancestors when expressing the honoring ancestors norm.

Situated just to the right of Asian Americans are Latinos. Many Latinos in the United States today are first- or second-generation immigrants, and research suggests members of these groups tend to be perceived as more foreign and less American than Black and White people in the United States. With their ethnicity regularly replenished and facing a constant othering from out-groups, Latinos may be more likely to situate their ancestors in other nations and through the lens immigration.

However, compared to Asian Americans, more Latinos may maintain strong panethnic identities that link them to racial ancestors in the United States. These group members may see their ancestors through narratives more closely paralleling that of Black Americans: early

Latinos in the United States faced the legal stripping of property and sustained barriers—formal and informal—to full political representation and integration (García Bedolla, 2015; Camarillo, 1990; Takaki, 2008). In response, Latinos have organized throughout history with well-known movements including the Chicano student movement, the labor union movement, and the nationalist movement, and this history may inspire ancestral honoring through political participation for some Latinos.

This theoretical arrangement of the groups leads to specific expectations about variation both across and within racial groups in the United States. We have moved now from the general tenets of the racialized norms model into specific expectations about group variation with regard to one particular norm. Our next task is to test these hypotheses empirically using nationally representative survey samples. Let's begin with a look at the prevalence of the honoring ancestors norm across groups in the United States.

Ubiquity and Variation in Honoring Ancestors

The Participatory Social Norms Survey introduces a four-item battery designed to measure the existence and strength of the honoring ancestors norm. Respondents were asked to what extent they agreed or disagreed with four statements, presented in random order and preceded by, "Let's begin with a few questions about the people who made it possible for you to be where you are today. This might include your parents, grandparents, leaders in your community, or historical figures." Respondents were provided with five response options that ranged from strongly agree to strongly disagree. The four statements were

- Honoring the struggles and traditions of my ancestors is a guiding principle in my life.
- I should respect the traditions and wishes of my family.
- I feel a debt to those who paved the way for me.
- Others made sacrifices so I could have the opportunities I do today.

These measures were constructed with both the familial and imagined elements of ancestry in mind and infused with norm-evoking words throughout. The statements gauge feelings of obligations toward family but also those in the past more generally. Race is not explicitly mentioned but likely figures prominently in respondents' conscious and subconscious imaginings. Words like "should," "duty," and "respect" are strung throughout to evoke the sense of morality, obligation, and guilt indicative of personal norms (Bicchieri, 2016; Schwartz, 1977; Thøgersen, 2006). When aggregated over group membership, the measures also elucidate patterns regarding descriptive and injunctive group-based norms in addition to these personal norms.

My hope was that these four statements would unite to measure a single, theoretically informed concept about ancestral honoring; empirically, they do so quite well. Cronbach's alpha tests confirm that the battery has high internal consistency: the items are highly correlated in the sample as a whole ($\alpha = 0.76$) and equally so across the four groups (White $\alpha = 0.74$, Black $\alpha = 0.79$, Latino $\alpha = 0.77$, Asian $\alpha = 0.76$).[3] Because of this, I can combine the four measures into a single index to assess the strength of the honoring ancestors norm. Averaging together an individual's responses to the four statements generates a score that ranges from 0 to 4. High scores on this scale identify individuals who have strong prescriptive commitments to honoring the sacrifices, stories, and traditions of those in the past; low scores represent individuals with weak commitments to the honoring ancestors norm. I call this measure the *honoring ancestors index*.

We can use this index to determine how prevalent the honoring ancestors norm is in the United States generally and for each racial group specifically. I plot the distribution of the honoring ancestors index for each group in figure 4.2. The *x* axis shows values of the honoring ancestors index, the *y* axis represents within-group proportions, and the vertical, dashed lines indicate means for each group.

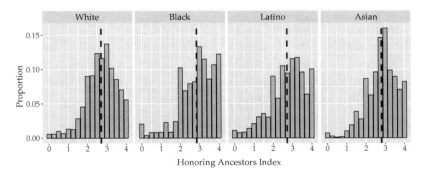

FIGURE 4.2 Distribution of honoring ancestors strength

The results demonstrate that, on average, Americans in the United States harbor strong commitments to honoring ancestors. Fully half the sample, or 56% of Black Americans, 50% of Asian Americans, 49% of Latinos, and 45% of Whites, fall between "somewhat agree" (3) and "strongly agree" (4) on the scale. Each distribution exhibits a clear left skew, and means range from 2.70 (White) to 2.85 (Black), which round to the affirmative category of "somewhat agree."[4]

While the honoring ancestors norm appears to be widely held in the United States, some variation across groups does appear. Statistically, Black and Asian American group means are indistinguishable (2.85 versus 2.80, respectively, $p > 0.05$), but both groups have, on average, slightly higher and statistically distinct evaluations compared to Whites and Latinos (2.70 and 2.72, respectively, $p < 0.05$). Only 6% of Whites strongly agreed with all four statements, but 12% of Black Americans, 10% of Latinos, and 8% of Asian Americans answered the same way. Variation is particularly clear for some of the items in the scale: only 14% of White Americans reported they strongly agree that "honoring the struggles and traditions of my ancestors is a guiding principle in my life," compared to a third of Black Americans (33%) and roughly a quarter of Latinos (23%).[5] The results suggest that the honoring ancestors norm may be especially strong and important for understanding the choices and behaviors of racial minorities in the United States.

Collectively, though, my measures reveal that a commitment to honoring the past is both common and relatively strong in the United States, despite some variation across groups. Very few Americans explicitly disagree with any of the components of the honoring ancestors scale. Rather, regardless of their race, most Americans believe to some degree that the struggles and traditions of their ancestors are a guiding principle in their lives, that it is important to respect the traditions and wishes of their families, that others have made sacrifices so they could have the opportunities they do today, and that they owe a debt to the past.

Interpretations and behavioral expressions of the honoring ancestors norm, however, likely diverge across groups. The PSNS includes a question designed to assess expression of the honoring ancestors norm. Respondents were asked to "think again about the people who made it possible for you to be where you are today." Then, "What do you think are the best ways to honor the legacy of these people?" Respondents examined a list of ten response options, randomly presented and accompanied with both "none" and "other" at the end of the list.

The list included three categories of behaviors my grounded theory suggested might be associated with honoring ancestors: political, cultural, and economic/educational expressions. For the political options, respondents could indicate whether they honor their ancestors by voting in elections, attending political rallies and protests, exercising their political rights, and fighting injustices when they see them. For the cultural options, respondents could choose celebrating cultural or religious holidays; continuing traditional practices around food, clothing, music, or marriage; and speaking a language other than English. And for the education/economic options, respondents could select working hard to support their families, pursuing certain educational opportunities, and pursuing certain career opportunities.

Each specific expression of the honoring ancestors norm was included in the list and phrased as such because it arose during my interviews. Although the list is not designed to capture *all* the ways Americans may honor the past, an examination of the "none" and "other" response categories suggests it does capture *most* of the ways people act on the norm. Across the whole sample, only 8% of respondents chose "none" and an additional 3% selected "other." Furthermore, selecting "none" was inversely correlated with the strength of the norm. That is, those falling into the lowest category of the honoring ancestors index were also those most likely to select "none" as a response option.[6]

To determine whether Americans of different races are more likely to connect political, cultural, or economic/education behaviors to the honoring ancestors norm, I first present the proportion of each group selecting at least one political, cultural, or economic expression in figure 4.3. In this plot, 80% confidence intervals are indicated, with vertical

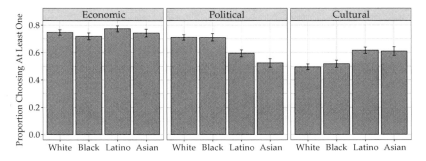

FIGURE 4.3 Ways to honor ancestors

lines surrounding point estimates to represent the rough equivalent of an across-group 0.05 statistical t-test (Cumming and Finch, 2005; Schenker and Gentleman, 2001).

The figure demonstrates that the honoring ancestors norm has a variety of behavioral interpretations, with many respondents selecting at least one economic, political, or cultural activity as a way to honor their ancestors. However, the plot also elucidates important variation with respect to each group's propensity to express the norm in specific ways.

Of the three categories, an economic expression of the norm shows the most stability across groups. Seventy-five percent of White Americans, 72% of Black Americans, 77% of Latinos, and 74% of Asian Americans see at least one economic option as a component of the honoring ancestors norm; none of these estimates are statistically distinguishable from the others at conventional levels.[7] This result is consistent with findings from the qualitative work and expectations developed from extant theory: regardless of race, Americans seem to connect educational and economic opportunities to the ancestors norm.

Important group variations emerge on both cultural and political expressions of the norm, however. Black and White Americans are significantly more likely than Latinos to choose at least one political act as a way to honor ancestors—71% of Black and White Americans selected at least one political act, compared to 59% of Latinos ($p < 0.05$). Furthermore, all three groups are significantly more likely than Asian Americans to believe political behaviors are required of the norm ($p < 0.05$). In fact, a nearly twenty-point chasm between Black Americans and Asian Americans emerges in the proportion of each group believing a political behavior is a central component of honoring the sacrifices and stories of ancestors. When looking at cultural expressions, roughly the reverse pattern appears. Half of White and Black Americans—50% and 52%, respectively—selected a cultural option as a way to honor ancestors, compared to 62% of Latinos and 61% of Asian Americans.

These results are again consistent with expectations. Black and White Americans—the two racial groups whose members are perceived as most American and that comprise primarily individuals with distant arrival histories—are more likely to connect democratic participation to norms of ancestral honoring. In contrast, Asian Americans and Latinos, whose racial groups are perceived as more foreign and whose membership is made up mostly of first- and second-generation immigrants, are

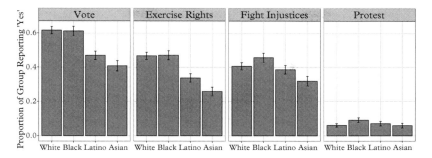

FIGURE 4.4 Political expression of honoring ancestors by group

more likely to connect the norm to traditions around marriage, music, holidays, and language.

Let's take a closer look at the specific participatory acts associated with honoring ancestors, as the political expression of this norm is our primary focus. Figure 4.4 shows the proportion of each racial group reporting that either voting, protesting, fighting injustices, or exercising political rights is a way to honor the legacy of those who came before them.[8]

Here again, a pattern consistent with expectations emerges across the groups. Black and White Americans are nearly identical in their likelihood to believe that voting in elections and exercising their political rights are required for honoring the past. Sixty-one percent of Black Americans and 62% of White Americans believe voting in elections is an important component of honoring the sacrifices of those who came before them, and 47% of both groups think that exercising their political rights is required by the norm. For Latinos and Asian Americans, however, the connection of the ancestors norm to traditional forms of political participation is less common. Only 47% of Latinos and 41% of Asian Americans select voting as an important component of the honoring ancestors norm; 34% of Latinos and 26% of Asian Americans see exercising their political rights as part of the norm.

These differences are both statistically and substantively important. Black and White Americans are statistically distinct from Latinos on both measures, and all three of these groups are statistically distinct from Asian Americans ($p < 0.05$). Substantively, more than half of Black Americans and White Americans believe the honoring ancestors norm demands participation in conventional forms of politics like voting, but only a quarter of Asian Americans feel the same. Despite high levels of commitment to the honoring ancestors norm generally, the behavioral expectations of the norm vary systematically by race.

A slightly different pattern appears in the final two measures—"Fight injustices when I see them" and "Attend political rallies and protests." These two measures are meant to capture evaluations of more grass-roots, disruptive, or outside-the-system forms of political participation (Conway, 2000). On these system-challenging forms of political activity, Black Americans pull ahead in believing the honoring ancestors norm demands such behaviors. Nearly half, or 46%, of Black Americans believe that honoring those in the past requires fighting injustices when they see them, compared to 41% of White Americans, 39% of Latinos, and 32% of Asian Americans. Unlike the previous measures, Whites and Latinos are statistically indistinguishable when it comes to system-challenging political action, but Asian Americans continue to trail in connecting these political acts to the honoring ancestors norm.

Although a relatively small number of respondents selected protesting and rally attendance as components of the honoring ancestors norm, a similar across-group pattern appears. Black Americans are statistically more likely than White or Asian Americans to believe that protesting and rally attendance are important ways to honor those from the past ($p < 0.05$). In fact, nearly 10% of Black Americans see protesting as a component of the honoring ancestors norm, compared to 6% of White and Asian Americans. Latinos, at 7%, are statistically indistinguishable from the other groups.

Together, the results demonstrate that despite the ubiquity of the honoring ancestors norm, its behavioral form is distinct across groups. Some racial groups are, on average, more likely to tie political behaviors to the honoring ancestors norm; other groups are more likely to tie cultural activities to the norm. Specifically, Black Americans consistently tie both system-affirming and system-challenging forms of political involvement to the honoring ancestors norm, seeing the norm as demanding participation in politics. White Americans connect the honoring ancestors norm primarily to system-affirming political participation. And Latinos and Asian Americans, on average, are less likely to connect the honoring ancestors norm to politics, instead linking cultural activities to the norm.

The Political Ancestors Index

Whether voting, protesting, exercising political rights, or fighting injustices is seen as required for honoring ancestors can be added together to create a single variable that indicates the strength of the political ancestors norm among respondents. I assign a point for each political act an individual selected as a way to honor ancestors and then add together the assigned points. Rescaled from 0 to 1, a score of 0 on the resulting index indicates that an individual did not select any political acts as ways to honor ancestors; 1 means they selected all of the political items when describing the best ways to honor ancestors.

I call this measure the *political ancestors index*. It indicates the degree to which an individual believes honoring ancestors requires political involvement. The political ancestors index is, importantly, a measure of attitudes, not behavior. It does not indicate whether people actually participate in politics or not (that will come later) but rather whether they think doing so is morally required to honor the past. This attitudinal index is going to feature prominently in the remainder of the book so, it is important that we spend some time now interrogating its properties.

First, we can assess whether it is appropriate to combine the four items together as I have. A Cronbach's alpha test confirms the political ancestors index has high internal consistency ($\alpha = 0.70$), and a confirmatory factor analysis shows the items load together on a single dimension consistently across the racial groups.[9] These two tests give us confidence that the components included in the measure—attitudes about voting in elections, protesting, exercising political rights, and fighting injustices as ways to honor ancestors—can be combined to produce a single index that reliably captures an underlying concept.

Second, the measure has suitable variability. Figure 4.5 shows the distribution of the political ancestors index for each of the four racial groups. The figure demonstrates both variation across and within groups. Black Americans, on average, show the strongest connection between ancestors and political participation ($x = 0.41$), followed by Whites ($x = 0.39$), Latinos ($x = 0.32$), and Asian Americans ($x = 0.26$). Thirty-two percent of Black Americans select at least three of the four political acts as ways to honor ancestors, compared to 28% of Whites, 22% of Latinos, and 15% of Asian Americans. On the opposite end of the spec-

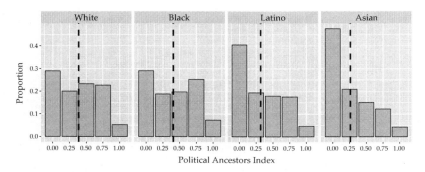

FIGURE 4.5 Distribution of the political ancestors index by group

trum, fully 48% of Asian American citizens selected none of the political act as a way to honor their ancestors, suggesting the norm is completely devoid of politics for nearly half the group; 40% of Latinos share this sentiment. The figure confirms the pattern of across-group variation we observed in the previous section: Black and White Americans are most likely to connect the stories, sacrifices, and traditions of those who came before them with political activity, with Black Americans on average edging out Whites ever so slightly for the group most likely to make this connection. Latinos, on the other hand, are significantly less likely to connect their commitment to honoring the past with political behaviors than Black and White Americans but are still more likely to do so than Asian Americans, who hold, on average, the weakest connection between beliefs about honoring the past and political involvement.

But even among these strongest and weakest on-average group assessments, variation occurs within the groups. Four percent of Asian Americans, for instance, selected all four political acts as part of the honoring ancestors norm, suggesting that for at least some of the population, political participation is strongly connected to ancestral honoring. Furthermore, 29% of Black Americans made no connection between the honoring ancestors norm and political participation. Although these individuals depart from their group's average, variation within as well as across racial groups can help us understand what contributes to norm development, which individuals are the most likely adopters, and the contexts where norms are the strongest.

Third, does the political ancestors index capture a unique concept, separate from extant predictors of political psychological engagement? That is, does it have *discriminant validity*? When confronted with the response option list, some may worry that individuals selecting the political options do so not because they believe voting or protesting is a way to honor the sacrifices of those in the past but because they simply like and care about politics. We can test the degree to which scores on the political ancestors index diverge from conventional measures of psychological investment in politics including political interest and partisanship to help alleviate these concerns. Furthermore, some may wonder whether the political ancestors index is theoretically distinct from its conceptual cousin, racial linked fate (Dawson, 1994; Masuoka, 2008). Racial linked fate has generally been conceptualized as a measure of attachment to ingroup members in the *present* but potentially could encompass attachment to group members in the *past*. If my measure is precisely, or even highly, correlated with racial linked fate, then I have added little conceptually to our understanding of politics; rather, the political ancestors index might simply be an old concept in a new package.

While we will examine the discriminant validity of the political ancestors index compared to political interest, partisanship, and racial linked fate, these measures can also give us a test of *predictive validity*; albeit distinct, the political ancestors index should be positively correlated with these three measures. Others have shown that involvement in politics can increase political knowledge and interest (Tolbert and Smith, 2005). If individuals believe honoring the past is important and their group demands they do so through political activity, we would expect individuals to become more interested and invested in politics as a result. Furthermore, considering the highly partisan context of the United States, involvement and interest in politics should lead to stronger partisanship (Iyengar et al., 2019; Westfall et al., 2015). And if an individual feels a sense of racial linked fate, driven by the perceived boundedness of a group, this feeling may increase a sense of connection to or knowledge about racial ancestors.

To examine the predictive and discriminant validity of the political ancestors index, I present in table 4.1 the Pearson's correlation coefficient for its relationship with four variables: strength of Republican or Democratic partisanship (compared to independents), political interest, and racial linked fate.[10] The table provides evidence that each of these four variables is statistically related to the political ancestors index, as expected, but none are correlated particularly well. Rather, each is only marginally related to the political ancestors index, providing us with confirmation that the newly constructed measure of ancestral honoring

TABLE 4.1 **Relationship between the political ancestors norm and political dispositions**

	Asian	Black	Latino	White
Political interest	0.36	0.36	0.39	0.41
	(418)	(1,000)	(995)	(999)
Republican partisanship	0.17	0.27	0.14	0.14
	(390)	(140)	(321)	(571)
Democratic partisanship	0.24	0.22	0.25	0.32
	(640)	(897)	(720)	(466)
Racial linked fate	0.08	0.23	0.15	0.05
	(1,013)	(986)	(988)	(990)

Notes: Table entry is the Pearson's correlation coefficient; number of observations appears in parentheses. Political interest is measured using a 4-point scale; Democratic and Republican partisanship are 4-point scales where 0 represents independents, 1 represents leaners, 2 represents weak identifiers, and 3 represents strong identifiers; racial linked fate is a 5-point scale.

through political involvement makes an independent contribution to our understanding of orientations to the political system. That is, the political ancestors index measures something distinct, although related to, other known measures of psychological investment in politics.

Specifically, political interest is positively related to the political ancestors index for each of the four racial groups with a more robust relationship than any of the other variables in the table. The correlation coefficient ranges from 0.36 for Asian and Black Americans to 0.41 for Whites. The strength of Democratic and Republican partisanship is also positively related to the political ancestors index for each of the four groups. On average, Democratic partisanship is more related than Republican partisanship; however, for Black Americans the opposite is true. The correlation between the political ancestors index and partisanship is slightly stronger for Black Republicans ($r = 0.27$) than for Black Democrats ($r = 0.22$). Finally, racial linked fate is weakly related to the political ancestors index for Asian and White Americans but more correlated among Black Americans and Latinos. As might be expected, the correlation between the political ancestors index and racial linked fate is strongest among Black Americans at 0.23.

The results confirm that while political interest, partisanship, and to some degree, racial linked fate are statistically related to the political ancestors index, they are not the same thing. The political ancestors index introduces a unique concept with discriminant validity. However, because these other predictors of political involvement are related to the measure, we will want to control for them in the subsequent analyses predicting political participation in chapters 6 and 7.

Demographic Predictors of the Political Ancestors Index

We have seen that the political ancestors index varies systematically in its prevalence across racial groups: Black Americans are, on average, most likely to embrace a political version of the norm, while Asian Americans are, on average, the least likely. But even within these strongest and weakest on-average groups, there is variation in the strength of the norm, as figure 4.5 demonstrates. We can use this variation to explore other correlates with a political expression of the honoring ancestors norm above and beyond race. Doing so sheds further light on why some individuals believe ancestral honoring requires political participation while others do not.

I examine within-group variation on four additional dimensions of salient social cleavage:

Generational status. I have suggested that expressions of the honoring ancestors norm develop in response to demographic variation in generational status and perceived foreignness. Individual-level nativity and generational status compared to group-level demographics provide an additional test of this claim: whether individuals are immigrants themselves or the children of immigrants may influence expressions of the honoring ancestors norm compared to those who are at least third-generation American. For testing this, I include in my analyses two indicator variables: one for first-generation citizenship (naturalized) and another for second-generation American (either or both parents born abroad). The suppressed reference category is third-generation American or more.

Gender. Within racial groups, gender may shape the relationship with the honoring ancestors norm, but the direction of this relationship is unclear. On the one hand, women may feel connected to ancestors who fought for the right to vote and, as a result, be at least as likely as men to connect the honoring ancestors norm to politics.[11] On the other, women may be excluded from politics in ways that produce a relatively low connection between the norm and political involvement. I examine within-group variation across gender by including in my analyses a binary variable for self-reported gender where women are the suppressed reference category.

Class. Like race, class often divides communities, shaping contact between individuals. I test the relationship between class and the political ancestors norm by including individual-level measures of educational attainment and yearly household income.

Age. The honoring ancestors norm may become more refined and stronger with age; the elderly may have clearer ideas of how honoring should happen or feel closer to ancestors who are further removed from the present. In my analyses, age is measured as a categorical variable, with cohorts separated roughly by ten-year increments.

I include each of these variables in a multivariate linear regression predicting the strength of the political ancestors index (0–1). To allow for the possibility—indeed, the expectation—that the predictors of the political ancestors index will vary by racial group, I model the relationship between the dependent variable and independent variables separately for Asian, Black, Latino, and White Americans (Crenshaw, 1989; Masuoka and Junn, 2013). Variables like gender and class have nuanced meaning in the context of the highly racialized United States, where race is a prism through which the rest of the world is experienced (Crenshaw, 1989). Gender, for instance, is a salient social cleavage across groups, but the content of the identity "woman" and the lived experience of women depart based on an individual's race (Bhattacharya, 2016; Dawson, 2003). As a result, the relationship between demographic variables and the participatory ancestors norm should be examined for each group separately (Masuoka and Junn, 2013).

Table 4.2 provides the results of these analyses.[12] It reveals a number of significant relationships. Looking first at nativity, the results show that some of the generational variables are related to a political expression of honoring ancestors—but *only* among Black and White Americans. For White Americans, those who are naturalized are 17% less likely than multigenerational Americans to connect the honoring ancestors norm to political participation, the equivalent of more than half of a standard deviation shift. For Black Americans, both first- and second-generational status are associated with a weaker political ancestors norm compared to third- or more generation Americans, but only the estimate for second-generational status is statistically significant. For Latinos and Asian Americans, neither indicator is related to the outcome.

Individual-level nativity status, then, does temper the political expression of the honoring ancestors norm among the two groups who, on average, harbor stronger commitments to the norm. However, longer generational residence in the United States among Latinos and Asian

TABLE 4.2 **Demographic correlates of the political ancestors norm**

	Asian	Black	Latino	White
1st generation	0.00 (0.03)	−0.04 (0.04)	0.04 (0.03)	−0.17 (0.07)*
2nd generation	−0.01 (0.03)	−0.08 (0.04)*	0.02 (0.02)	0.05 (0.04)
Male	0.03 (0.02)	−0.03 (0.02)+	0.05 (0.02)*	0.01 (0.02)
Age	0.04 (0.01)*	0.05 (0.01)*	0.03 (0.01)*	0.02 (0.01)*
Income	0.00 (0.00)	0.00 (0.00)	−0.01 (0.00)*	0.01 (0.00)
Education	0.00 (0.01)	0.02 (0.01)*	0.02 (0.01)*	0.01 (0.01)*
(Intercept)	0.10 (0.04)*	0.25 (0.03)*	0.20 (0.04)*	0.25 (0.03)*
N	1,008	955	926	963
R^2	0.04	0.09	0.04	0.03

Notes: Results produced from four linear regression models, one for each racial group. The dependent variable, the political ancestors index, ranges from 0 to 1. Income is a 9-point scale ranging from $0 to $200k+ by $25k; education is a 6-point scale ranging from no high school degree to advanced degree; age is a 7-point scale separated by roughly ten-year increments.

*$p < 0.05$; +$p < 0.1$.

Americans—two groups dominated by recent immigrants—does not seem to *increase* a political expression. Why? The results likely reflect how group variables constrain the expression of the norm above and beyond individual-level traits. Jiménez (2010) suggests that a constant flow of immigrants has led even multigenerational Latinos to have strong ethnicities, replenished continually with traditions and cultural practices from home countries. Further, members of both groups are more likely to experience discrimination from out-groups on the dimension of perceived Americanness, which may shape in-group beliefs about the nature of ancestors regardless of timing of arrival (Zou and Cheryan, 2017). And without concentrated efforts to politically integrate newcomers (Wong, 2008), descriptive group prototypes who are first- or second-generation citizens may set the group's norms, connecting cultural and economic behaviors to honoring ancestors.[13]

Next, gender. Identifying as male rather than female is unrelated to the political ancestors index for Asian and White Americans, but inversely related for Latinos and Black Americans. Latino men are significantly more likely than Latino women to connect the honoring ancestors norm to political involvement; Black women, on the other hand, are significantly more likely than their male counterparts to have a strong political ancestors norm. The effect among Black Americans is especially interesting considering extant work that shows Black women are more participatory than Black men (Ansolabehere and Hersh, 2013; Harris, Sinclair-Chapman, and McKenzie, 2005). Some have noted that gender differences in participation among Black Americans may be driven in part by institutional constraints imposed by the modern criminal justice system that directly affect men more than women (Pettit, 2012; Western, 2006). This contact may depress attitudes about governmental participation (Lerman and Weaver, 2014). Regardless, the finding suggests that Black women may have particularly strong participatory norms, channeled through a commitment to honor the sacrifices and struggles of those in the past.

Age, interestingly, is the only variable that is consistently related to the political ancestors index across groups. Although varying to some degree in its strength depending on racial group membership, on average, older Americans are more likely than younger Americans to see honoring ancestors as requiring political involvement.

Finally, class—including both education and income—is variably related across the groups. Income is negatively related to the political ancestors index for Latinos (an 8% shift from the lowest to highest category), but unrelated for Asian, Black, and White Americans. In contrast, education is positively related for Latinos as well as Black and White Americans. Individuals who have an advanced degree, compared to those who did not complete high school, are between 5 and 10 percentage points more likely to connect the honoring ancestors norm to political involvement.

Together, the results provided in table 4.2 demonstrate additional within-group heterogeneity along the dimensions of age, gender, class, and generational status. Black, well-educated women who are at least third-generation American have some of the strongest ancestors norms in the United States; high-earning but relatively young Latinos, on the other hand, have some of the weakest. Furthermore, with the exception of age, the relationship between these variables and the outcome of interest—participatory expressions of the honoring ancestors norm—is variable depending on the group. This suggests that demographic indicators vary in how they contribute to racial identity and the norms forged within it.

Racial Group Embeddedness and the Political Ancestors Norm

The more embedded individuals are in a group, the more likely they should be to adopt the group's norms. Embeddedness intensifies a number of variables important for norm creation and enforcement. It increases the clarity of signal with regard to both what is prescriptive and what is common; it boosts the flow of information by garnering trust; it allows for greater levels of observation and enforcement; and it affects the degree to which individuals care about a group's acceptance (Cialdini and Trost, 1998; Enos, 2017; Larson and Lewis, 2017; Oliver, 2010; White and Laird, 2020). As a result, geographic, social, and psychological embeddedness in one's own racial group should increase compliance with, and internalization of, group-specific norms.

The PSNS is uniquely set up to examine the relationship between norms and geographic, social, and psychological racial group embeddedness, as it includes measures of each. To capture geographic embeddedness, I collect indicators of the residential census block for respondents and match this information with data from the 2010 census on racial composition at the block level (Manson et al., 2018). I then calculate the proportion of each respondent's census block that is coracial by dividing the number of coracial residents by total residents. This measure of *geographic embeddedness* indicates the degree to which an individual's proximal geographic space is coracial and may capture primarily the effect of descriptive norms on behavior.

For *social embeddedness*, I measure the degree to which a respondent's close social ties are coracial, a measure that primarily relates to injunctive norm formation and enforcement. To develop this measure, I use a two-step name-generator process (e.g., Marsden, 1987; McPherson, Smith-Lovin, and Brashears, 2006). Respondents were asked to provide the first name or initials of up to five individuals with whom they talk regularly about matters important to them. Then respondents were asked about the race of each of these individuals. From these two questions, I calculate the proportion of each respondent's close ties who are coracial.

Finally, I measure *psychological embeddedness* using a question aimed at racial group closeness (Wong, 2010). Respondents in the PSNS were asked, "Some groups of people you may feel close to, while others less so. How close do you feel to people in the United States who are (White/Latino or Hispanic/Asian/Black)?" Although respondents evaluated each of the groups, here I focus on their answer for coracials. This measure should affect both how important acceptance in that group is and also the internalization of a group's norms.

I examine the relationship between each of these embeddedness measures and the political ancestors index to determine whether the likelihood of connecting the ancestors norm to politics is more or less likely depending on geographic, social, and psychological embeddedness in one's own racial group.[14] To do this, I use four linear regression models—one for each racial group—where the political ancestors index is the dependent variable and the three embeddedness measures serve as the primary independent variables. I also include a number of possible covariates. These control variables are selected based on their likelihood to vary across embeddedness measures by racial group. Including them allows us to isolate the effect of racial group embeddedness compared to, say, class embeddedness. Specifically, I include census tract median income, the proportion of a respondent's census tract older than age twenty-five that has at least a high school degree, the proportion of citizens who are either naturalized or noncitizens, and, finally, individual-level controls for income, education, and nativity status. If the creation and enforcement of the honoring ancestors norm—specifically, its political form—are tied to racial group context rather than simply an individual's race, then their strength should vary by embeddedness.

This is indeed what I find. Many of the embeddedness measures are related to political ancestors strength. However, the direction and magnitude of these relationships are variable by group. Figure 4.6 plots the coefficients for the three embeddedness measures—psychological,

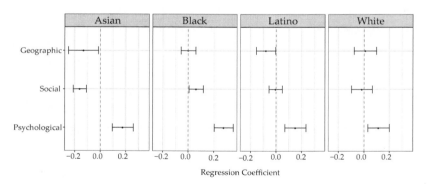

FIGURE 4.6 Relationship between racial group embeddedness and the political ancestors index

Notes: The figure plots the results of four multivariate linear regression models, one for each group. Point estimates show the effect of going from the smallest to the largest category in the independent variable, and 90% confidence intervals are plotted around point estimates. The dependent variable, the political ancestors index, is scaled from 0 to 1, with 1 representing the strongest possible commitment to ancestral honoring through political involvement.

social, geographic—for Asian, Black, Latino, and White Americans separately.[15] Because the independent variables are scaled from 0 to 1, each point estimate represents the equivalent of a full-scale change, moving from the lowest level of coracial embeddedness to the highest.

The results show that both geographic and social embeddedness are *negatively* related to a political expression of honoring ancestors among Asian Americans. Asian Americans who live in the most coracial census blocks in the United States are significantly less likely to believe the way to honor ancestors is through political participation compared to their counterparts embedded in less Asian-populated geographic spaces (-0.13, $p < 0.1$). Social embeddedness is similarly negatively related. Asian Americans with entirely coracial social networks score, on average, 16 percentage points lower on the political ancestors index than Asian Americans with entirely non-coracial social ties ($p < 0.05$). These results confirm that geographic and social embeddedness are associated with increased norm compliance at the group level for Asian Americans.

The result for geographic embeddedness among Latinos is similar. Individuals living in an entirely Latino census block, compared to an entirely non-coracial block, exhibit a weaker attachment of participation to the ancestors norm, an 8% shift ($p < 0.01$). Social embeddedness, though—the proportion of respondents' close social ties who are coracial—is unrelated to a political expression of the ancestors norm.

Black Americans exhibit a reversed pattern with respect to social embeddedness compared to Asian Americans. Social embeddedness, a variable negatively related to the political ancestors norm for Asian Americans, is associated with an increased connection between political participation and honoring ancestors for Black Americans. On average, Black Americans with entirely Black social networks score 6 percentage points higher on the political ancestors index than their counterparts who maintain entirely non-Black networks. Geographic embeddedness, however, when netted of other embeddedness effects, is unrelated to the political ancestors index.

Finally, White Americans show the weakest relationship between group embeddedness and the political ancestors norm with respect to social and geographic embeddedness in coracial contexts. Higher levels of geographic embeddedness and social embeddedness lead to neither stronger nor weaker commitments to the political ancestors index; these two embeddedness variables are simply unrelated to individual norm strength.

While social and geographic embeddedness in group produces variation in the strength of the political ancestors index depending on race, psychological embeddedness produces a consistent pattern—a positive relationship—across all four racial groups. Respondents who feel very close to other members of their racial group—whether it be other Blacks, Whites, Latinos, or Asians in the United States—are significantly more likely to report a political expression of the honoring ancestors norm ($p < 0.05$). The estimated relationships range from 0.12 for Whites to 0.28 among Black Americans.

In general, these results for minority Americans align with the expectations of the racialized norms model: the more embedded in one's group an individual is—with respect to either social or geographic embeddedness—the more an individual aligns with the group's norm. In the case of Black Americans, social embeddedness in one's own group produces a stronger expression of the political honoring ancestors norm. For Asian Americans and Latinos, geographic embeddedness and, to some degree, social embeddedness create a weaker connection. The results suggest that these groups have norms, and the clarity of these norms, along with the internalization of them by individuals, is stronger in contexts dominated by fellow group members.

Second, the most consistent pattern across the four racial groups is the positive relationship between coracial psychological embeddedness and the political ancestors index. Whether a respondent is White, Black, Latino, or Asian, feeling close to one's fellow group members is related to a stronger political expression of the honoring ancestors norm than not feeling close. For Black Americans, this finding is in line with the directional relationship of social embeddedness, but for the other groups, it stands in contrast to the either negative or nonrelationship with the other embeddedness measures.

The positive finding among Asian Americans and Latinos is particularly noteworthy in that it runs counter to the other measures of embeddedness. Rather than producing convergence toward the group's mean, more psychological embeddedness increases a political expression of the honoring ancestors norm for members of these groups.

This finding suggests two things. First, there may be an asymmetry in what geographic and social embeddedness versus psychological embeddedness means for Latinos and Asian Americans. As measured here, social and geographic embeddedness may more precisely capture *ethnic* group embeddedness. Rather than identifying contact with a range of Asian Americans of different ethnicities, ethnic enclaves may produce social and geographic contact that is primarily with individuals of the same ethnicity.

This phenomenon was obvious in my qualitative interviews. Twenty-five-year-old Aisha, for instance, explained, "My community has pretty much been our family-friends circle, all of the Indians pretty much around the Bay Area. . . . It feels like we're living in India almost, I mean, despite living in America. . . . We're all very close knit." On my measure of social and geographic group embeddedness, Aisha would score quite high as a deeply embedded Asian American but her connections are primarily with other Indian Americans, not with Asian Americans broadly. There is ambiguity here in what the social and psychological embeddedness measures are capturing.

In contrast, psychological embeddedness explicitly measures a sense of connectedness to a multiethnic Asian community. Others have shown that such an identity can increase political involvement (Masuoka, 2006, 2008; but see Beltrán, 2010); my findings imply that this increase may follow from, at least in part, how a sense of panethnic group closeness produces a reconceptualizing and politicizing of one's ancestors. Feeling connected to one's racial group—rather than simply one's ethnic group—in the context of the United States requires seeing similarities in history, experience, and fate among group members. This process of reconceptualizing the group within a specifically American context may bring to the fore exactly the types of considerations that animate a connection between honoring ancestors and political participation among Black Americans.

Finally, the lack of a relationship between the political ancestors index and White social and geographic embeddedness but the positive relationship with psychological embeddedness for members of this group alludes to how in-group racial categorization may be simultaneously salient and invisible for Whites in America (e.g., Jardina, 2019; Haney Lopez, 2006). The nonrelationship between social and geographic context and White political expressions of the honoring ancestors norm suggests that other dimensions of heterogeneity—possibly religion, class, or region—may create stronger boundaries of "group" cohesion for White Americans, shaping expressions of honoring ancestors. Still, a sense of psychological connectedness to other White Americans is positively related to a political expression of the norm. This implies that White racial group identity may serve to crystallize beliefs about the past and its relationship to political participation. This is an idea we'll come back to a few times in this book.

The Past and Political Participation

Collectively, the results suggest that a normative commitment to honoring the past is widespread in the United States, but a connection between honoring the past and political participation is highly dependent on racial community. Black and White Americans, on average, are much more likely to conceptualize the honoring ancestors norm through a political lens; Asian Americans and Latinos, on the other hand, more often express ancestral honoring through commitments to continuing religious and cultural traditions. These connections, which produce equally valuable but divergent behavioral expectations, likely shape the incentives individuals face when deciding how to spend their time.

Because the political ancestors index demonstrates positive properties with respect to divergent and predictive validity, reliability, and variation, our next step is to determine whether it can predict who chooses to spend their time engaged in politics. Right now, what we have in the political ancestors index is a measure of attitudes. We have learned who is most likely to believe that honoring the past requires political participation, that this normative commitment varies within and across groups, and that its strength is influenced by embeddedness in a group. Still to determine is whether this normative belief influences political behavior. Do the varying constructs of the honoring ancestors norm help us understand who turns out and who stays home? What can we learn about the antecedents of political participation once we consider the underlying normative concepts connected to it?

We'll turn to these questions in chapters 6 and 7 when we use the political ancestors index to predict behaviors like voting and protest attendance. But first we have one more norm to explore: the helping hands norm. That's the work of the next chapter.

CHAPTER FIVE

Taking Care of Those in Need

Acommitment to helping those in need was a common thread in my discussions with Black and Asian Americans across the country who often identified helping behaviors as a core component of self, career, and relationship to family and society. A prescriptive commitment to help those in need intersected with political participation for some I talked with, drawing it to my attention as a norm with relevance for politics. The primary way these individuals helped those in need was by engaging in the political arena to change policy. Black Americans, more than Asian Americans, discussed this interpretation of the helping hands norm and described how their choices to help others in this way were often rewarded and reinforced by their community.

In this chapter, I use empirical data from the Participatory Social Norms Survey to examine the strength of the helping hands norm in the United States and its behavioral variations across racial groups. I begin by diving into a robust literature in social psychology that examines why, when, and how people help one another. Combining this literature with insights from the qualitative interviews presented in chapter 3, I develop a set of hypotheses about why racial groups in the United States might vary with respect to this particular norm. Specifically, I argue that differences in experiences with and perceptions of structural disadvantage that vary systematically across groups shape beliefs about the causes of need in the United States and the norms that emerge around solutions. In line with the racialized norms model, group-based norms with respect to helping behavior should be clearest in segregated contexts where the signal and enforcement of norms are strongest.

Developing and examining unique empirical measures of the helping hands norm, I find that a prescriptive commitment to helping those in need is widely endorsed in the United States but that both the strength of the norm and how one goes about complying with it vary moderately across racial groups. Black Americans both exhibit stronger commitments to the helping hands norm in general and are more likely to couple the norm with participatory behaviors. Furthermore, social and psychological coracial embeddedness increases the strength of a participatory commitment to the norm for this group. Other racial minorities, too, show some increased coupling of the norm with participatory behaviors compared to Whites, and racial embeddedness again influences the strength and direction of this connection.

The collective evidence suggests that political participation is a behavior sometimes connected to the helping hands norm and that the propensity to make this connection varies somewhat across groups. Yet the magnitude of this cross-group variation is significantly smaller than we observed for the honoring ancestors norm in the previous chapter. The findings suggest, then, that while a political expression of the helping hands norm may influence an individual's propensity to engage in politics, it may be less important for explaining cross-group variation in participation compared to the political ancestors norm.

The When, Why, and How of Helping Behavior

The beauty of the scientific method lies in its ability to create unbiased knowledge, but scientists themselves are far from dispassionate observers. Their choices about how to apply the scientific method—which questions to ask, which measures to use, how to interpret results—reflect everything from the epistemology of their discipline to personal life experiences. As a result, when salient events occur, including war, recession, or protest, the whole trajectory of a discipline can change suddenly as a new set of questions captures the attention of scientists all at once.

This is what happened in the wake of World War II. As the Allied powers made headway against the German forces in the mid-1940s, Soviet, American, and British troops began to uncover mass graves and concentration camps, informing the world of the genocide that had occurred. Millions of German officials, soldiers, and citizens it turned out had systematically tortured and killed the young, the elderly, and the disabled alike. Shocked and horrified, moral theorists and social scientists were left wondering how seemingly ordinary people were convinced to do such terrible things. A burgeoning field of research emerged on *antisocial behavior*, or acts of hostility and violence against others (Ross, Lepper, and Ward, 2010). This research revealed a complicated mix of dispositional and situational factors that led many people to obedience, even under conditions that clearly made them uncomfortable. In some of the most well-known studies ever conducted in the social sciences, scholars began to understand and explain the "banality of evil" (Adorno, 1950; Arendt, 1963; Zimbardo et al., 1971; Milgram, 1963).

As work on antisocial behavior proliferated through the midcentury, some scholars responded by challenging science to think not just about why people do bad things but also why they do good. Stories emerged about those who hid the persecuted and aided in the escape of strangers during the Holocaust, putting their own lives on the line for the sake of others (Monroe, 2013; Oliner and Oliner, 1988). These scholars argued that doing good was not simply the opposite of doing bad, as some had previously assumed. Rather, *prosocial* behavior had its own origins, pushing some individuals from neutrality to altruism and self-sacrifice. On the heels of the antisocial literature, a prosocial scholarship was born as scientists across disciplines began to map the why, when, and how of helping behavior (Batson, 1998; Dovidio, 1984; Penner et al., 2005).

To a lay observer, the question of why some people help others may seem to have an obvious answer: because it is the right thing to do, clearly. But for social scientists, this question challenged a central assumption held widely in economics, political science, and psychology at the time: that people are fundamentally motivated by their own self-interest (Mansbridge, 1990; Monroe, 1994). Theories of human behavior often hinged on the belief that people were universally motivated by the desire to increase their personal well-being, especially with respect to material resources; attitudes and actions followed from this singular goal. But if people were prosocial, sometimes engaging in acts of altruism or even self-sacrifice, what did this mean for the foundational assumption of humans as self-interested actors?

This question led many to quibble over whether human action was ever, really, self-sacrificing, but natural scientists skipped this theoretical conundrum entirely. Informed by the theory of natural selection, these scholars asked, What evolutionary advantage might prosocial behavior produce or be the product of? From this work, an evolutionary theory of prosocial behavior emerged, one that helped explain the cross-cultural tendency to help others (Batson, 1998). Individuals are more

likely to survive and reproduce when they can cooperate with and anticipate the actions of others, evidence suggested, and so tools that aid in
this process proliferate (Dawkins, 1976; Iacoboni, 2009; Petersen, 2011;
Wilson, 2000). Empathy may be one such tool, allowing people to literally feel and mirror the thinking and emotions of those around them
(Batson and Coke, 1981; Iacoboni, 2009). Research suggests that when
observing others in need, many experience psychological distress in response, which can prompt them to action (Batson, 1998; Betancourt,
1990; Dovidio, 1984).

Evolutionary theory then, can help explain the *why* of helping behavior but not necessarily the *when*. Psychological tension following the
observation of someone in need provides a prerequisite for helping behavior, as once a person feels this tension, he or she is motivated to resolve it and can do so through prosocial, helping behavior (Batson, 1998;
Dovidio, 1984). But there are alternatives. Some will chose to flee, es-
caping the situation and person all together if the opportunity presents
itself (Batson, 1998; Darley and Batson, 1973). Others will provide aid,
although this can take on a variety of forms (Diekman and Clark, 2015;
Gilligan, 1993; Luria, Cnaan, and Boehm, 2014). Still others will see
their distress transform into contempt and blame the person in need for
the situation (Batson, 1998).

To understand when a person's psychological tension will manifest in
helping behavior, we must turn to the social features of a situation. This
turn from universal predisposition to contextualized behavior should
be a familiar one by now. In the previous chapter, we learned the desire to honor the past is a near universal concept, appearing in countries, cultures, and religions across the world, but how one goes about
honoring the past is highly context dependent. Helping behavior seems
to follow a similar pattern. Many humans experience psychological tension when observing someone in need, but deciding how to act following this emotional response is heavily driven by context. Beliefs about
who is deserving of help, situational factors that distract or allow for easy
escape, and past experiences that systematically vary across groups all
drive an individual's propensity to decide whether and how to help (Batson, 1998; Darley and Batson, 1973; Diekman and Clark, 2015; Gilens,
2009; Wright, 2001). A basic neurological predisposition to feel tension
when observing someone in need is followed by an environmentally influenced reaction regarding whether helping is the appropriate response
to the observed situation.

So what are the contextual features that lead someone to help ver- sus resolve their psychological tension some other way? Timing and ease of escape are two important factors (Batson, 1998; Darley and Batson, 1973), but so too are beliefs about the attributes of the person needing help and the cause of his or her situation (Betancourt, 1990; Petersen, 2011; Ross, 1977). Research has shown that if an individual believes a person's distress is caused by his or her own doing—that is, the person either has dispositional flaws like laziness or has made bad choices lead- ing to his or her need—a potential helper is more likely to reject the needy person. In contrast, if the problem is perceived as caused by the situation—say, a structural malfunction or bad luck outside of the per- son's control—then empathy is more likely to follow, leading to helping behavior. Beliefs about worthiness and the cause of one's problems de- termine whether an individual responds to a person in need with empa- thy and prosocial action or contempt and rejection (Betancourt, 1990; McMahon, Wernsman, and Parnes, 2006).

Unlike the predisposition to help itself, the manifestation of *attribu- tion*, then, is far from unified. But neither is it random. Structural fea- tures of a society or group that shape exposure to need or beliefs about agency can create group-level patterns in attributional tendencies (Wright, 2001; Zucker and Weiner, 1993). Research suggests that per- sonal experiences with suffering as well as occupying a low-status posi- tion can lead to greater empathy and a higher propensity toward proso- cial action under certain circumstances (Gilens, 2009; Piff et al., 2010; Vollhardt, 2009).[1] Perceived similarity between oneself and the person in need also triggers stronger empathetic reactions and an increased pro- pensity to help (Fowler and Kam, 2007; Penner et al., 2005; Sirin, Valen- tino, and Villalobos, 2016a, 2016b). Macrostructural features of a society that unequally distribute resources, create inequalities in exposure to in- justice, or build status differences between groups, then, can lead to sys- tematic variations in the perceived causes of need.

Not only are beliefs about attribution context dependent, but so too are the actions individuals choose to engage in when trying to help oth- ers (Brickman et al., 1982). *How* one helps, that is, once one has decided to do so, is shaped by the opportunities and constraints imposed by soci- ety and the situation. Men and women, for instance, have been shown to help differently, with their behaviors reflecting the skills and social roles imposed upon them (Diekman and Clark, 2015; Gilligan, 1993). Struc- tural constraints with respect to the pathways available for helping also influence the form of prosocial behavior. Volunteering, for instance, is possible only in societies with robust civic organizations (Luria, Cnaan, and Boehm, 2014). The menu of options in America ranges from direct and voluntary organizational assistance to structural change (Poppendieck, 1999), but context affects one's choice.

Because beliefs about the causes of need are responsive to structural elements of society and opportunities to provide aid are similarly constrained by structural forces, descriptive norms about what the average person thinks and how he or she acts can diverge based on group membership. If benefits exist to sustain these descriptive norms, then prescriptive norms are likely to follow (Morris et al., 2015). Beliefs about deservingness and the behaviors associated with helping transform into group-level social norms that are defined, justified, and reinforced over time by the micro mechanisms of social expectation, socialization, and elite framing. Those socially embedded in a group, or highly identified with its members, will be more likely to conform to these norms (Conover, 1988; Huddy, 2013), and with enough reinforcement, external norms are integrated into core concepts of self and morality, leading to the rise of powerful personal norms (Batson, 1998; Schwartz, 1977; Thøgersen, 2006).

Thus, much like the honoring ancestors norm, the tendency to help people in need likely has its foundation in evolutionary biology, but the exact ways people help others and the conditions for action are group specific and highly variable. The selection of genes that lubricate social relations gives rise to a broad, psychological predisposition to feel empathy and help others, shared by many around the globe. But the specific content of the *helping hands norm*—who is deserving, how best to help—mirrors the contextual features of a group. Macrostructural forces constrain the development of these norms, but group members have agency in defining their essence and maintaining their cohesion.

Expectations about Variation in Helping Behavior

Extant theory on prosocial behavior suggests that normative commitments to help those in need are widespread, but the *when* and *how* of helping behavior is variable. My qualitative work in chapter 3 suggested that variation might exist across groups in the propensity to link political participation to the helping hands norm. Black Americans were more likely than Asian Americans to identify political involvement, especially localized and grassroots political activity, as a way to help those in need. Asian Americans were more likely to identify individual acts of generosity. My analysis of these interviews suggested that differences stemmed from variation in individual-level material status and individual- and group-level exposure to injustice; the prosocial literature confirms that this may be the case, highlighting how these factors likely affect beliefs about the structural causes of need and influence prosocial responses. We can use these insights to develop a set of hypotheses about how and why political participation as a helping behavior may vary across racial groups in the United States.

When discussing why and how they help, many Black Americans I interviewed cited their own experiences with poverty, racial injustice, and violence—or mentioned the experiences of those close to them. Tisha provides an example. A Black woman and resident of Oakland, Tisha discussed the murder of her childhood friend, the poor representation her father received in a trial for attempted robbery, and her time spent in foster care when I asked about her decision to pursue a law degree. These experiences shaped her interest in working for policy change in the criminal justice system. "I came in with the goal of being a youth lawyer," she said, but now, "a lot of people are trying to push me into going into politics. . . . I want to effect change on the policy level, because that's really where the change happens in terms of laws."

Scholars have long documented the ways that Black Americans are "disadvantaged and devalued" compared to Whites, who "are positioned as the dominant and most advantaged group in American society" (Zou and Cheryan, 2017, 696; see also Hochschild, Weaver, and Burch, 2012; Masuoka and Junn, 2013; Pettit, 2012; Sidanius and Pratto, 1999). This position in the racial hierarchy affects the treatment of Black Americans across a wide range of economic, political, and legal institutions (Alexander, 2012; Pager, 2003; Sidanius and Pratto, 1999) and manifests in striking income and wealth gaps. As of 2017, the median Black household was estimated to have $28,000 less in income and $100,000 less in assets than its non-Hispanic White counterpart (Fontenot, Semega, and Kollar, 2018; Kochhar and Fry, 2014). Furthermore, Black Americans report a high level of discrimination centered around their perceived social and intellectual worth (Zou and Cheryan, 2017).

The fact that Black Americans, as a group, are situated lower in the American racial hierarchy, are more likely to experience poverty first-hand or through proximal means, and face continuing constraints with respect to the perceived porousness of their group likely affect the average group member's beliefs about why people are in need and the best ways to help them. Experimental research in social psychology has shown that awareness of one's low status shifts beliefs about desert (Piff et al., 2010) and that individuals who experience suffering or injustice respond more empathetically when observing others in parallel situations (Sirin, Valentino, and Villalobos, 2016b; Vollhardt, 2009). These factors should produce an observable group-level pattern among Black Americans with regard to the causes of need in the United States. Indeed, evidence from the General Social Survey (GSS) suggests that Black Americans are more likely than Whites to believe coming from a wealthy family is key to getting ahead in America, are less likely to believe hard work alone leads to success, and more commonly cite racial discrimination as the cause of Black social and economic status.[2]

An increased likelihood to see need as the product of structural malfunction may lead Black Americans not only to attitudes that encourage redistributive policies (Dawson, 2003; Gilens, 2009) but also to helping behaviors aimed at changing what is perceived as an unjust political system (Brickman et al., 1982). Social identity theory suggests that when the boundaries of groups are tightly constrained, the most well-off members of low-status groups will press for social change (Tajfel and Turner, 1986). This dynamic is well captured in my interview with DeMarkus, a Tennessee resident who works on a college campus. He and his wife have advanced degrees, collectively make six figures, and own their home. He told me, "I promise you, if I had all the stuff I needed and I was sure that my family was gonna have for the next few years, I might not give two cares about this political system. I may not care, 'cause I have that privilege and that luxury. And I kind of have it now, a little bit. [But] I'm still Black. That's the only problem." Even middle- and upper-class Black Americans, then—individuals who make up a growing segment of the population (Hochschild, Weaver, and Burch, 2012)—may tie the helping hands norm to political participation. Group elites, too, may actively tie political activity to norms about helping those in need as a way of advancing group interests.

Societal constraints in the form of Black Americans' minority status in a majoritarian democracy may further shape the expression of the helping hands norm. Politically oriented helping behavior may be channeled into local electoral politics, where minority groups sometimes make up a larger share of the voting population (Hajnal and Trounstine, 2005), and into nonvoting political activities, which do not require access from a gatekeeper (Gillion, 2013). Thus, while we are likely to observe a number of behaviors associated with helping those in need—reflecting the proliferation of charitable, religious, and direct service options— Black Americans might be more likely than others groups to name political activism that is local or nonelectoral as a way to address need in the United States.

In contrast, a consideration of group status and experiences with disadvantage suggests that White Americans, on average, may be less likely to connect the helping hands norm to political activism. White Americans have dominated the top of the racial hierarchy for as long as the nation has existed (Haney Lopez, 2006; Masuoka and Junn, 2013; Omi and Winant, 2014), and a smaller percentage of White Americans live below the poverty line than any other racial group (Fontenot, Semega, and Kollar, 2018). This positioning likely affects beliefs about the causes of and solutions for need. Humans are inclined to down-weight situational factors when explaining others' behavior (Ross, 1977; Ross, Amabile, and Steinmetz, 1977), ascribe success to self but disappointments to external causes (Bradley, 1978; Pettigrew, 1979), and assign trait-based explanations for need to out-groups (Hewstone, 1990). These proclivities assist in a process of justifying White social, political, and economic domination, attitudes that are further crystallized and activated by elites (Gilens, 2009; Mendelberg, 2001).

Others have shown that many White Americans identify helping people in need as normatively important but believe that the government is likely to help those who are undeserving (Cramer, 2016; Katz, 2013)—namely, Black people (Bobo and Kluegel, 1993; Gilens, 2009; Snowden and Graaf, 2019). Evidence from the GSS shows that White Americans, on average, rate Black people as significantly lazier than their in-group.[3] Those inclined to help, as a result, may turn to prosocial behaviors where the recipient of the help is more closely within their direct control, like charitable giving or volunteering. However, a connection between the helping hands norm and politics may diverge significantly by partisanship for White Americans, with Democrats more likely to perceive structural disadvantage and seek political solutions for need as a result.

Work on the racial hierarchy in the United States generally situates Latinos and Asian Americans between White and Black Americans—

although the arrangement of these two groups relative to each other depends on the scholar (e.g., Lee, 2005; Masuoka and Junn, 2013; Zou and Cheryan, 2017). Asian Americans have, on average, the highest level of yearly family income of the four largest racial groups in the United States and are lauded as a "model minority" (Fontenot, Semega, and Kollar, 2018; Junn, 2008). With their socioeconomic status framed as reflecting positive, internal traits of the group's members, Asian Americans are commonly placed in juxtaposition to Black Americans—by White elites but also by Asian Americans themselves—despite radically different group histories (Junn, 2008; Masuoka and Junn, 2013; Osajima, 2005; Paek and Shah, 2003; Wong et al., 1998; Wong and Halgin, 2006).[4]

These factors may lead Asian Americans, on average, to situate the causes of need in the dispositions of individuals rather than in structural malfunction, leading to helping behaviors expressed through means other than politics. However, I expect this pattern to be tempered compared to White Americans. Many have argued that the model-minority myth produces a number of negative externalities, including the continuation of the perception of Asian Americans as "forever foreigners," a stereotype that has historically constrained the political and economic rights of Asian Americans (Junn, 2008; Lee, 2005; Takaki, 2008; Wong and Halgin, 2006; Wong et al., 2011). Jonathan, a medical student at an elite private university I interviewed, echoed the social science research on this topic. He explained, "The model-minority myth, in a lot of ways, in really kind of bad ways, has been internalized by the Asian American community as a form of flattery, even though it's used as a cultural bludgeon. . . . They said, 'Oh, see these Japanese Americans and these Chinese Americans, they don't need rights, 'cause they have good family values, and hard work, and focus on education.' . . . Bill O'Reilly used [this line of reasoning] last week." As a result, members of this group who are highly aware of their minority status and see commonality across Asian Americans may be more likely to identify political activism as a way to help those in need.

Latinos similarly face ambiguity in status. Noting the categorization of Latino/Hispanic as an ethnicity rather than a race on official government forms like the US Census and efforts to incorporate Latinos into conservative, primarily White coalitions, some have argued that this racial group in particular is more poorly defined in the United States, leading to porousness and attempts to "Whiten" its members (Beltrán, 2010; Gans, 2012; Mora, 2014; Waterston, 2006). Others argue that the focus on immigration policy in the United States along with the recent criminalization of border crossings is increasingly racializing the group and defining the experiences of even third-, fourth-, and fifth-generation Latinos (Jiménez, 2010; Waters and Kasinitz, 2015). As a result, some theoretical models position Latinos between Black and White Americans at a level commensurate with Asian Americans, while others place them below both Asian Americans and Whites but above Black Americans (e.g., Lee, 2005; Masuoka and Junn, 2013; Omi and Winant, 2014).

Regardless of their potential status as honorary Whites, Latinos in the United States more closely resemble Black Americans with respect to poverty and resources. Thirteen percent of Latinos in the United States have at least a bachelor's degree, compared to 29% of Whites and 18% of Blacks (Ogunwole, Drewery, and Rios-Vargas, 2012). Furthermore, an estimated 18% of Latinos live below the poverty line, 3% fewer than Black Americans but almost 10% more than White Americans (Fontenot, Semega, and Kollar, 2018). Evidence suggests that Latinos are more likely than Asian Americans or Whites to experience discrimination and stereotyping with respect to their perceived cultural, economic, and intellectual qualities (Zou and Cheryan, 2017). The relatively low levels of socioeconomic resources among Latinos combined with the racialization of the group should lead to stronger helping hands norms compared to White Americans and a stronger propensity to situationalize poverty, leading to grassroots political action rather than charitable solutions to American need. However, this commitment may be tempered compared to Black Americans, with more heterogeneity within the group.

My expectations about variations in the helping hands norm are displayed visually in figure 5.1. The figure arrays groups along a continuum that encompasses positioning with respect to experiences with and perceptions of structural disadvantage, based on extant literature and hypotheses about the likelihood of expressing the helping hands norm through political involvement below. White Americans are situated to the far left of the spectrum, reflecting how the group's high status and resources are expected to produce a weak connection between the helping hands norm and political participation. Black Americans, in contrast, are situated on the opposite end of the spectrum, reflecting their historical anchoring at the bottom of the American racial hierarchy and beliefs about the structural disadvantage targeted at their group.

Asian Americans and Latinos are centrally arranged between these two groups, with Asian Americans shifted slightly to the left of the

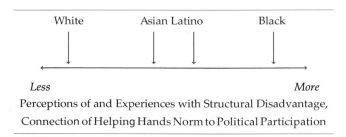

FIGURE 5.1 Expected group variability in the helping hands norm

continuum. While I expect all three minority groups to be more likely than White Americans to connect the helping hands norm to political involvement, especially grassroots action that is local and system challenging and champions community-based leadership, this commitment should be tempered among Latinos and Asian Americans, for whom the boundaries of racial group are more porous.

Commitments to and Expressions of Helping Others

Having defined specific expectations about the direction and strength of the helping hands norms in the United States, I turn to testing these hypotheses using the PSNS. This data set includes a novel four-item battery designed to measure prescriptive commitments to helping the needy. Each respondent in the PSNS was asked to think about "those in need. This might include people who are struggling to get by or are experiencing hardship," then indicate the degree to which they agreed or disagreed (0–4) with four randomly presented statements:

- Helping those in need is a guiding principle in my life.
- I should make sacrifices of my own—time, money, or other things—to help people in need.
- I feel a moral duty to help those who are struggling.
- I should pursue what is best for me and my family even if it comes at the expense of people in need (reverse coded).

These four items were designed to capture an underlying propensity to prioritize helping those in need, gauging attitudes about prosocial behavior aimed at strangers rather than kin. Each statement is laden with normative language, orienting individuals to evaluate helping behavior within the framework of what is right and good (Bicchieri, 2016; Thøgersen, 2006). Although these measures most accurately represent the strength of personal norms, when aggregated together they provide insight into group descriptive or injunctive norms as well (Thøgersen, 2006).

I hoped that these items would load together to measure a single concept and the empirical evidence suggests they do. A Cronbach's alpha test confirms that the battery has high internal consistency both in the sample as a whole ($\alpha = 0.71$) and across groups (Asian $\alpha = 0.71$, Black $\alpha = 0.66$, Latino $\alpha = 0.68$, White $\alpha = 0.78$). I average responses to these four items, producing a single score for each respondent that indicates the strength of his or her personal helping hands norm. Ranging from 0 to 4, high scores on this scale identify individuals who have strong prescriptive commitments to help those in need; low scores represent individuals with weak commitments to the helping hands norm. I call this measure the *helping hands index*.

Figure 5.2 shows the distribution for each racial group with respect to the helping hands norm. Low values along the x axis represent weak commitments to the norm, while higher values represent stronger commitments. The y axis plots within-group proportions, and a vertical dashed line indicates the mean for each group.

The results show distributions that are skewed to the left, suggesting a general endorsement of the norm both in the sample as a whole and across racial groups. Fewer than 4% of the entire sample register a score

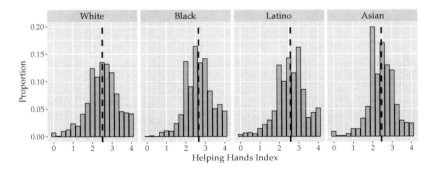

FIGURE 5.2 Distribution of helping hands strength

below 1, indicating they "somewhat disagree" to "strongly disagree" with the provided statements. Furthermore, the sample mean of 2.55 is statistically distinct from the scale's midpoint. However, compared to the honoring ancestors norm, commitments to help those in need are tempered. In chapter 4, I showed that nearly 50% of the PSNS sample scored between the top two categories of the honoring ancestors index (figure 4.2); comparatively, only 20% of the sample register the same strong commitment to the helping hands norm. Furthermore, the helping hands index sample mean is statistically lower than that of the honoring ancestors index ($p < 0.01$). The results suggest that while many Americans seem to embrace the helping hands norm, a commitment to honor the struggles and sacrifices of those in the past is more widespread than is a commitment to help those in need.

Turning to each of the individual groups, the results show variation with respect to endorsements of the helping hands norm. Of the four groups, Black Americans demonstrate the strongest commitment to helping those in need, with a sample mean of 2.66, followed by Latinos at 2.59, White Americans at 2.51, and Asians at 2.45. All sample means are statistically distinct from one another at levels of $p < 0.07$. Within-item variation also appears across groups (appendix C, figure C.3). For instance, 28% of Black Americans and 24% of Latinos strongly agree that helping those in need is a guiding principle in their lives, compared to only 16% of Whites and 14% of Asians. These results suggest that moderate but statistically significant differences appear across the groups with respect to the strength of the norm. Many believe that helping those in need is normatively required of them, but Black Americans are most likely to embrace this commitment.

How do Americans go about expressing these commitments to help the needy? A question from the PSNS allows us to explore this. Respondents were asked to "think again about people who are in need. What do you think are the best ways to take care of these people?" The question was followed by a list of eight response options presented in random order with the addition of "none" and "other" anchored at the end. Drawing from my qualitative interviews, these response options fell into three theoretical categories: political expressions of the helping hands norm, charitable or personal service expressions, and religious expressions. For the political expressions, respondents could indicate that the best way to help those in need was through voting or engaging in politics to change policy, giving money to political causes, or participating in po-

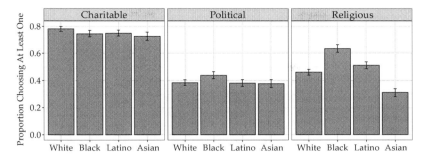

FIGURE 5.3 Ways to help those in need

litical organizations. For the charitable and personal service expression, respondents could select giving money to charitable causes, participating in charitable organizations, or acts of service to strangers. Finally, for the religious expression of the norm, respondents could select praying for those in need or helping those in need find a religious community.[5]

Figure 5.3 plots the proportion of each racial group that selected at least one behavior from each of the three categories. Eighty percent confidence intervals surround the point estimates, indicating roughly a 0.05 statistical t-test between groups (Cumming and Finch, 2005; Schenker and Gentleman, 2001). The plots show that of the three categories, charitable activities are the more common behaviors tied to the helping hands norm for all four groups. Seventy-eight percent of White Americans, 75% of Black Americans and Latinos, and 73% of Asian Americans suggest charitable activity is the best way to care for the needy. White Americans, however, are statistically more likely than the three minority groups to select at least one charitable activity as an ideal way to help those in need ($p < 0.05$).

Wider variation appears with respect to the connection between religious behaviors and the helping hands norm. Here, 63% of Black Americans, 51% of Latinos, 44% of White Americans, and 31% of Asian Americans connect at least one religious behavior to helping those in need. All group point estimates are statistically distinct from one another ($p < 0.05$) and substantively quite large.

Finally, all four groups are significantly less likely to select at least one political activity as a way to help those in need compared to charitable activities, but the connection between political activities and prosocial helping is still relatively common. More than a third of the sample identify political participation as part of the helping hands norm, but variation occurs with respect to the prevalence of this connection. As hypothesized, Black Americans are significantly more likely than the three other groups to select at least one political behavior as a way to care for those in need. The other three groups—Asian, Latino, and White Americans—are statistically indistinguishable. Forty-four percent of Black Americans connect political involvement to the helping hands norm, compared to 38% of Asian, Latino, and White respondents. This six-point gap between Black Americans and other racial groups is statistically significant at $p < 0.05$.

These results only partially confirm expectations. While Black Americans are statistically more likely than other groups to connect at least one political behavior to the helping hands norm, there is no variation between Asian, Latino, and White Americans. However, variation may still appear with respect to the specific political behaviors attached to the helping hands norm for each group.

To examine this possibility, figure 5.4 shows the proportion of each racial group selecting specific political behaviors associated with the helping hands norm: vote or engage in politics to change policy, give money to political causes, and participate in political organizations.[6] Although some nuance emerges with respect to how groups go about bundling political behaviors into the helping hands norm, significantly less variation appears than with respect to the honoring ancestors norm (figure 4.4). Across groups, the most common political behavior associated with helping those in need is to "vote or engage in politics to change policy." Black Americans are more likely than the other racial minority groups to consider this activity an ideal way to help those in need. Forty-

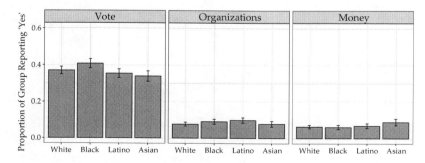

FIGURE 5.4 Political expression of helping hands by group

one percent of Black Americans select this option as the best way to help the needy, compared to 35% of Latinos, 34% of Asian Americans, and 37% of White Americans ($p < 0.05$ for the Black/Latino-Asian comparison and $p < 0.1$ for the Black/White comparison).

Differences in the other two political behaviors show only marginally significant variation across groups. Latinos are most likely to report participating in political organizations as a way to help those in need at 10%, compared to 9% of Black Americans and 8% of White and Asian Americans. The two-point gap between Latinos on one hand and White and Asian Americans on the other is substantively small and only marginally significant ($p < 0.1$). Finally, Asian Americans are significantly more likely than both White and Black Americans to report giving money to political causes as a way to help those in need ($p < 0.05$) and marginally more likely than Latinos to do so ($p < 0.1$).

Similar to the honoring ancestors norm, then, the results show that a number of behaviors can and do get bundled into the helping hands norm. Americans can show compliance with the norm through charitable, religious, and even political behaviors, but some groups are more likely than others to endorse one way of helping compared to another. Although the variation is less pronounced than with the honoring ancestors norm, White Americans are more likely than racial minorities to endorse charitable giving as the best way to help those in need. Black Americans are more likely than other groups to believe political activity is the best way to care for those in need. Furthermore, specific racial minority groups are occasionally more likely to attach political behaviors to the helping hands norm. This variation, though, is significantly muted compared to the honoring ancestors norm explored in the previous chapter. Analyses of the PSNS there revealed relatively large gaps of up to 15 percentage points between groups with respect to the propensity to couple political participation to the honoring ancestors norm in general and to specific political behaviors in particular.

The Political Helping Index

We can combine the three political items connected to helping those in need to make a single measure gauging the strength of a personal political expression of the helping hands norm for each respondent. I assign a point for each political act an individual selected, then add together

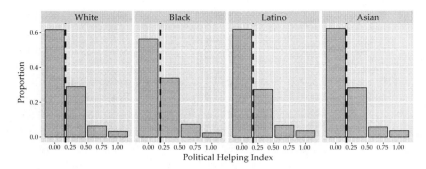

FIGURE 5.5 Distribution of the political helping index by group

these three items and rescale the measure from 0 to 1. Zero signifies the individual did not select any political acts as ways to help those in need, and one means they selected all of the political items when describing the best ways to care for the needy. The distribution of this measure, which I call the *political helping index*, is plotted in figure 5.5 for each of the four racial groups.

The figures show distributions heavily scaled to the right, suggesting a strong connection between the helping hands norm and political activity are relatively rare in the United States. Only 3%–4% of any racial group connect all three political behaviors to taking care of those in need, while fully 62% of White Americans, Asian Americans, and Latinos and 56% of Black Americans make no connection between political participation and helping those in need.[7]

The relative rarity of a strong political helping hands norm does not suggest that it is inconsequential for political participation. Rather, high-cost grassroots political actions—the types of behaviors most commonly coupled with the helping hands norm during interviews—are relatively unusual in the United States, suggesting the variable that explains these behaviors should also be relatively rare. However, the consistent means in the political helping index across groups ($x = 0.17$–0.19) suggest that this variable may be less important for explaining variation across groups than the honoring ancestors norm. As a result, we may find that a political interpretation of the helping hands norm is important for predicting engagement in politics among individuals but does relatively less to explain across-group differences in engagement.

I will use the political helping index later to predict engagement in politics, so it is important we confirm that this newly constructed mea-

sure is distinct from other known political variables. If the political helping index is simply a reiteration of other measures already known to matter in the political world, it does little to grow our understanding of the
dynamics of politics. For instance, critics might wonder whether the political helping index simply captures one's interest in political affairs
rather than measuring the unique bundling of the helping hands norm
with political behavior or may be concerned that the political helping index is a reiteration of the well-known concept of racial linked fate among
low-status group members. Before we start using our measure to predict
political behavior, then, we want to establish that the political helping index has *discriminant validity* from other possible confounds.

I examine the relationship between the political helping index and
four political variables—political interest, racial linked fate, and Democratic versus Republican partisanship compared to independents—as
I did for the political ancestors index using Pearson's correlation coefficients.[8] I also examine the relationship between the political helping index and the political ancestors index to further determine whether the
two measures capture distinct norm expressions rather than simply a latent interest in political participation.

Table 5.1 shows the results of these analyses. The tests confirm that
while the political helping index is correlated with each alternative measure of political and group investment, the relationships are far from
perfect. Rather, most of the variables are only weakly correlated with
the political helping index, providing us with confirmation that our

TABLE 5.1 **Relationship between the political helping norm and political dispositions**

	Asian	Black	Latino	White
Political interest	0.39	0.38	0.37	0.36
	(418)	(1,000)	(995)	(999)
Republican partisanship	0.16	0.03	0.06	0.09
	(390)	(140)	(321)	(571)
Democratic partisanship	0.22	0.15	0.25	0.36
	(640)	(897)	(720)	(466)
Racial linked fate	0.13	0.19	0.16	0.01
	(1,013)	(986)	(988)	(990)
Political ancestors index	0.51	0.52	0.55	0.49
	(1,020)	(1,001)	(1,000)	(1,000)

Notes: Table entry is the Pearson's correlation coefficient; number of observations appears in parentheses.
Political interest is measured using a 4-point scale; Democratic and Republican partisanship are 4-point scales
where 0 represents independents, 1 represents leaners, 2 represents weak identifiers, and 3 represents strong
identifiers; racial linked fate is a 5-point scale; the political ancestors index is a 4-point scale developed in the
previous chapter.

newly constructed measure of helping others through political involvement makes an independent contribution to our understanding of orientations to the political system. That is, the political helping index measures something distinct, although related to, other known measures of psychological investment in politics and one's racial group.

Specifically, political interest is positively related to the political helping index for each of the four groups, with an *r* ranging from 0.36 (White) to 0.39 (Asian). This positive relationship suggests that those with a strong political helping index are also more likely to be interested in politics, an expected outcome. It also provides confirmation that the two measures capture distinct variations in attitudes, giving us confidence that the political helping index is not simply an indication of those high in political interest.

Similarly, the strength of Democratic and Republican partisanship is positively related to the political helping index for each of the four groups, although the relationship tends to be stronger for Democratic partisans. While a strong Republican identifier is more likely than a partisan independent to see helping those in need as requiring political action, the relationship ranges from only 0.03 (Black) to 0.16 (Asian). Among Democrats, the strength of partisanship is positively related at rates of 0.15 (Black) to 0.36 (White). The relatively stronger connection between Democratic partisanship and the helping hands norm, especially among White Americans, is expected given the theoretical centering of structural disadvantage in the party's current platform. I have argued that perceptions of and experiences with structural disadvantage within a group help to couple the helping hands norm with political participation. White coalitions within the Democratic Party tend to be low-status members of the American social system on dimensions other than race (e.g., women, LGBTQ individuals, low socioeconomic status individuals) and as a result, may be more likely to perceive and experience such disadvantage. Alternatively, the relationship may capture the underlying ideology of the party that centers structural solutions for problems like poverty and discrimination.

Racial linked fate is similarly related to the political helping index but only weakly so and at rates variable across groups. The strength of this relationship increases as we move from the highest-status racial group (White Americans, *r* = 0.01) to the lowest (Black Americans, *r* = 0.19).

Finally, the results show a correlation between the political helping index and the political ancestors index ranging from 0.49 (White) to 0.55 (Latino). Although larger than the other correlation coefficients in the table, the relationship still falls well below the conventional threshold of 0.85 for determining discriminant validity (Campbell and Fiske, 1959). Collectively, the results confirm that while other variables of political and group interests are statistically related to the political helping norm, they are not the same thing. Rather, the political helping index introduces a unique concept with discriminant validity, one we'll use in the next two chapters to predict and explain political involvement in the United States.

Racial Group Embeddedness and the Political Helping Norm

The racialized norms model suggests that group-based norms will be most evident in highly racialized contexts. It is within these settings that norm signal is the strongest and enforcement is most potent (Larson and Lewis, 2017; Oliver, 2010). The results so far suggest that only moderate variation exists across groups with respect to the political behaviors bundled into the helping hands norm, but does racial embeddedness intensify this variation?

I use the PSNS to examine whether geographic, social, or psychological embeddedness in a racial group leads to a weaker or stronger interpretation of the political helping norm. I rely on the same measures developed and discussed in the previous chapter. Geographic embeddedness measures the degree to which a respondent's census block is coracial. Social embeddedness represents the proportion of respondents' close social ties that are coracial. And psychological embeddedness is a measure of in-group feelings of closeness.

I use four linear regression models—one for each racial group—to estimate the relationship between group embeddedness and a political expression of the helping hands norm. For each of these regressions, the dependent variable is the political helping index, and the primary independent variables are the measures of geographic, social, and psychological coracial embeddedness, scaled from 0 to 1. I include controls in these models for variables that likely covary with racial context and may be associated with helping norms: census tract median income; the proportion of a respondent's census tract older than age twenty-five who has

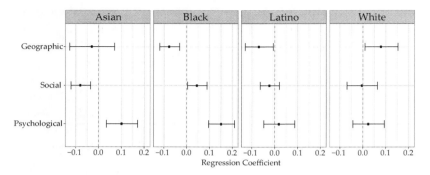

FIGURE 5.6 Relationship between racial group embeddedness and the political helping index

Notes: The figure plots the results of four multivariate linear regression models, one for each group. Point estimates show the effect of going from the smallest to the largest category in the independent variable, and 90% confidence intervals are plotted around point estimates. The dependent variable, the political helping index, is scaled from 0 to 1, with 1 representing the strongest possible commitment to helping those in need through political involvement.

at least a high school degree; the proportion of citizens who are either naturalized or noncitizens; and individual-level controls for income, education, and nativity status.

Figure 5.6 plots the coefficients for geographic, social, and psychological coracial embeddedness, drawn from each of the four linear regression models available in appendix C, table C.4. By including each of the embeddedness measures in a single model, these coefficients estimate the independent effect of each level of context on the political expression of the norm. Since these independent variables are scaled from 0 to 1, we can interpret the plotted points as the estimated full-scale change in the strength of the political helping index when moving from the lowest to the highest level of coracial embeddedness.

The results show that the strength of the political helping index often varies with racial embeddedness, especially for Asian and Black Americans. Specifically, social embeddedness has a negative effect on the strength of the political helping norm for Asian Americans, but psychological embeddedness has a positive effect. Maintaining a network of close ties that is entirely coracial versus not doing so produces an 8% decrease in the strength of the political ancestors norm among Asian Americans ($p < 0.05$). In contrast, psychological embeddedness in the group—that is, a feeling of closeness with other Asian American panethnics—increases the political helping index for Asian Americans by 10% ($p < 0.05$). Geographic coracial embeddedness, however, has no discernible effect on Asian American beliefs about whether the helping hands norm demands political participation.

For Black Americans, both social and psychological embeddedness lead to an increase in a political expression of the helping hands norm. Specifically, psychological closeness with other Black Americans increases the strength of the political helping index by 15%, and coracial social embeddedness creates a 5% increase in the politicization of the norm ($p < 0.05$ and $p < 0.1$, respectively). Geographic embeddedness, however, is negatively associated with the politicization of the norm, producing a 7% decrease in the strength of the political helping index, an unexpected finding.

While racial embeddedness—especially social and psychological embeddedness—affects the strength of the political helping norm for Asian and Black Americans, it has little effect on the dispositions of Latino and White Americans. For both groups, social and psychological embeddedness are statistically unrelated to a political expression of the helping hands norm, and geographic embeddedness is related to a marginally significant—but contrasting—effect. For Latinos, increased geographic embeddedness decreases the strength of the political helping index by 6% ($p < 0.1$). For White Americans, geographic coracial embeddedness increases the political expression of the norm by 8% ($p < 0.1$).

In many ways, the results mirror the broader pattern of variation with respect to a political expression of the norm across groups: while some variation exists in the racialization of the norm, it is significantly smaller and less consistent than what we observed for the honoring ancestors norm in the previous chapter. While racial embeddedness shapes the propensity to link the helping hands norm to political participation among Black and Asian Americans, it often does so in contrasting directions and with less potency than for the honoring ancestors norm, where effect sizes were often between ten and twenty points. Thus, while a politicization for the helping hands norm does seem to vary across racial contexts, the degree of the variation is less pronounced.

Helping Those in Need through Political Action

Beliefs about deservingness, propensities toward empathy, and the effect of both on prosocial policy positions have held growing interest among political scientists in recent years (e.g., Cramer, 2016; Gilens, 2009; Piston, 2018; Sirin, Valentino, and Villalobos, 2016a). These scholars argue that race, group position, and perceptions about who the government is inclined to help influence a range of political attitudes, including partisanship, redistribution, and immigration. To this literature, I add the measurement of a new political attitude: a normative belief that political participation is a way to help those in need.

My results demonstrate that prescriptive beliefs about the importance of helping those in need are quite common in the United States, echoing those who have engaged with this question from a policy perspective (Gilens, 2009; Piston, 2018). However, the behaviors associated with helping—that is, how one goes about showing compliance with the prescriptive norm—are many. Helping those in need can take the form of charitable action, religious work, and even political involvement. Furthermore, the likelihood of elevating political participation as a way to help those most in need varies slightly across groups, with Black Americans in particular, and minority Americans in general, more likely than White respondents to make this connection. Drawing from a rich literature in social psychology on prosocial behavior, I argue that this variation comes from differences in status and resources between the groups that alter perceptions of deservingness and the causes of suffering.

The results also indicate that racial variation in the political helping index is significantly smaller than what we observed for the political ancestors norm discussed in the previous chapter. This finding suggests that while a prescriptive commitment to help those in need through political action may shape motivations to engage in politics broadly, it may be less important for explaining across-group likelihood to engage. I turn next to examining this possibility, determining whether our newly constructed measures of political social norms—the political helping index and political ancestors index—explain turnout in large, salient elections above and beyond extant theories.

CHAPTER SIX

Norms and National Turnout

We have now identified, defined, and measured the honoring ancestors and helping hands norms, two widely shared social norms that vary in their connection to political participation across racial groups in the United States. As we've seen, these two norms are consequential in the formation of *political attitudes*, influencing group beliefs about whether political participation is important, useful, respected, required. But do these norms also affect *political behavior*? Are they consequential in the decisions individuals make when deciding whether to engage?

In this chapter, I turn to testing the influence of participatory social norms on turnout in high-salience national elections—or those years when either a president or members of the US Congress are elected. I again use data from the PSNS. I find that the honoring ancestors norm is of central importance for explaining who shows up at the polls and who stays home during presidential and midterm elections. Across groups and in a variety of years, my novel political ancestors index predicts validated voter turnout at rates outpacing alternatives, including degree of political recruitment, political interest, racial linked fate, income, and education. Further, accounting for norm prevalence helps explain variation in minority turnout behavior and demonstrates that the honoring ancestors norm helps Black Americans participate at rates similar to Whites.

Two experiments further show how peers and elites together mobilize others to the polls. I find that Black Americans reward neighbors for voting to a greater degree than other racial groups and are more likely to respond to ancestor-themed turnout messages. This is especially true for Black Americans who live in predominantly Black neighborhoods or who are lower-propensity voters themselves.

Collectively, my results help to explain a participatory puzzle frequently cited in the American politics literature: the fact that Black Americans often outperform other racial minorities in national election year turnout and even, occasionally, show up at rates higher than Whites. My findings demonstrate that the honoring ancestors norm serves as a particularly potent mobilizing resource in Black communities. When the honoring ancestors norm is coupled with politics, it predicts turnout in national elections for all Americans, regardless of race, but Black Americans are significantly more likely than other groups to embrace this expression of the norm and enforce it on community members. As a result, even Black Americans who do not personally believe that the honoring ancestors norm requires political participation face social incentives to engage and can be mobilized by elites who invoke the norm.

The Uniqueness of National Election Years

So far we've seen that norms vary in their connection to politics across groups, but this is inconsequential if these norms do not also influence behavior, motivating action in the political sphere. Our focus in this chapter is on political behavior in national elections—specifically, whether an eligible individual choses to vote when presidential nominees or congressional representatives appear on the ballot. Voting in these elections is the most commonly undertaken form of participation among Americans and occupies the central theoretical and empirical space of most scholarship on political participation (e.g., Fraga, 2018; Leighley and Nagler, 2013; Verba, Schlozman, and Brady, 1995). This is because the franchise is thought unique in a number of ways. Voting is often cited as a basic building block for democracy, allowing a regular and direct path for citizens to select who governs them and influence policy formation. But federal elections, in particular, are unique even from other opportunities to vote because they are *high salience*. With billions of dollars spent each cycle by campaigns to inform individuals of the impending election and nonprofit organizations across America similarly contacting and mobilizing potential voters, voting in federal elections is arguably relatively low in cost compared to other forms of political participation.

And yet an in-depth study of national-level turnout requires some justification if the primary focus of this book is the political participation of racial minorities. While the evidence is quite persuasive that more equitable state and local turnout, as well as nonelectoral participation, produces better representation for the poor and racial minorities (e.g., Avery and Peffley, 2005; Gillion, 2013; Hajnal and Trounstine, 2005; Hill and Leighley, 1992), turnout at the national level is more of a mixed bag (e.g., Ellis, Ura, and Ashley-Robinson, 2006; Griffin and Newman, 2005, 2007; Sides, Schickler, and Citrin, 2008). Still, with the demography of America rapidly changing and with non-White Americans expected to make up a majority of the population by midcentury (US Census Bureau, 2012), the outcomes of federal elections are increasingly influenced by the engagement of non-White people. These changes may fundamentally alter the landscape of electoral representation and the importance of minority coalitions for winning elections (Bowler and Segura, 2011; Judis and Teixeira, 2004). Apart from changes in representation, electoral participation too has a number of positive externalities, leading to higher levels of political efficacy, citizen education, and engagement through other means (Finkel, 1985, 1987; Tolbert and Smith, 2005). Understanding why groups do or do not turn out, then, is consequential for a host of substantive reasons.

Norms Predict National Election Year Turnout

Our first task is to determine whether the participatory norms we've identified predict political involvement at the individual level. Our honoring ancestors and helping hands measures are new to political science, so before we test whether these indexes can explain variation across groups, we want to see if they have any relationship to political behavior generally. I use data from the PSNS to test the independent effect of the political ancestors index and political helping index on turnout in congressional and presidential election years, controlling for a variety of known alternative predictors.

In these analyses, my primary independent variables are the political ancestors index and political helping index developed and validated in the previous two chapters. Recall that in the PSNS, respondents were asked to select the behaviors they believed best honored the legacy of those who made it possible for them to be where they are today and the best ways to care for people in need. For each question, the selection of political responses are added together and rescaled from 0 to 1, where 1 indicates a strong connection between the norm and political participation and 0 indicates no connection at all.[1] A significant relationship between these indexes and turnout suggests that the strength of participatory personal norms affects the likelihood that an individual votes in high-salience elections.

I also include in my analyses other known predictors and correlates of turnout.[2] Their inclusion allows me to both isolate the effect of the norms indexes on political behavior and compare the magnitude of my novel measures to known predictors of engagement. They are

Socioeconomic resources. Some have argued that socioeconomic resources including income and education are the strongest and most consistent predictors of turnout (e.g., Nie, Powell, and Prewitt, 1969; Verba, Schlozman, and Brady, 1995), although others show that when using validated voter data as the outcome, this relationship is significantly reduced (Ansolabehere and Hersh, 2012). I include in my analyses a measure of individual educational attainment (five categories) and yearly family income, measured in increments of $25,000 up to $200,000 or more. Both measures are rescaled from 0 to 1.

Generational status. Generational status has been tied to turnout by a number of scholars (e.g., Tam Cho, 1999; Pantoja, Ramirez, and Segura, 2001) and, we have learned, is related to a political expression of the honoring ancestors norm. To control for generational differences across racial groups, I include indicator variables for whether an individual is either a first-generation American citizen or second-generation American citizen compared to at least third-generation (suppressed category). First-generation American citizens are defined as those who were born abroad but naturalized into American citizenship, and second-generation American citizens are those with at least one parent who was born abroad.

Age. Recently enfranchised young voters have notoriously low turnout compared to their counterparts approaching or recently passing retirement age (Highton and Wolfinger, 2001a; Niemi, Stanley, and Evans, 1984). Further, age is related to a political expression of the honoring ancestors norm across racial groups. To control for age, I include a seven-category variable for age ranging from eighteen to twenty-four up to over seventy-five by roughly ten-year increments, rescaled from 0 to 1.

Gender. Evidence suggests that gender is sometimes related to turnout and especially so for some minority groups (e.g., Ansolabehere and Hersh, 2013; Burns, Schlozman, and Verba, 2001; Verba, Schlozman, and Brady, 1995). I include an indicator variable for self-reported gender, where "woman" is the reference category.

Political interest. In chapters 4 and 5, we saw that political interest is correlated with my novel norms measures, and others have shown it is strongly related to political participation (Verba, Schlozman, and Brady, 1995). If I wish to isolate the effect of norms on turnout from this predictive juggernaut, I must control for it in these analyses. To measure political interest, respondents were asked, "In general, how interested are you in politics and public affairs?" and then provided with four response options ranging from "not at all interested" to "very interested." I rescale answers from 0 to 1.

Political efficacy. Both *internal* and *external efficacy*—the beliefs that one can influence the political system and that the government is responsive, respectively—affect the likelihood to participate in politics (Campbell, Gurin, and Miller, 1954; Soss, 2002; for a review, see Abramson, 1983, chapter 8). To measure internal and external efficacy, respondents were asked the strength of agreement with the statements "I don't think public officials care much about what people like me think" and "I consider myself well qualified to participate in politics." The five categories of response options are rescaled from 0 to 1.

Political recruitment. For decades, scholars have shown both observationally and experimentally the strong relationship between being asked to turn out and actual participation (e.g., García Bedolla and Michelson, 2012; Green, Gerber, and Nickerson, 2003; Rosenstone and Hansen, 1993; Verba, Schlozman, and Brady, 1995). To measure recruitment, respondents were asked whether they have been contacted on behalf of a political candidate in the past two years (0–1).

Racial linked fate. In chapters 4 and 5, we saw that racial linked fate is related to the norms measures for some groups. I control for strength of racial linked fate by including in the analyses the degree of respondent agreement with the statement "What happens generally to [respondent's race] people in this country will affect what happens to me" (Dawson, 1994). Five responses range from strongly disagree to strongly agree and are rescaled from 0 to 1.

In addition to these known predictors of political participation, I include in my analyses novel measures of alternative interpretations of the honoring ancestors and helping hands norm. By including these measures, I am able to assess whether other interpretations of the norms are similarly related to political participation—either positively or negatively. If individuals see acts of honoring as mutually exclusive or in competition for precious time and resources, then a strong nonpolitical interpretation of these norms may lead to lower levels of engagement. I create an *economic ancestors index, cultural ancestors index, charitable helping index,* and *religious helping index* by adding together the selection of behaviors within each category when respondents were asked about the best ways to honor those in the past and, separately, the best ways to take care of those in need. I then rescale each from 0 to 1. For a further discussion of these measures, return to "Ubiquity and Variation in Honoring Ancestors" (chapter 4) and "Commitments to and Expressions of Helping Others" (chapter 5).

Table 6.1 uses each of these variables to predict validated turnout in 2016. I purchased vote history from the data firm Catalist, which worked

TABLE 6.1 **Relationship between norms and validated voting record in 2016**

	Asian	Black	Latino	White
Political ancestors	0.35 (0.10)*	0.28 (0.06)*	0.23 (0.07)*	0.17 (0.06)*
Political help	−0.13 (0.10)	−0.03 (0.07)	−0.01 (0.07)	0.09 (0.06)
Income	−0.06 (0.07)	0.08 (0.04)	0.08 (0.04)	0.02 (0.04)
Education	0.04 (0.06)	−0.02 (0.04)	−0.01 (0.04)	−0.06 (0.03)
1st generation	−0.11 (0.05)*	0.01 (0.08)	0.04 (0.04)	0.17 (0.10)
2nd generation	−0.09 (0.08)	−0.06 (0.05)	0.01 (0.04)	−0.03 (0.05)
Age	0.21 (0.10)*	0.32 (0.06)*	0.33 (0.06)*	0.22 (0.05)*
Male	0.03 (0.05)	−0.06 (0.03)*	0.03 (0.03)	−0.02 (0.03)
Interest politics	−0.07 (0.08)	0.13 (0.05)*	0.17 (0.06)*	0.09 (0.05)
External efficacy	−0.10 (0.10)	0.01 (0.06)	−0.08 (0.06)	−0.02 (0.05)
Internal efficacy	−0.01 (0.09)	0.09 (0.05)	−0.02 (0.06)	0.03 (0.05)
Recruitment	0.28 (0.05)*	0.08 (0.04)*	0.13 (0.04)*	0.24 (0.04)*
Linked fate	0.07 (0.10)	−0.02 (0.05)	−0.07 (0.05)	0.00 (0.05)
Cultural ancestors	−0.20 (0.07)*	0.07 (0.06)	−0.06 (0.05)	−0.09 (0.05)
Economic ancestors	−0.00 (0.09)	0.04 (0.05)	0.00 (0.06)	0.02 (0.05)
Charitable help	0.28 (0.08)*	0.04 (0.05)	0.04 (0.05)	0.04 (0.05)
Religious help	−0.19 (0.07)*	−0.13 (0.04)*	0.05 (0.04)	0.05 (0.04)
Intercept	0.41 (0.13)*	0.24 (0.07)*	0.25 (0.06)*	0.29 (0.06)*
N	351	866	834	886
R^2	0.27	0.19	0.16	0.17
Adj. R^2	0.23	0.17	0.14	0.16
RMSE	0.47	0.41	0.45	0.39

Notes: Table shows OLS regression coefficients with standard errors in parentheses. All predicting variables are scaled from 0 to 1. The smaller sample size among Asian Americans reflects the missing political interest information for respondents recruited off of the GfK panel. I replicate these analyses for Asian Americans without political interest in the online appendix (see appendix A for the URL) and find that in the larger sample of 881 respondents, the coefficients on the political ancestors index (0.32) and political helping index (−0.04) are virtually unchanged.

*$p < 0.05$.

with GfK to merge the PSNS with publicly available voting records and return to me a deidentified file that included the turnout history of each of my respondents. The outcome variable in these analyses, then, is a confirmed measure of behavior: whether an individual actually voted or not in the 2016 election based on publicly available records. Using a linear regression, I model the equations separately for each group, as others have shown many of the standard, included predictors vary in their relationship to political outcomes by race (e.g., Barreto and Segura, 2009; Masuoka and Junn, 2013). Further, in this test, we care primarily about the relative significance of effects *within* groups rather than *across* them.[3] Each predictor is scaled from 0 to 1 and so the coefficients in this table can be interpreted as the effect of moving from the lowest possible category to the highest for each variable.

The results demonstrate that the political ancestors index is substantively and statistically related to turnout in 2016 for all four racial groups. The magnitude of the effect, which ranges from 17% to 35%, is particularly striking for the three racial minority groups. For Asian Americans, the political ancestors index is in fact the *strongest* predictor of propensity to vote compared to any of the other variables included in the model; for Black Americans and Latinos, only age is more strongly related to turnout.

The substantive ability of the political ancestors index to predict voting in the 2016 election is best demonstrated by comparing its effect sizes to the other known predictors included in the model. The analyses show, for instance, that individuals reporting they were contacted by a political campaign increases the propensity to vote by 8% among Black Americans, 17% among Latinos, and 28% among Asian Americans. Being not at all interested in politics versus being very interested increases turnout among Black Americans by 13%, among Latinos by 17%, and among White Americans by a statistically unreliable 9%. In contrast, maintaining the personal belief that honoring those in the past who sacrificed for you requires political involvement increases the likelihood to turn out by 17% for White Americans, 23% for Latinos, 28% for Black Americans, and 35% for Asian Americans. Put into direct comparison for Black Americans, the relationship between the political ancestors index and Black turnout is more than double that of political interest and triple the effect of self-reported recruitment.

In chapter 4, we learned that Asian Americans and Latinos were significantly less likely than Black Americans and Whites to believe that honoring their ancestors requires political involvement. Even within these least likely groups, though, some individuals did connect the honoring ancestors norm to politics. The results in table 6.1 demonstrate that Asian Americans and Latinos who do make this connection are significantly more likely to turn out than their coracial peers, indicating an opportunity for mobilization. If political entrepreneurs are able to connect already strong honoring ancestors norms that exist in these communities to politics, their efforts would likely pay dividends.

In contrast to the political ancestors index, the political helping index proves entirely unrelated to turnout in the 2016 election. Table 6.1 shows that believing helping those in need is best done through political involvement does not significantly predict turnout in 2016 for any of the four racial groups. The results suggest that the honoring ancestors norm is uniquely tied to national-level elections. While both the honoring ancestors norm and helping hands norm are widely shared and while both can have participatory interpretations, beliefs about honoring the past are especially important for motivating turnout in high-salience elections like those for president.[4] But this is not to say that the helping hands norm is *unimportant* for political participation. In fact, as we'll see in the next chapter, the political helping index matters significantly for higher-cost participatory acts and turnout in local elections. When it comes to national election year turnout, however, it is only a participatory interpretation of the honoring ancestors norm and not the helping hands norm that matters for who shows up at the polls.

The analyses also show that the other interpretations of the honoring ancestors and helping hands norm are generally either unrelated or negatively related to turnout. For instance, a strong cultural interpretation of the honoring ancestors norm significantly *decreases* the propensity to vote among Asian Americans. A strong religious interpretation of helping hands significantly decreases voting for both Asian and Black Americans.[5] The result provides some initial empirical evidence that the honoring ancestors norm is sometimes perceived as a zero-sum game. Time spent on activities in the political sphere can be seen as reducing time available for activities alternatively connected to honoring one's past or helping those in need (see also Wong et al., 2011, on opportunity costs). If this is the case, we might imagine that priming the honoring ancestors norm might actually *reduce* political participation for some groups instead of increasing it, as we'd expect it to do for others. We'll test this idea later in this chapter.

TABLE 6.2 **Relationship between norms and turnout in 2012, 2014, and 2016**

	Asian	Black	Latino	White
2012 voting turnout (validated record)				
Political ancestors	0.30 (0.10)*	0.14 (0.07)*	0.19 (0.07)*	0.30 (0.10)*
Political help	−0.06 (0.11)	0.03 (0.07)	−0.02 (0.08)	−0.06 (0.11)
2014 voting turnout (validated record)				
Political ancestors	0.47 (0.10)*	0.28 (0.07)*	0.13 (0.07)⁺	0.10 (0.06)
Political help	−0.09 (0.10)	0.08 (0.08)	0.05 (0.07)	0.08 (0.07)
2016 voting turnout (self-report)				
Political ancestors	0.22 (0.07)*	0.19 (0.05)*	0.17 (0.06)*	0.11 (0.04)*
Political help	−0.03 (0.07)	−0.10 (0.06)	0.02 (0.06)	0.03 (0.04)
Controls	✓	✓	✓	✓

Notes: Table shows OLS regression coefficients with standard errors in parentheses. Income, education, generational status, age, gender, interest in politics, political efficacy, recruitment, linked fate, cultural ancestors index, economic ancestors index, religious helping index, and charitable helping index are all included as controls, mirroring table 6.1.

*$p < 0.05$; ⁺$p < 0.1$.

In table 6.2, I replicate these analyses for an additional presidential election year (2012), extend them to a midterm election year (2014), and show the relationship between my predictors and a self-reported turnout measure (2016).[6] The results show that the relationship between the political ancestors norm and turnout in presidential elections extends back through time, holds in a midterm congressional election, and replicates in self-reported turnout data. Specifically, the strength of an individual's political ancestors norm in 2018—when the PSNS was collected— remains a substantively large and statistically significant predictor of validated turnout six years earlier in the presidential contest between Mitt Romney and incumbent Barack Obama. The political ancestors index is also an important predictor of validated voting among racial minorities in a midterm congressional election year. In 2014, a strong political interpretation of the norm increased chances of turning out by 47% among Asian Americans ($p < 0.05$), 28% among Black Americans ($p < 0.05$), and 13% among Latinos ($p < 0.1$). And analyses of self-reported turnout in the 2016 election show a similar pattern between predictors, although the magnitude of the effects is attenuated compared to the validated vote model. A full-scale change in the political ancestors index produces a 17% to 35% shift in the propensity to vote when the dependent variable is *validated* vote history but between only 11% and 22% when the dependent variable is *self-reported* turnout in the same year.

This attenuated effect compared to the validated voting model teaches us something important about how social norms operate theoretically and empirically in the political sphere. Discrepancies almost always emerge between self-reported political participation and validated engagement in politics, with data that relies on self-reported measures regularly producing inflated estimates. For instance, in the PSNS, 59% of respondents are confirmed voters in 2016, but fully 86% of the sample report having voted in the same election. Most scholars argue that this phenomenon of *overreporting* is the product of *social desirability bias*, whereby individuals know voting is normatively appropriate and so falsely report their behavior in the desirable direction (Ansolabehere and Hersh, 2012; Holbrook and Krosnick, 2009). The attenuated strength of the political ancestors index in the self-reported voting model suggests that the honoring ancestors norm is precisely one of the expectations considered when people lie about their voting choices. It also tells us that when scholars rely on self-reported political participation data to estimate the effect of norms, they will likely *underestimate* the size of the relationship.

Through the political ancestors and political helping indexes measures, we have included in our models personal norm strength. These personal norms are thought to operate on their host primarily through psychological expectations about what is good behavior, invoking pride, guilt, and sense of self (Cialdini and Trost, 1998; Thøgersen, 2006). But this is not the only way norms generate behavioral outcomes. In addition to internalization, norms create behavioral compliance by promising social rewards and sanctions from other group members. If individuals of different groups variously reward engagement in politics, we may see norms motivating political participation above and beyond just the effect of the personal norms captured here. We'll return to this idea in a moment, but first, let's look at how personal social norms alone may shape racial turnout trends in the United States.

Norms and the Turnout Gap

I opened this book with an oft-cited puzzle in scholarship on American political behavior. Drawing from the Current Population Survey (CPS)—a common data source for examining turnout across racial groups—I showed that after controlling for resources, Black Americans consistently turn out at rates significantly higher than other minority racial groups and at levels comparable to White Americans. Calculating the predicted probability of turnout in presidential elections for each of the four racial groups and controlling for income, education, and nativity status, those results revealed that between 2000 and 2008, turnout among Black Americans was either equal to or higher than similarly resourced Whites, but Latinos and Asian Americans were significantly less likely than both groups to cast a vote for president (figure 1.1). A 23% to 28% gap emerged between the predicted turnout of Black Americans, the most participatory minority group, and Asian Americans, the least participatory group, depending on the year.

We know now that a political expression of the honoring ancestors norm predicts turnout in national elections at the individual level; we've also learned that groups vary in the degree to which their members connect norms to politics (chapters 4 and 5). As a result, while a participatory interpretation of the honoring ancestors norm is correlated with involvement in politics *across* groups, it may not mobilize the same proportions of citizens *within* those groups. Rather, because the number of Black, White, Latino, and Asian Americans with strong participatory social norms varies, including norms in analyses of national-level turnout may account for at least some of the variation in participation.

I use data from the PSNS to test this assertion. In these analyses, I model turnout two ways. First, I calculate the predicted probability of voting for each of the racial groups in 2014 (a midterm election year) and 2016 (a presidential election year) using validated voting record as the outcome variable. I include in these models controls for income, education, and nativity status—covariates also available in the CPS and on which I relied in those opening analyses. In the second set of models, I repeat this analysis but add both the political ancestors index and political helping index into the equations.

Figure 6.1 plots the predicted probability of turning out for Asian, Black, Latino, and White Americans controlling for income, education, and nativity status at either their sample median or mean. The top two panels show predicted turnout in 2014 and 2016 from the *base* models—those that parallel our opening CPS analyses. The bottom two panels show estimates for the same years but include the political ancestors and political helping indexes set at 0, or no connection between the norm and political participation (*norms* models).

The results from the base models show roughly the same relative

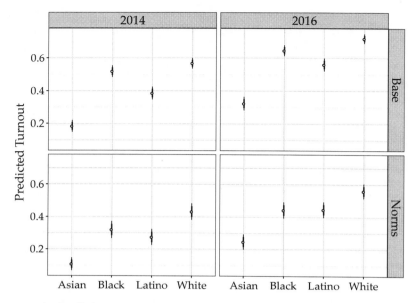

FIGURE 6.1 Predicting turnout rates with and without norms

Notes: Point estimates are predicted probabilities derived from appendix C, table C.5. Income and nativity status are each set at the sample median; education is set at the sample mean. The political ancestors and helping indexes are fixed at o.

turnout pattern between groups observed in the CPS. Asian Americans are the group least likely to turn out, with middle-class US-born citizens predicted to vote at rates of 18% in the midterm election and 32% in the presidential election. Latinos, with a predicted turnout rate of 39% in 2014 and 56% in 2016, are the next least likely to vote in both election years. After controlling for resources, Black and White Americans turn out at roughly similar levels in 2014 (52% and 57%, respectively) and at rates of 65% and 72% respectively in 2016.

The bottom two panels show important changes in the relative rates of turnout between groups when norms are added to the models.[7] The relatively large turnout gap between Black Americans and the other two racial minority groups is decreased substantially. Between Black and Asian Americans, an initial difference of 32 percentage points in predicted turnout in 2016 is reduced by more than a third, as is the 33-point difference between these groups in 2014. For Black Americans and Latinos, the gap in 2016 is reduced to zero when differences in norms are controlled for and the remaining 5-point gap between the groups in 2014 is no longer statistically significant. In contrast, once norms are controlled for in the model, the gap between Black and White Americans *increases* substantially. The 5-point gap in 2014 and the 7-point gap between the two groups in 2016 increases to 12 points for both election years when norms are neutralized at zero.

The implication of these results is that personal, participatory social norms shape turnout trends across racial groups in the United States. Black Americans, as a group, are more able to overcome the inherent costs involved in participating to turn out at rates roughly equal to White Americans because of the strong participatory norms many of these group members possess. In the absence of these normative incentives, Black Americans would turn out at rates significantly lower than we otherwise observe—and at rates substantively lower than White Americans because of the enhanced costs and persistent inequities in the structural elements of engagement (Fraga, 2018; Philpot and Walton, 2014; Ramírez, Solano, and Wilcox-Archuleta, 2018).

Furthermore, in a counterfactual world where the honoring ancestors and helping hands norms are completely unconnected to politics, we would observe much more similarity in rates of turnout across racial minority groups than we currently do, after controlling for income, education, and nativity status. Participatory social norms lead to higher rates of turnout for individual Asian Americans, Black Americans, and Latinos who internalize these norms. But because the strength of these norms varies across groups, differences in the overall effect on group turnout rates follows. Once the relatively strong personal norms of many Black Americans are accounted for, the three racial minority groups look much more similar to one another with respect to predicted turnout. The results suggest that while all racial minorities in the United States face enhanced costs beyond simple demographics when deciding whether to vote, norms that add intrinsic value to the process of voting can increase turnout even in the face of these costs.

Social Rewards for Turnout Vary by Racial Community

Our focus up to this point has been on how personal participatory norms shape voting choices across and within racial groups, but as we have learned, norms do not operate only at the individual level.[8] Rather, *injunctive norms* guide community-level expectations individuals have for each other. Through the promise of social rewards, including respect and group acceptable for compliance—or sanctions for deviance—injunctive norms alter the incentive structures for action and shape the behavior of individuals and communities. Considering how social norms vary in their connection to politics across racial group membership and embeddedness (see chapters 4 and 5), I expect that the social rewards individuals dole out for participation also vary along these dimensions.

To examine racial variation in participatory injunctive social norms, I designed an online experiment that was fielded outside of the Participatory Social Norms Survey in 2014.[9] In this study, I ask respondents to evaluate four hypothetical individuals who are "interested in moving to your community." Respondents viewed a table of information about each individual on separate survey pages with entries about the individual's name, age, occupation, and community involvement.[10] Embedded in these tables was a treatment aimed at assessing rewards for national-level turnout. Respondents were asked to evaluate an individual who "votes in every presidential election." Immediately following the tables, respondents were asked to evaluate the individual on two measures of social desirability: likability and respectability. Both measures follow from previous experimental work (Byron and Baldridge, 2007; Gerber et al., 2016; Hamilton and Fallot, 1974; Ridgeway and Cornell, 2006; Snyder and Haugen, 1994) and are designed to estimate the relative social incentives attached to political actions. Thus, the average in evaluations of these hypothetical voters can be compared across groups, adjusting the estimates to a control—evaluations of a perspective neighbor who "annually attends neighborhood potluck dinners"—to determine the degree to which social incentives for turnout vary across racial groups.[11]

This experiment was administered on three omnibus surveys using the online platforms YouGov/Polimetrix and Latino Decisions between the months of April and October 2014.[12] The first survey, conducted through YouGov/Polimetrix, yielded a nationally representative sample of two thousand Americans drawn from a panel of US adults.[13] To supplement the minority sample available in this pool, I joined these data with two racial minority-specific samples conducted through Latino Decisions and YouGov/Polimetrix. The resulting sample included 1,254 White respondents, 1,229 Black respondents, and 748 Latino respondents.[14]

To evaluate variations in the social rewards made available to the politically active by members of different racial communities, I use a difference-in-difference design. First, I calculate the difference in the averages for the social desirability variables between the treatment and control conditions for each of the racial groups. Then I subtract this average treatment effect for White Americans and Latinos from the average treatment effect for the Black sample. Formally, this assessment of cross-racial heterogeneity reads:

(1) $DiD = (\bar{y}_T - \bar{y}_C|\text{White/Latino}) - (\bar{y}_T - \bar{y}_C|\text{Black})$

This calculation allows me to determine whether White Americans and Latinos, on average, evaluate politically active individuals differently than do Black Americans.

Figure 6.2 plots the results of these calculations, showing the effect of evaluating a prospective neighbor who votes among Whites and Latinos compared to Black Americans for the two dependent variables— likability and respectability—averaged together. Movement away from the zero line represents the difference in the treatment effect for the two racial groups compared to Black Americans. Each point estimate is displayed with a 95% confidence interval around it.

The results show that Black Americans provide, on average, more social rewards to voters than do either Latinos or White Americans. The effect sizes of −0.29 for White respondents and −0.23 for Latino respondents represent roughly 25% of a standard deviation in the dependent variable, and both point estimates are statistically significant ($p < 0.01$).

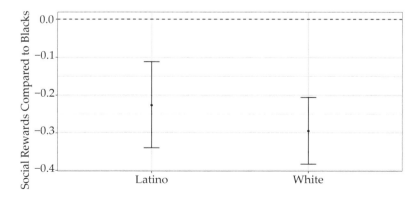

FIGURE 6.2 Differences in social rewards for voters

Just as personal norms about the value of voting are variable across racial groups, these results reveal that so too are levels of social incentives group members distribute for turnout. Black Americans in particular incentivize voting through the distribution of social rewards at higher rates than do either White Americans or Latinos. This ascription of socially desirable characteristics adds an additional layer of considerations to the voting calculus. Black Americans are more likely to vote not only because of the psychological rewards that follow from complying with group-based personal norms but also because voting bestows social rewards in the form of respect and likability.

Group *membership*, then, shapes the distribution of social rewards for turnout in high-salience elections, but the RNM further suggests that racial group *embeddedness* should influence the enforcement of participatory social norms. We learned in chapters 4 and 5 that a participatory expression of the honoring ancestors and helping hands norms are positively related to social and geographic embeddedness for Black Americans, negatively related to embeddedness for Latinos, and primarily unrelated for White Americans. Considering this, I expect social rewards for turnout to vary in parallel ways. We should observe increased social rewards for voting when Black Americans are embedded in contexts that are primarily coracial, decreased rewards from Latinos under the same circumstances, and no relationship between embeddedness and social rewards for White Americans.

To test these hypotheses, I merge my survey data with neighborhood demographic data from the American Community Survey. Specifically, I calculate the proportion of each respondent's zip code that is coracial using data from the 2009–13 American Community Survey: 5-Year Data Set (Manson et al., 2018). In earlier instantiations of geographic and social embeddedness presented in this book, I have focused on the racial composition of census block and intimate social ties. However, neither of these data points is available in this data set, so I settle on something approximate: zip code. Recent work by Velez and Wong (2017) shows that across an array of measures, zip code most closely approximates people's perceptions of the racial composition of their "local" community. In fact, zip code even outperforms respondent-constructed boundary maps (cf. Wong et al., 2012), providing a justification for its usage here as a measure of racial group embeddedness.

With this value as the primary independent variable, I use a linear regression model to predict the strength of participator likability and respectability, averaged together and standardized from 0 to 1. In addition, I include in the model four individual-level controls that may vary with both social rewards and geolocation—income, education, gender, and age—and one contextual-level control—the percentage of residents who are foreign born, either noncitizens or naturalized, in the zip code.[15] Separate models are run for each racial group.

Table 6.3 shows the outcomes of these analyses. Our primary interest is in the first row of this table, which shows the relationship between racial group embeddedness and the level of social rewards distributed to individuals who vote. Because our independent variable is coded from 0 to 1, these coefficients can be interpreted as the effect of moving from an entirely non-coracial zip code to an entirely coracial one—that is, a full-scale change in the predictor—while controlling for neighborhood nativity composition, individual income, education, gender, and age.

The results show that the level of social rewards conferred to voters by Black Americans is significantly and positively related to the racial composition of their neighborhood. Moving from an entirely non-coracial zip code to an entirely coracial one produces a 6% increase in the strength of social rewards conferred to voters ($p < 0.05$). This shift, which is the equivalent of 33% of the dependent variables' standard deviation, suggests that when Black Americans dole out social incentives to participate, other Black people are the primary recipients.

TABLE 6.3 **Social rewards for voting by racial composition of zip code**

	Black	Latino	White
Proportion zip coracial	0.06 (0.02)*	−0.09 (0.04)*	0.00 (0.04)
Proportion zip foreign born	−0.01 (0.04)	0.23 (0.06)*	0.00 (0.06)
Income	0.00 (0.00)	0.00 (0.00)	0.00 (0.00)
Education	−0.01 (0.00)	0.01 (0.01)	−0.01 (0.00)*
Gender	−0.02 (0.01)	−0.03 (0.01)*	−0.04 (0.01)*
Age	0.00 (0.00)*	0.00 (0.00)*	0.00 (0.00)
(Intercept)	0.67 (0.02)*	0.64 (0.03)*	0.74 (0.04)*
N	1,218	736	1,245
R^2	0.02	0.04	0.04
Adj. R^2	0.02	0.04	0.03
RMSE	0.15	0.16	0.20
SD of DV	0.20	0.20	0.17

Notes: Table shows OLS regression with weights predicting social value of voting. Social value calculated by averaging likability and respectability scores and standardizing from 0 to 1. A value of 1 represents "extremely likable and respectable" and a value of 0 means "not at all likable and respectable." Standard errors in parentheses.

*$p < 0.05$.

In contrast, the relationship between social rewards for voting and racial group embeddedness is, as expected, negative among Latinos and zero for White Americans. Moving from an entirely non-coracial neighborhood to one that is composed entirely of Latino residents produces a 9% decrease in the strength of social rewards for voters ($p < 0.05$). Again mirroring findings with respect to the strength of the honoring ancestors and helping hands norms in the previous two chapters, embeddedness in coracial Latino contexts is associated with weaker normative incentives to turn out.[16] For White Americans, racial group embeddedness is entirely unrelated to social rewards conferred to voters.

We have learned in previous chapters that racial group membership influences the form and strength of personal participatory social norms; to this, we can now add that racial group membership and embeddedness also influence the distribution of social rewards and sanctions for voting that follow from injunctive norms. Black Americans are more likely than Latinos and White Americans to provide social rewards to individuals who vote in presidential election years. And when they live in neighborhoods composed of primarily Black residents, those incentives increase. In contrast, Latinos who live in primarily Latino neighborhoods provide fewer rewards to voters than their nonracially embedded peers. These results suggest that when Latinos experience high levels of geographic or social group embeddedness, they are not only less likely to have strong internalized norms of political participation—a key ingredient of engagement—but are also less likely to confront external social rewards that can incentivize turnout in the face of costs. In contrast, if Black Americans live in segregated spaces, they likely face strong social rewards for engaging in politics even if they personally have weak norms. For White Americans, the social incentives doled out for engagement are unaffected by coracial neighborhood embeddedness.

Elite-Norm Priming and Turnout

In addition to personal and peer-level incentives to turn out, norms might influence voting trends through elite-level mobilization. In an effort to "get out the vote," elected officials, candidates, community leaders, organizations, activists, and cultural icons all weigh in with messages and contacting strategies designed to get citizens to the polls on election day. Sometimes these messages feature the honoring ancestors norm—as the opening epigraph of this book demonstrates[17]—and serve to remind or teach citizens about what is expected of them with regard to honoring the past. Considering what we know about how interpretations of the honoring ancestors norm vary across racial communities, it is unlikely these messages mobilize equally, though. Rather, groups who connect the honoring ancestors norm to political participation should be more likely to respond positively to these elite-level evocations.

I use an experiment embedded in the PSNS to test the effects of elite priming of the honoring ancestors norm on turnout intention. Respondents read a vignette in which an imaginary but respected community leader delivered a specific message to them. This message took on one of four possible conditions, shown in table 6.4. In the first condition, the *control*, respondents read a politically neutral statement delivered by the community leader about the importance of exercising. In the second condition, *traditional*, a parallel but explicitly political message is presented. Respondents in this condition read a general appeal to participate, mimicking language that might be used in a classic civic duty bid. The third condition, *ancestors*, removes the explicit reference to politics and instead invokes the honoring ancestors norm in a general sense. In this condition, political participation is not mentioned; rather, "rights and opportunities" speak to the broader set of behaviors encompassed in the norm's meaning and identified through interviews. This includes pursuing economic or educational opportunities ancestors fought hard for their descendants to have or continuing religious and cultural traditions condemned in other nations or during certain historical periods. Finally, the fourth condition, *interaction*, explicitly ties ancestral honoring to political participation, explaining that participation is a way to honor the past.

TABLE 6.4 **Experimental conditions for elite priming study**

Condition	Text
Control	"We must exercise. We all should take care of our body and mind."
Traditional	"We must participate in politics. We all should seize the right to vote, attend political protests, even give money to political groups."
Ancestors	"We must honor the legacy of our ancestors. We all should claim the rights and opportunities those in the past fought so hard—even died—for us to have."
Interaction	"We must participate in politics to honor the legacy of our ancestors. We all should seize the right to vote, attend political protests, even give money to political groups. These are rights and opportunities those in the past fought so hard—even died—for us to have."

   The conditions replicate the kinds of messages Americans likely hear from political entrepreneurs, community leaders, and organizers. In fact, a manipulation check administered to a pretest sample confirmed that the vast majority of Americans have heard these types of messages before. Further, each condition is designed to invoke the sense that a social expectation exists within the group. The vignette's messenger is "a respected community leader," identifying this person as a group prototype and someone able to set injunctive, normative standards. Words like "must" and "should" communicate the prescriptive nature of the statement. And the use of "we," "our," and "us" focuses the vignette on the in-group.

   However, unlike in the real world, where actual esteemed leaders deliver these messages, here the treatment is deployed by an imaginary social referent. This simplicity is good from an experimental standpoint: it allows us to assess the effect of just the messages, holding characteristics about the messenger constant. But from the standpoint of external validity, we might think of this experiment as a rather hard proof of concept. If we observe effects from priming the ancestors norm in this least likely case, where the setting is manufactured, where there are no opportunities for social observation, where the message is brief, and where the messenger is relatively undefined, we might expect the actual effects to be magnified in the real world.

   Immediately following the treatment, respondents were told, "It is difficult for people to find time to do everything they want to do, and most people have to make choices about what activities are most important to them. Considering the message you just read, please tell us how important it is to make time for each of the following activities." Respondents then answered a randomized battery of questions about four activities, rating each on a scale of not important at all (0) to extremely important (4). Included in this battery was a question about voting, asking respondents to rate how important it is to "Find time to vote."[18] This dependent variable may be thought of as a measurement of respondents' willingness to prioritize voting given other obligations. Others have suggested that such a measure of *behavioral intention* is a key mediator in the process of manifesting actual behavioral outcomes (Bagozzi, Baumgartner, and Yi, 1989; Kim and Hunter, 1993a, 1993b; Randall and Wolff, 1994).

   I examine variation in the effect of my mobilizing messages on prioritization of voting compared to the control across two dimensions of intersecting categories: race and voter propensity. We have learned that the connection between the honoring ancestors norm and politics varies across racial group membership, with Black Americans most likely to make this connection and Asian Americans least likely to do so. As a result, Black Americans who confront a message about the sacrifices and struggles of those in the past should be most likely to then think of the expectations their community has for them around voting and increase their prioritization of this activity. In contrast, when confronting a message about honoring the past, groups who bundle other activities into the honoring ancestors norm should show no effect on prioritizations of voting or, possibly, a deprioritization because they are reminded of other demands on their time.

These effects should appear primarily among individuals for whom voting is not already driven by internalized norms that lead to habitual voting. For these individuals, a prioritization of voting is already quite high, and additional normative messages from outside mobilizers will likely have little effect. Unlike a survey environment where quite a lot is known about respondents, organizers and activists in the real world who deploy these messages rely primarily on voter rolls to identify these high-, medium-, and low-propensity voters. These rolls, derived from statewide voter registration and turnout data, are increasingly available to on-the-ground organizations through the Voter Activation Network and companies including Catalist and TargetSmart (Hersh, 2015).

Like these voter rolls, the PSNS includes information about respondents' voting history. I use validated voter information regarding participation in the past three presidential elections—2008, 2012, and 2016—to create three categories of voter propensity. Low-propensity voters are those individuals who have not voted in any of the three previous presidential elections. Medium-propensity voters are inconsistent voters, people who have voted in some but not all of the previous three elections. And finally, high-propensity voters are those individuals who have voted in all of the last three elections. This final group might be thought of as habitual voters—individuals who have internalized a strong set of norms and habits that bring them repeatedly to the polls (Denny and Doyle, 2009; Fowler, 2006; Gerber, Green, and Shachar, 2003).

Based on what we've learned about norms, my presumption is that priming the honoring ancestors norm—or bringing it to the "top of the brain" (Druckman and Chong, 2009)—will positively increase the prioritization of voting among low-propensity Black voters. These individuals should recognize the honoring ancestors prime and be reminded of the normative connection to voting common in their community. In contrast, for low-propensity Asian Americans and Latinos, priming the same norm should either reduce or have no effect on prioritization of voting compared to the control. For these groups, for whom the honoring ancestors norm is more commonly attached to cultural or economic interpretations, priming the ancestors norm may instead increase a sense of obligation to behaviors other than voting. Further, across groups, the priming of the honoring ancestors norm should do little to change the voting prioritization of high-propensity voters, for whom incentives to vote of various kinds have likely already been internalized.

Figure 6.3 shows the average treatment effect on prioritization of voting for the traditional, ancestors, and interaction conditions compared to the control separately for low-, medium-, and high-propensity voters in each racial group.[19] Ninety-five percent confidence intervals are displayed as vertical lines around the point estimates.

The results show the importance of thinking about group-based norms as well as within-group variation when designing mobilizing interventions. Specifically, both the magnitude and direction of norms-based messages (honor your ancestors, honor your ancestors by participating) vary depending on an individual's propensity to vote and the group's underlying distribution of norm interpretations. Taking low-propensity voters first, I find that both of the honoring ancestors messages have a positive and statistically significant effect on low-propensity Black voters' prioritization of turning out. Specifically, Black citizens who have not voted in the past three elections move from a low prioritization of voting—1.57, or a score falling between "slightly important" and "moderately important"—to a significantly stronger prioritization of voting in both ancestors conditions (+1.07 for both, $p < 0.05$). The average treatment effect equates to more than a full category change and 87% of a standard deviation shift in the dependent variable. The traditional participation message, devoid of any call upon ancestors, on the other hand, has no statistical effect.

We can conclude from this finding that injunctive reminders to honor the past and legacy of ancestors can increase a commitment to voting among those familiar with the participatory interpretation but who may not have personally internalized the norm. These individuals may be suspicious of the voting process or skeptical of voting's effectiveness—a sentiment I observed often during my qualitative interviews with many Black Americans—but by focusing on a group-based norm that presents

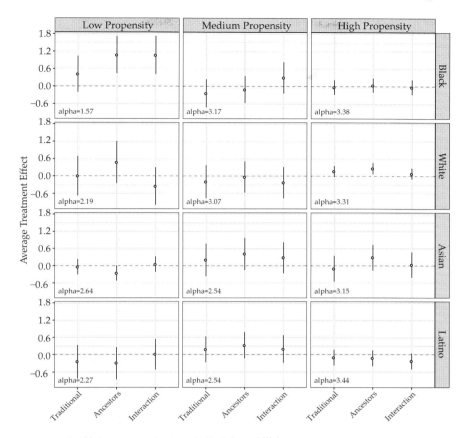

FIGURE 6.3 Heterogeneous treatment effects in mobilizing messages

Notes: The plot shows average treatment effects for the three treatment conditions minus the control. The mean of the dependent variable—prioritization of voting—for each subgroup in the control condition is displayed as the α in each plot. Ninety-five percent confidence intervals are plotted around point estimates.

an intrinsic benefit to voting, or at least reminds individuals that their community views it as intrinsically valuable, low-propensity Black voters may be mobilized in ways that traditional civic duty messages cannot replicate.

In contrast, priming the honoring ancestors norm devoid of any mention of political participation has no effect on low-propensity Latino voters and produces a negative effect among low-propensity Asian American voters (-0.3, $p < 0.05$). Based on our earlier findings, we might presume this is because both groups are more likely to bundle other types of behaviors into the act of honoring. Further, Asian Americans may see these demands as in competition with voting for their time (see Wong et al., 2011). As a result, reminding Asian Americans that it is important to honor their ancestors—a message that mobilizes low-propensity Black voters—appears to have the opposite effect within this group. The direct coupling of ancestors with political participation in the *interaction* treatment, too, produces no observable effects.

Medium- and high-propensity Black voters are similarly unresponsive to the treatments, but examining the control condition may help to explain why. Both subgroups place a high priority on voting to begin with, falling between the top two categories on the importance scale. The results suggest that a ceiling effect may limit possible movement; these groups have already internalized norms that value and prioritize voting. With or without entrepreneurs and activists making claims about the value of the vote, these individuals consistently show up. The results suggest that appeals like Oprah Winfrey's, presented at the beginning of this book, likely do not change turnout rates among consistent Black voters who already believe, personally, that voting is a normative requirement; rather, these appeals likely serve to mobilize low-propensity Black voters to go to the polls.

Treatments are similarly ineffective for Latino and Asian medium- and high-propensity voters, but the *ancestors* condition does positively increase expected turnout among high-propensity White voters by 0.3. This small but statistically significant ($p < 0.05$) effect suggests that messages like Donald Trump's campaign slogan—"Make America Great Again"—or other messages that prime White Americans to think about their forebears, may lead to higher levels of White turnout.

Collectively, the results reveal that classic civic duty appeals deployed in many get-out-the-vote messaging studies are ineffective; however, thinking more specifically about the underlying normative concepts that guide turnout in salient national elections introduces possibilities for broadening the electoral base. Burgeoning get-out-the-vote scholarship often concludes that low-propensity voters cannot be moved, and message does not matter (e.g., Arceneaux and Nickerson, 2009; Enos, Fowler, and Vavreck, 2014; Michelson, 2006). In contrast, my results show that the *right* message may matter quite a lot and that low-propensity voters may be most affected by norm interventions. But these normative messages must be deployed strategically. A message about honoring the past that mobilizes Black voters may have the opposite effect among Asian Americans.

Further, attempts to explicitly connect social norms to politics among groups for whom such a connection is not already prevalent may prove a challenging task. Norms are sticky, built over time, and entrenched in communities in ways that reflect group history and structural constraints. But some scholarship suggests that norms are also malleable and can be changed with creative interventions (e.g., Paluck and Green, 2009; Perkins, Craig, and Perkins, 2011; Tankard and Paluck, 2015). The findings here in the *interaction* condition suggest that such interventions will require more than a two-sentence message linking the norm to political participation. How organizers might use norms to increase political participation among Latinos and Asian Americans is an idea we'll come back to at the end of this book.

Understanding Norms to Understand National Turnout Trends

It should be clear now that community-based social norms matter not only for attitudes toward the value and meaning of political participation but also for individual- and community-level political behavior and mobilization. The honoring ancestors norm, it turns out, is of particular importance for explaining voting in high-salience federal elections and accounts for a large portion of the difference in turnout among minority Americans. After controlling for both the prevalence and predictive abilities of participatory social norms, the gap in validated national-level turnout between Black Americans and other racial minorities is significantly reduced. But in the absence of these norms, all three minority racial groups turn out at rates significantly below that of White Americans.

Personal participatory social norms that vary by racial group shape turnout in national elections but so too do social incentives from peers and mobilization techniques of elites that center social norms (e.g., Gerber, Green, and Larimer, 2008; Rosenstone and Hansen, 1993; Sinclair, 2012). We have learned that racial group membership and embeddedness affect these dimensions of mobilization, influencing the likelihood an individual will confront incentives to turnout and respond to mobilizing messages by increasing their intention to vote. Black Americans specifically provide high levels of social rewards to peers for voting compared to others groups and are more likely to do so when they are embedded in their racial group. Further, mobilization messages that prime the honoring ancestors norm increase the prioritization of voting among low-propensity Black voters. The results help explain why Black Americans often turn out at rates far exceeding other racial minority groups, despite facing continued disadvantages and barriers to engagement. The findings also suggest pathways through which other groups might be mobilized in the future.

CHAPTER SEVEN

Norms and High-Cost Participation

Voting in federal elections may be the most common form of political participation in the United States (Verba, Schlozman, and Brady, 1995), but it is not necessarily the most important. Rather, casting a single ballot in the context of a nationwide election is a rather ineffective tool for influencing politics (Blais, 2000). In contrast, other forms of engagement like voting in local elections or engaging in system-challenging actions can have decisive and lasting effects on political representation (Anzia, 2011; Gillion, 2013; Hajnal and Trounstine, 2005; Hill and Leighley, 1992). These forms of engagement are theoretically distinct from voting in federal election years not only in their possible effectiveness but also because they impose *higher costs* on the participant. Local and nonvoting participation is generally more time intensive, requires more information seeking, and can demand extensive planning, compared to voting for the president or congressional representatives (Conway, 2000; Verba, Schlozman, and Brady, 1995).

In this chapter, I take up precisely these forms of participation: high-cost acts of political involvement, including voting in local elections; attending political protests; and speaking out at community meetings. Using data from the PSNS, I examine whether norms shape an individual's likelihood to engage in these types of political participation. I find that a political expression of the honoring ancestors and helping hands norms are strongly associated with voting in local elections and other high-cost forms of engagement for most Americans. Two experiments further reveal that members of different racial groups distribute social rewards to those engaged in high-cost political participation differently and that elites can prime norms to increase a commitment to participate in local politics and political protests. Together, the results demonstrate that the honoring ancestors and helping hands norms are crucial components of individuals' motivations to engage in high-cost political participation.

Rates of Engagement in High-Cost Participation

In chapter 1, I engaged with the question of whether political participation ever really matters. An exploration of existing research suggested that while turnout equity in federal elections is only precariously related to representation (e.g., Ellis, Ura, and Ashley-Robinson, 2006; Griffin and Newman, 2005, 2007; Highton and Wolfinger, 2001b; Sides, Schickler, and Citrin, 2008), participation in local elections can have lasting consequences, especially for racial minorities. In local and state elections, racial groups who account for a minority of the population at the federal level sometimes make up significantly larger voting blocs (Camarillo, 2007; Hajnal and Trounstine, 2005),[1] and as a result, more equitable turnout in these contexts has measurable impacts on policy outcomes and descriptive representation (Avery and Peffley, 2005; Fellowes and Rowe, 2004; Franko, 2013; Hajnal and Trounstine, 2005; Hill and Leighley, 1992).

Contentious political activities like protests, marches, and rallies too can have measurable and lasting effects on policy. These forms of political participation communicate demands and apply pressure in ways that voting cannot, allowing minority groups to set the agenda and influence justice-oriented attitudes (Enos, Kaufman, and Sands, 2017; Gillion, 2013; McAdam and Su, 2002). Individuals can decide when, where, and how to engage in nonvoting participation (Conway, 2000), making it an avenue of representation even for those without access to the franchise (Barreto and Muñoz, 2003; García Bedolla, 2015; Earl, Maher, and Elliott, 2017; Leal, 2002; Owens, 2014). As a result, nonvoting political participation has often been the steam engine of large-scale social change in America (Gillion, 2013; Harris and Gillion, 2010; Hogan, 2007; Takaki, 2008), especially when it is system challenging rather than system affirming.

Despite the potential instrumental value of these types of political involvement, participation through means other than voting in federal elections is relatively uncommon in the United States. Figure 7.1 shows self-reported frequency of local voting and the number of completed nonvoting participatory acts in the previous twelve months for

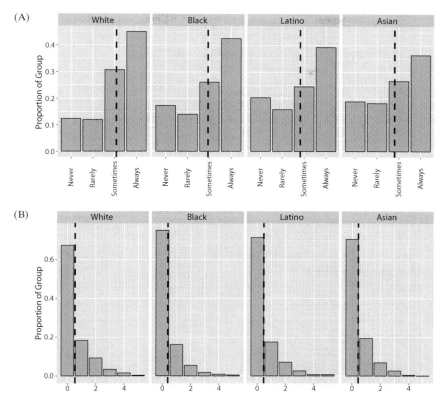

FIGURE 7.1 Frequency of high-cost political participation. (A) Voting in local elections; (B) Number of nonvoting acts completed in the past twelve months

respondents in the Participatory Social Norms Survey. The index of non-voting acts includes self-reported attendance at a protest or political rally; contacting a government official; volunteering or working for a political campaign, party, issue, or cause; signing a petition; and sharing an opinion about a town or community issue at a public meeting.

Figure 7.1A shows the distribution of local voting habits across racial groups in the United States. The figure demonstrates that regardless of race, the majority of Americans are at best inconsistent voters in elections like those for mayor or school board. Across groups, White Americans are most likely to report always voting (45%), followed by Black Americans (43%), Latinos (39%) and Asian Americans (36%).[2] On the opposite end of the spectrum, 24% of White Americans report rarely or never voting in local elections, followed by 31% of Black Americans, 36% of Latinos, and 37% of Asian Americans.

Rates of participation through nonvoting action are similarly low. Figure 7.1B shows the proportion of each racial group reporting completion of zero, one, two, three, four, or five nonvoting participatory acts in the last twelve months. Just over a quarter of the entire PSNS sample reports completing at least one such act. Thirty-three percent of White Americans report participating in politics through a nonvoting action at least once in the last twelve months, compared to 29% of Asian Americans, 28% of Latinos, and 25% of Black Americans.

These low levels of participation likely reflect the high-cost nature of voting in local elections and engaging through nonvoting behaviors compared to federal election year turnout. Campaigns and other organizations pour billions of dollars into informing eligible voters of impending national elections and mobilizing citizens to the polls (*Cost of 2018 Election to Surpass $5 Billion, CPR Projects*, 2018). Selecting a candidate to vote for in these national elections is a relatively simple task with limited options and clear partisan heuristics (Kirkland and Coppock, 2018; Popkin, 1995). In contrast, voting in local elections or participating through other means often takes place in lower-information environments, involve a broader degree of issues and choice, and are more time intensive. The visibility of actions like protesting, petition signing, or speaking at a public meeting, compared to casting a private ballot, further increases the expected risk involved. As a result, voting in local elections or completing other nonvoting acts are relatively high-cost forms of political participation compared to voting in a national election.

Norms may be especially influential, then, in encouraging engagement in these types of participation. With social and psychological rewards (and sanctions) at stake, individual- and community-level beliefs about the value and meaning of political participation may shape who overcomes these costs to participate in local politics and other community-based political activities.

Norms Predict High-Cost Participation

The Participatory Social Norms Survey provides a unique opportunity to examine the relationship between norms and political participation through means other than federal turnout. With multiple measures of high-cost participation included and a wide range of control variables captured, I am able to test whether a political expression of the helping hands norm and honoring ancestors norm have an independent effect on involvement. Furthermore, leveraging the large, representative samples of Asian, Black, Latino, and White Americans included in the PSNS, I am able to do so separately for each racial group.

I use linear regression models—one for each racial group—to test the relationship between the political ancestors index, political helping index, and two outcome measures of high-cost political participation: self-reported frequency of voting in local elections and number of nonvoting political acts completed in the last twelve months. Voting in local elections was measured with the question "This question is about LOCAL elections, such as for mayor or a school board. Do you: 1. Never vote in local elections; 2. Rarely vote in local elections; 3. Sometimes vote in local elections; 4. Always vote in local elections?" I rescale this measure to run from 0 to 1 so that a higher value represents more regularity in reported turnout. To gauge nonvoting participation, I add together the number of acts a respondent reported completing in the previous twelve months out of a list of five: attended a protest or political rally; contacted a government official; volunteered or worked for a political campaign, party, issue, or cause; signed a petition; and shared an opinion about a town or community issue at a public meeting.[3] These five behaviors represent relatively visible and high-cost forms of political participation.

In these models, my primary independent variables are the *political ancestors index* and *political helping index*. These two attitudinal measures, coded from 0 to 1, capture the degree to which an individual believes that honoring the past and helping those in need demand political involvement. Chapters 4 and 5 discuss the design and validation of these measures; here we examine their ability to predict high-cost participatory behavior.

In addition, I include in each model an array of variables known to predict political participation and that likely covary with our primary independent variables. These include a measure of political recruitment, political interest, racial linked fate, external and internal political efficacy, yearly family income, highest level of completed education, generational status, age, and gender. Each of these variables is discussed at length in chapter 6, where parallel analyses are performed to predict voting in nationwide election years. By including these variables, I am able to identify the unique contribution of norms to high-cost participation and further, benchmark the magnitude of any observed relationship to extant predictors.

Lastly, I include in my equations measures of the four nonpolitical interpretations of the helping hands and honoring ancestors norms I outlined in chapters 4 and 5. These indexes, scaled from 0 to 1, represent the degree to which individuals believed the honoring ancestors norm should be expressed through cultural and economic means and the degree to which the helping hands norm was tied to charitable and religious expressions. Inclusion of these measures allows me to test whether these alternative expressions of the helping hands and honoring ancestors norm depress or encourage political involvement.

Turnout in Local Elections

Let's start with the relationship between the political ancestors norm, political helping norm, and frequency of turnout in local elections. Drawing from the full regression results available in appendix C, table C.9, figure 7.2 plots the predicted relationship between the two primary independent variables—the political ancestors index and political helping index—and the outcome measure, turnout in local elections. Because these predictors are scaled from 0 to 1, the plotted point estimates can be interpreted as a full-scale change in the variable, or the increased predicted frequency of turnout in local elections if a respondent moved from no connection between these norms and political participation to the strongest possible connection, holding constant the other included variables.

The results show that much like the national election analyses presented in the previous chapter, the political ancestors index is often positively related to turnout. The estimates range from 0.08 to 0.21, with the relationship not reaching statistical significance only among Latinos. For Asian Americans, a political interpretation of the honoring ancestors norm increases the frequency of voting by 21% of the scale, or almost a full category change in frequency ($p < 0.05$). The size of this effect surpasses the predictive ability of political interest, racial linked fate, education, income, and generational status, which are also estimated in the model. For Black Americans, a full-scale change in the honoring ancestors norm produces a 16% shift in local turnout frequency ($p < 0.05$). This estimate again blows past most conventional predictors of politi-

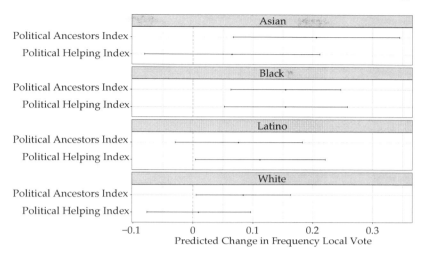

FIGURE 7.2 Relationship between norms and frequency of participation in local elections

cal engagement included in the model with the exception of age and reported political recruitment. For White Americans, a strong political honoring ancestors norm increases the likelihood to engage by 8%, or one-third of a category shift, representing a weaker, albeit statistically significant relationship ($p < 0.05$).

The plots also show that for two of the four racial groups, the political helping index emerges as an important predictor. For Latinos and Black Americans, the political helping index is positive and significantly related to frequency of turnout in local elections ($p < 0.05$). In fact, for Black Americans, the political helping index is just as strong a predictor of turnout as the political ancestors index, with an effect size of 0.16. The predictive power of this variable exceeds that of political interest, racial linked fate, internal and external efficacy, income, and education for Black respondents. For Latinos, the political helping index is also related to local turnout, with an effect size of 11%, or roughly half a category shift in the variable.

This finding stands in contrast to my results presented in the previous chapter, where the political helping index was completely unrelated to turnout in federal elections. Those analyses showed that of the two norms, only the political ancestors index was predictive of turnout, suggesting a special link between it and the federal franchise. In shifting

from turnout in nationwide elections to voting in local elections, however, the helping hands norm and its political manifestation become
relevant. As we will see shortly, this is also the case for nonvoting acts,
suggesting the helping hands norm may be uniquely tied to high-cost political participation compared to nationwide voting.

The analyses from chapter 6 also revealed that the positive relationship between the honoring ancestors norm and political participation
was even larger when validated vote was the outcome rather than self-
reported turnout. This should assure those who may worry that the findings are a product of the self-reported nature of our dependent variable.
While the frequency of self-reported local voting is likely inflated due
to pernicious overreporting (Ansolabehere and Hersh, 2012; Silver, Anderson, and Abramson, 1986), the results in the previous chapter suggest
that if anything, the positive and significant coefficients reported here on
norms are likely an underestimate of the true values.

Despite the higher-cost nature of local voting compared to federal
voting, norms remain consequential for galvanizing individuals to go to
the polls. Believing that honoring the sacrifices of those before you requires political participation or that political involvement is the best way
to help those in need—two attitudinal measures—have a behavioral effect on involvement in local elections. These internalized norms incentivize individuals to seek out information about candidates and timing of
elections and arrive at the polls to cast a ballot. And they do so at rates
equal to or outpacing other structural and resource variables. Personal
norms about the value and meaning of political participation shape even
high-cost voter involvement.

Nonvoting Participation

Next, I turn to the relationship between participatory social norms and
involvement through nonvoting behaviors. Figure 7.3 plots the effect of
moving from the lowest to the highest category of the political ancestors
index and political helping index on political participation for the four
racial groups, based on the regression parameters outlined above.[4]

The results demonstrate the importance of norms in mobilizing political action across racial groups. The political ancestors index is a significant and positive predictor of participation for three of the four groups.
For Latinos, moving from a weak to a strong political interpretation
of the norm increases the number of political acts completed by 0.27,

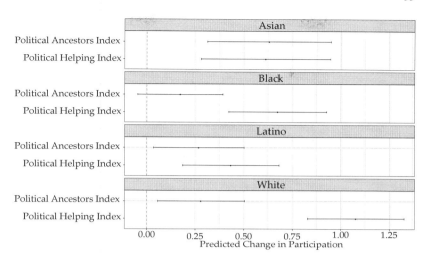

FIGURE 7.3 Relationship between norms and nonvoting participation

or roughly a third of a standard deviation. For White Americans, the change is similar at 0.28. For Asian Americans, the effect size is large, at 0.63, or 80% of a standard deviation.

Again, though, the political ancestors norm is not the only social norm of consequence for understanding engagement in high-cost action. Rather, the political helping index is positive and statistically related to political involvement for all four racial groups. For these higher-cost, more grassroots-based actions, a participatory interpretation of helping those in need sometimes even exceeds in magnitude the effect of the political ancestors index. For Asian Americans, a full-scale change in the political helping index increases the predicted number of nonvoting political acts completed in the previous year by 0.61—more than half an act and 78% of a standard deviation. For Latinos, the point estimate is 0.43, or 49% of a standard deviation. For both Black and White Americans, the effect of the political helping index—0.67 for Black and 1.08 for White Americans—exceeds the predictive power of the political ancestors index. In fact, the political helping index is the strongest predictor of political participation among White Americans included in the model, increasing the predicted number of acts completed by more than a standard deviation and outpacing political interest and internal efficacy, the two other strongest predictors at 0.71 and 0.35, respectively.

Helping Hands and High-Cost Political Participation

Why is the helping hands norm so important for motivating individuals to participate in nonvoting ways and turnout in local elections for some groups? Why is it completely unrelated to turnout in federal elections? The distinct relationship between the helping hands norm and more grassroots and localized political behavior may be tied to a few factors. First, the connection may reflect the instrumental policy demands embedded in the helping hands norm compared to the honoring ancestors norm. While the very act of voting fulfills a mandate to honor the past for those embracing its participatory expression, helping those in need may require individuals to have an actual and observable impact on policy. Because of the increased effectiveness of political participation in local elections and through nonvoting acts compared to federal turnout, those who feel compelled to help those in need through political participation may turn to involvement in these domains.

The localized nature of many high-cost forms of political participation may also evoke the helping hands norm. Scholars have shown that individuals feel a stronger commitment to help those in their immediate social environment like those in their community or neighborhood (Wong, 2010). When one thinks of those in need, then, they may be likely to invoke those in their proximal geographic space and turn to local political participation as a way to care for them. Thus a politicized helping hands norm may be a more fundamental driver of turnout in local elections than in federal elections.

These considerations manifested in my interview data. Often, the helping hands norm was discussed not in the context of voting but in relationship to local politics and political organizing. Doreen, a county worker living in Nashville, Tennessee, provides an example of this. When I talked with her in the winter of 2017, Doreen had recently established a 501(c)(3)—now a thriving community organization—to educate, organize, and mobilize members of the Black community in Nashville for progressive legislation. I asked Doreen about the impetus for founding her organization and she explained,

> We kept finding ourselves [saying], "Man, we got to do something. . . . Why are the police shooting us all the time? And why are we getting a bad rap? Why are we always dehumanized as people?" . . . So I called these ladies up. It was about six of them, all Black women, like I said. And I said, bring your

kids if you need to. And we went out to eat, went to Chili's. And I just presented my idea. . . .

So [our organization] is gonna be this advocacy group to really give African Americans and other minorities a voice because we just don't have that representation right now, especially at the state level. . . . We need to make sure that they hear us out and we're not being left behind, especially with the growth that's happening in Nashville. Communities are being gentrified and so it's like, what about us? You know, what about what we want?

In her discussion, Doreen draws attention to the local nature of her concerns: Nashville is gentrifying, state and local level representation is abysmal, and a recent shooting of a Black man, Jocques Clemmons, in the back by a White police officer in Nashville had brought the issues of the Black Lives Matter campaign front and center in the city. Doreen's concern is that her community—the African American community in Nashville—is being left out of the policy-making process, and she is turning to local collective activism as a way to help those she sees as most in need in her city.

The more politically involved Asian Americans I talked with, too, coupled their desire to help others with localized forms of nonvoting political participation. In response to my question about the ways Samaira, a thirty-two-year-old Asian American author, tries to help others, she explains,

I think that some amount of community building and community advocacy are definitely important to me. . . . I have this conversation a lot because I think that for my community who feels we're very politically active, there's always the sense of like, well, what can we do? You know, what is it that we can actually do? And for some of my friends it has meant actually going into government and really feeling like that's how they want to participate. And for some of my friends it has been becoming lawyers and advocating for people who can't advocate for themselves. . . . For me, it means that I have to use my skill set, so I have to be able to do it by writing or editing or speaking.

Here, Samaira explains that she and her peers have turned to higher-cost forms of participation like advocacy, running for office, and public writing as a way to have an instrumental effect on the issues that concern them most. Feeling normatively committed to help those in need—those "who can't advocate for themselves"—Samaira's social circle has ruminated on the best ways to do this. Rather than turning to voting, they have found themselves enmeshed in community advocacy and activism.

Thus, while only the honoring ancestors norm motivated voting in federal elections for individuals of any race, the helping hands norm takes special significance in nonvoting political participation and, to some degree, participation in local elections. When individuals feel personally committed to take care of those in need and believe political involvement and policy change are the best ways to do this, they do not turn to voting in high-salience federal elections. Rather, they start working in their community—organizing, advocating, and agitating.

Social Rewards for High-Cost Participation Vary by Racial Community

Social norms like beliefs about how to help those in need or honor the past can influence individuals through their internalization into personal norms—as we've seen so far in this chapter—but norms also influence behavior through social enforcement. When the promise of social rewards or sanctions is invoked, individuals are more likely to participate not just in voting but in other forms of nonvoting political participation as well (Gerber, Green, and Larimer, 2008; McClendon, 2014). Considering the distinct usefulness and historic importance of high-cost nonvoting forms of political participation among minority Americans compared to White Americans (Gillion, 2013), we might expect that social rewards for involvement in participation like this will vary across racial group membership and racial group embeddedness in the United States.

The racialized norms model anticipates that the combination of segregation and distinct histories leads to norm variation. Theses histories can provide insight about the anticipated direction and magnitude of variation. Consider, for instance, the historic importance of nonvoting participation for minority empowerment. Locked out of the ballot box through both de jure and de facto disenfranchisement, and with considerably less voting bloc power due to their minority status, non-White Americans have often used contentious forms of nonvoting political participation to seek policy change at various consequential moments in history (Harris and Gillion, 2010; McAdam, 1988; Takaki, 2008). The American civil rights movement and the 2006 immigration protests provide just two notable examples (Barreto et al., 2009; Branton et al., 2015; Gillion, 2013; Pantoja, Menjívar, and Magaña, 2008).

Our previous chapters on the content of the helping hands and honoring ancestors norms suggested that Latinos and Black Americans might be more likely than Whites to see value in nonvoting political involvement. Chapter 4, for instance, showed that Black Americans were consistently more likely than other groups to connect the honoring ancestors norm to high-cost political involvement like protesting and fighting injustice. It also showed that Latinos were significantly more likely than White Americans to believe helping those in need required participation in political organizations. We might expect, then, that these two racial groups will provide more social rewards to individuals engaged in high-cost nonvoting political participation than White Americans. As norms about political participation vary not just by racial group membership but also by racial group embeddedness, we should expect this cross-group variation to be intensified by geographic racial context.

In chapter 6, I used a survey experiment to show that social rewards for voting in presidential elections vary across groups. We can use this same experiment, but with a different treatment variable, to examine variation in social rewards for high-cost participation as well. In this online study, Black, White, and Latino respondents viewed profiles of hypothetical neighbors engaged in different types of community activities.[5] Included in this list of activities was a high-cost political act—"annually attends political rallies"—as well as a control—"annually attends neighborhood potluck dinners." Immediately after reading the profiles, respondents were asked to evaluate these individuals with respect to two social characteristics: likability and respectability.[6]

Drawing from this experiment, I plot in figure 7.4 the average treatment effect for Latino and Black respondents compared to White respondents. This difference-in-difference comparison allows us to examine whether minority Americans statistically and substantively differ with respect to the level of social rewards provided to political rally attendees compared to the majority group. Ninety-five percent confidence intervals are plotted around the point estimates.

The results show that while Black Americans and Latinos are statistically indistinct from each other with respect to levels of social rewards distributed to political rally attendees, both groups, on average, provide significantly more rewards to these individuals than do White

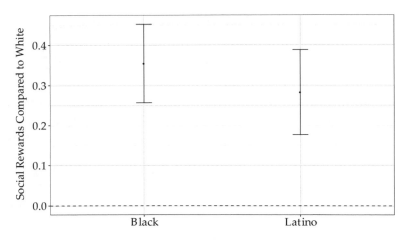

FIGURE 7.4 Differences in social rewards for rally attendees

Americans. The average treatment effect for evaluating a political rally attendee compared to the control is significantly larger for Black Americans than for White Americans (β = 0.35; p < 0.01). The same is true for Latinos compared to White Americans (β = 0.28; p < 0.01). In contrast, Latinos provide statistically the same level of social rewards to rally attendees as Black Americans. The results suggest that nonvoting participation is more normatively valuable to Black Americans and Latinos compared to Whites, and as a result, these groups distribute higher levels of social rewards to participants to encourage these behaviors.

Group membership, then, moderates the distribution of social rewards for high-cost participation, but what about racial group embeddedness? I use data from the 2009–13 American Community Survey: 5 Year Data Set to create a variable for the proportion of each respondent's zip code that is coracial. Using this value as my primary independent variable, I run a linear regression for each racial group predicting rally attendee likability and respectability, averaged together and standardized from 0 to 1. I also include in these models a number of individual- and contextual-level controls that may covary with geolocation: yearly family income, the respondent's highest level of completed education, gender, age, and the proportion of the respondent's zip code that is either naturalized or noncitizens.

Table 7.1 shows the results of these analyses. The first column provides the results for Black Americans, which show that the likability and

TABLE 7.1 **Social rewards for rally attendance by racial composition of zip code**

	Black	Latino	White
Proportion zip coracial	0.06 (0.02)*	−0.07 (0.04)+	−0.07 (0.04)+
Proportion zip foreign born	0.00 (0.05)	0.20 (0.07)*	−0.12 (0.07)+
Income	0.00 (0.00)	0.00 (0.00)	−0.01 (0.00)*
Education	0.00 (0.00)	−0.01 (0.01)*	0.00 (0.00)
Gender	0.00 (0.01)	−0.02 (0.02)	−0.02 (0.01)+
Age	0.00 (0.00)*	0.00 (0.00)	0.00 (0.00)
(Intercept)	0.63 (0.02)*	0.69 (0.03)*	0.76 (0.04)*
N	1,218	736	1,245
R^2	0.01	0.02	0.02
Adj. R^2	0.01	0.02	0.01
RMSE	0.15	0.18	0.22
SD of DV	0.21	0.21	0.18

Notes: Table shows OLS regression with weights predicting social value of political rally attendance. Social value calculated by averaging likability and respectability scores and standardizing from 0 to 1. A value of 1 represents "extremely likable and respectable" and a value of 0 means "not at all likable or respectable." Standard errors in parentheses.

*$p < 0.05$; +$p < 0.1$.

respectability of political rally attendees increase significantly with coracial embeddedness. Black Americans living in entirely Black zip codes are predicted to evaluate individuals engaged in this high-cost activity 6% more positively than those living in non-coracial neighborhoods. Of all the predictors included in the model, only coracial embeddedness is related to the distribution of social rewards for nonvoting political participation.

In contrast, the coefficient on coracial geographic embeddedness is negative for Latinos and White Americans. For both groups, moving from a zip code that is 0% coracial to 100% coracial is predicted to produce a 7% decrease in social rewards for political rally attendees. The results suggest that while Latinos and Black Americans, on average, distribute roughly the same levels of social rewards to those attending political rallies, coracial embeddedness only increases the distribution of social rewards for the latter.

However, the results also suggest that a different dimension of social embeddedness may importantly structure social rewards for high-cost participation among Latinos: the proportion of an individual's zip code that is foreign born. While the coefficient on this variable is insignificant for Black respondents and negative for White respondents, the estimated relationship is positive and significant for Latinos. The larger the share of one's community that is composed of naturalized citizens or noncitizens, the more positive are evaluations of political rally attendees for Latinos. This finding suggests that community context shapes the distribution of social rewards for high-cost participation; however, among Latinos, it is not necessarily racial embeddedness that matters. Rather, reflecting the fundamental fault line of inclusion and exclusion into the American citizenry, the proportion of foreign-born citizens is more influential in the perceived social value of grassroots political participation for this group.

Together, the results show that racial groups systematically vary in their distribution of social rewards for nonvoting political acts like political rally attendance. Minority Americans—specifically, Latino and Black Americans—are significantly more likely than White Americans to reward high-cost political action. Furthermore, social embeddedness of various kinds influences the distribution of these rewards. When geographically embedded among coracial neighbors, Black Americans reward political rally attendees at higher rates. For Latinos, rewards for political rally attendance increase when individuals are more embedded among foreign-born individuals.

Elite-Norm Priming and High-Cost Participation

Peers are not the only people who can incentivize participation through social norms. Rather, elites are also actively involved in this process. Political organizers, elected officials, and cultural leaders all play a role in drawing individuals into collective action and local politics (e.g., Rosenstone and Hansen, 1993). We've seen that personalized, internal norms about honoring ancestors and helping those in need are central in shaping an individual's choice to be active, but can messages that prime and evoke these norms also bring new participants into the fold?

A growing body of evidence on the psychology of social norms shows that giving individuals information about what is common or priming people to think about broadly shared expectations in their community can influence their behavior (Goldstein, Cialdini, and Griskevicius, 2008; Tankard and Paluck, 2015). Even novel messages can lead to new behavioral patterns when delivered by salient social referents (Paluck and Green, 2009; Paluck and Shepherd, 2012). In shaping the *perception* of expected or common actions, these social norms interventions can influence behavioral outcomes before more fundamental attitude change occurs (Tankard and Paluck, 2015).

Interventions designed to prime norms, though, must resonate with the listener (Tankard and Paluck, 2015). In chapter 4, we learned that a commitment to honoring the past is widely shared in the Unites States but that some racial groups are more likely than others to infuse this honoring ancestors norm with political expectations. In chapter 6, we further discovered that because of this variation in group-based social norms, messages that prime ancestral honoring were effective only on turnout intentions among Black and White Americans for whom the connection between this norm and political action is already prevalent. Here we turn to testing whether elite-level priming of the honoring ancestors norm can increase a willingness to engage in high-cost political participation like protesting or involvement in local politics while paying careful attention to possible heterogeneity in treatment effects by race and previous levels of political involvement.

To do this, we'll return to a survey experiment first presented in chapter 6. In this study, PSNS respondents were randomly assigned to view one of four messages delivered by an imaginary, "respected community leader." These four messages follow:

The *control* condition: "We must exercise. We all should take care of our body and mind."

The *traditional* civic duty condition: "We must participate in politics. We all should seize the right to vote, attend political protests, even give money to political groups."

The *ancestors* condition: "We must honor the legacy of our ancestors. We all should claim the rights and opportunities those in the past fought so hard—even died—for us to have."

The ancestors and traditional *interaction* condition: "We must participate in politics to honor the legacy of our ancestors. We all should seize the right to vote, attend political protests, even give money to political groups. These are rights and opportunities those in the past fought so hard—even died—for us to have."

Each of these messages is delivered in the context of normative language (*must, should*) and designed to invoke a sense of community (*we, all*) but the core content of the messages varies. In the first, the respondents read a completely apolitical control about the need to exercise. In the second, respondents are confronted with a basic plea to vote, mirroring the types of standard civic duty messages used in get-out-the-vote scholarship. In the third, we get a message designed to prime the honoring ancestors norm, but in its neutral form. The message does not explicitly call for political involvement; rather, it reminds individuals to consider the sacrifices of those in the past and the broad set of opportunities—educational, economic, religious, and so on—that these efforts afford them. Because this message invokes the honoring ancestors norm but without explicitly connecting it to politics, we might expect its effect on political participation will only be observed among groups for which a connection is already common. Finally, in the last condition, we get a norms intervention message that explicitly links the honoring ancestors norm to political participation in an attempt to increase political involvement even among individuals and groups that might be unaware of this interpretation of the norm.

We'll examine the effects of these messages on the intention to participate in high-cost political activities with two dependent variables. In the first, respondents were asked shortly after the treatment to evaluate how important it is to "find time to attend political protests for issues I care about" on a scale of not important at all (0) to extremely important (4). For the second dependent variable, respondents were told, "Many local organizations are trying to get people more involved in politics" and then asked, "Would you like information at the end of this study about organizations in your area?" These two dependent variables can be interpreted as measuring respondents' willingness to prioritize political participation in both protest activities and local politics, given other obligations.[7]

We'll test whether the three treatment conditions—traditional, ancestors, and interaction—shape respondents' willingness to engage in high-cost political participation, compared to the control. We'll do this focusing on two dimensions of heterogeneity: race and previous political activity. This second dimension is important for the application of these results to political organizing. Much of the work that organizers, campaigns, and community leaders do to mobilize groups in politics is divided into two camps. Political entrepreneurs can work to contact and activate those who are already politically involved, including, for instance, high-propensity voters, or they can work to expand the capacity of their organizations by reaching out to new participants and bringing them into the fold. Norms messages designed to increase political participation may be more or less effective depending on whether the individual is already politically active—and embedded among individuals with strong participatory norms—or considering high-cost political involvement for the first time. As a result, we'll consider the treatment effects separately for individuals who reported having completed at least one high-cost political act in the previous year (*active*) versus those who have completed zero political acts (*inactive*). These analyses mirror the subsetting of respondents on propensity to vote discussed in the previous chapter.

Figure 7.5 shows the average treatment effects of the traditional, ancestors, and interaction conditions, compared to the control on the first dependent variable, prioritizing time to protest. The results show that

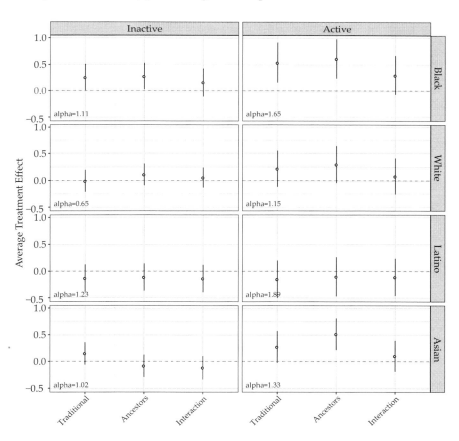

FIGURE 7.5 Priming effects on prioritization of protesting

priming the honoring ancestors norm has a significant and positive effect on intention to participate in high-cost activities among Black respondents. This is true for both inactive and active individuals. Among Black Americans who have been inactive in the previous year, receiving the apolitical ancestors prime increases their prioritization of protesting by 0.28 ($p = 0.03$). The effect of this nonpolitical norm treatment is comparable in magnitude to the explicitly political message about the importance of participation in the *traditional* condition ($\beta = 0.26$; $p = 0.05$). The effect of the treatment is even larger among Black Americans who were active in the previous year, increasing the prioritization of protesting by more than half a category of importance ($\beta = 0.61$; $p < 0.01$). Again, the effect size is similar to the *traditional* condition at 0.53.

Putting aside Black respondents, priming the honoring ancestors norm is generally ineffective at increasing prioritization of protesting with two exceptions. First, priming the honoring ancestors norm for White, active respondents produces a marginally significant increase in the dependent variable (0.30, $p = 0.09$). The result mirrors the experimental findings in the previous chapter on prioritization of voting. There, too, priming the honoring ancestors norm produced an increased commitment to participate in politics, but only among high-propensity White voters. This suggests that inactive, nonvoting White Americans are generally unaware of the participatory honoring ancestors interpretation, unlike both Black inactive respondents and active White respondents. Second, the honoring ancestors norm successfully increases the prioritization of protesting among already active Asian Americans. The effect size of 0.51 represents half a category shift in the prioritization of protesting for these individuals, a substantively large and statistically significant effect ($p < 0.01$).

Across groups, though, the norms intervention treatment—the *interaction* condition—which is designed to explicitly couple the honoring ancestors norm with political participation, is ineffective at increasing a commitment to attend political protests. The same is not true for the second dependent variable, willingness to learn more about local political organizations. Figure 7.6 shows that again the honoring ancestors norm is successful at mobilizing active Black respondents, increasing the willingness to learn more about local political organizations by 24%. For this dependent variable, though, the interaction condition also successfully changes an intention to participate in local political organizations for otherwise inactive Latino and Asian respondents. Learning

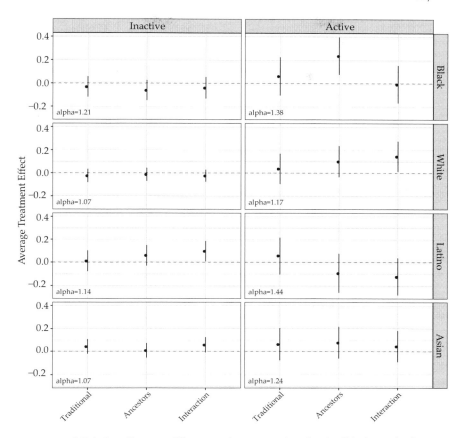

FIGURE 7.6 Priming effects on willingness to learn more about local political organizations

that a respected community leader is urging them to honor their ancestors through political participation increases inactive Latino respondents' willingness to learn about local political organizations by 10%
(p = 0.03). The comparable figure is 6% for otherwise inactive Asian
Americans (p = 0.09).

These results provide a promising first look at how two traditionally inactive groups—Latinos and Asian Americans—might be enticed
into local political participation. From an asset-based organizing approach, the honoring ancestors norm is widespread and especially strong
in communities of racial minorities (chapter 4). Organizing and other
intervention-based approaches that attempt to mobilize around this
norm, especially by explicitly connecting it to participatory behaviors,

may be a fruitful avenue for getting otherwise inactive individuals invested in local political organizations.

Structural Pulls and Strongly Held Beliefs

In his seminal book on the Mississippi Freedom Summer, sociologist and movement scholar Doug McAdam argues that two elements are essential for participation in high-risk political activism: "an intense ideological identification with the values of the movement . . . [and a] network [that] acts as the structural 'pull' encouraging the individual to make good on his or her strongly held belief" (McAdam, 1988, 64). My findings add details regarding the content of these "values," "pulls," and "beliefs." A deep sense of duty to participate, derived from beliefs about the ways one honors the past and helps those most in need, is essential in the process driving individuals to engage in high-cost actions like voting in local elections or through nonvoting means. Furthermore, social incentives to participate are distributed unequally depending on racial group membership and community context. Racial minorities are more likely than White Americans to reward those engaged in high-cost political action. This is especially true for Black Americans living in coracial contexts or Latinos surrounded by foreign-born citizens. And finally, the effectiveness of elite priming of "strongly held beliefs" varies depending on the underlying distribution of norms in a society. My findings show that the "structural pull" of elite and peer-level social pressure varies systematically across racial groups in the United States, shaping the incentives and sanctions individuals in different communities face when deciding whether or not to engage.

CHAPTER EIGHT

The Present and Future
of Participatory Social Norms

My intention for this book was to determine whether social norms about political participation in the United States diverge by racial group membership and embeddedness. The evidence overwhelmingly suggests that they do. Two norms—the honoring ancestors and helping hands norms—shape beliefs about the value and meaning of political participation across race in America. But because of divergent histories and continued racial segregation, the form, strength, and enforcement of these norms vary. Some groups are more likely to connect these norms to politics; others primarily express them through economic, cultural, or religious behaviors. Because the coupling of these norms to politics is strongly related to political participation, group-based beliefs about how best to honor the past and take care of people in need have widespread implications for who selects the American president, who votes in local elections, and who takes to the streets during a protest.

Yet, the state of the world I have described with respect to the distribution of participatory social norms is anything but inevitable. Rather, precisely because norms rely on context, they are dynamic. They can and do change (Bicchieri, 2016; Tankard and Paluck, 2015). In this chapter, I detail what we have learned about participatory social norms in the present moment but also how these norms might change and be changed in the future. As we are nearing the end of our time together, my hope is to leave you with a set of ideas—let's call them possibilities—about how organizers, activists, educators, and community members might leverage norms for a more equitable distribution of political participation in the United States.

Participatory Norms at This Moment in Time

The foundation of this book is a theory. I have proposed that participatory social norms should vary across racial groups in America because of divergent group histories and continued racial segregation. This is a theory fashioned on wisdom that spans social science disciplines. Psychologists teach us that norms shape much of human behavior, sociologists demonstrate that macro forces divide and define groups, and political scientists have recounted how selective benefits encourage political participation even in the face of costs. What I have done in the racialized norms model is draw together insight from these three literatures, which when combined, produce an expectation that is really very intuitive: racial groups likely have different participatory norms, which creates variation in political involvement.

But in many ways, the racialized norms model is devoid of specifics. It says that participatory social norms should vary across racial groups but does not tell us which norms are of consequence or identify the historical components of groups that will influence their expression. To find these details, I turned to the insights of regular Americans who live immersed in these norms. Using the method of grounded theory development, I conducted and analyzed interviews with Black and Asian Americans. My ambition was to identify norms tied to political participation and develop hypotheses about the direction and scope of their variance. This work uncovered two norms—the honoring ancestors and helping hands norms—that orient the lives of members of both groups but seemed differentially tied to political participation. Black Americans were more likely than Asian Americans I talked with to see honoring the past and helping those in need as demanding political involvement, and Black Americans discussed how these actions were valued and rewarded in their social communities.

With these insights in hand, I turned back to existing scholarship. Literatures ranging from evolutionary biology to cultural anthropology helped me translate my qualitative findings into a set of expectations about the political attitudes and behaviors of the four largest racial groups in America: Asian, Black, Latino, and White Americans. My goal was to build a cross-group theory, one that used the same moving parts to explain divergent outcomes. I hypothesized that a political expression of the honoring ancestors norm should vary in its strength and propensity across race in response to the proportion of recent im-migrants comprising a group and the group's location on the perceived foreignness dimension of the American racial hierarchy. A political ex-pression of the helping hands norm should similarly vary, but based on group members' perceptions of and experiences with structural disad-vantage; these factors are again shaped by position in the American ra-cial hierarchy.

The Participatory Social Norms Survey was designed to test these ex-pectations empirically. This data set innovates in a number of ways. It measures the strength and expressions of the honoring ancestors and helping hands norm, has numerous measures of political involvement, and includes questions designed to tackle the multidimensional nature of racial group embeddedness. And it does do equally for the nation's four largest racial groups, allowing for within- and across-group tests with representative samples of Asian, Black, Latino, and White Americans.

My analyses of the PSNS generate several findings that unveil the content of racial identities, describe the nature of norms in America, and demonstrate their relevance to political participation. Normative com-mitments to honor the past and help those in need are strong and wide-spread in the United States. But the expression of these two norms are multifold, with political participation comprising just one possible in-terpretation of the norms' demands. The political expression of these norms varies systematically across racial group membership and racial group embeddedness. Black Americans are most likely to believe hon-oring those in the past requires political involvement, followed by White Americans, Latinos, and then Asian Americans. The political expres-sion of the helping hands norm, too, varies to some degree, with minor-ity Americans more likely than White people to make this connection.

Further, those who believe the honoring ancestors and helping hands norms demand political participation are significantly more likely to engage in politics. That is, their beliefs about the content of these two widely shared social norms influence their political behavior. My novel political ancestors index predicts validated turnout in presidential elec-tions above and beyond a respondent's income, education, gender, gener-ational status, political interest, political efficacy, and racial linked fate. And it does so across racial groups. Accounting for both differences in norm strength within groups and their predictive ability across groups shows that strong participatory social norms help Black Americans over-come the inherent costs involved in national election year turnout. I find that Black turnout is on par with that of White Americans precisely because the group embraces strong participatory norms that reward and reinforce the value of engagement. In the absence of these norms, all three minority racial groups would turn out in national elections less than White Americans.

The political ancestors index also predicts voting in local elections for Asian, Black, and White Americans and participation through nonvoting acts for Asian, Latino, and White Americans. When it comes to these higher-cost forms of political participation, a political expression of the helping hands norm also emerges as essential. It predicts local turnout for Black Americans and Latinos and nonvoting political acts for all four racial groups. Again, the magnitude of these relationships is large, outperforming most other predictors included in the models. In fact, for White Americans, a political expression of the helping hands norm is the single largest predictor of nonvoting political participation.

My descriptive and correlational results are complemented by two experiments. The first shows that racial groups vary in the degree to which they assign social rewards to individuals engaging in both low- and high-cost political participation. The second shows that when community leaders activate the honoring ancestors norm, they can increase a commitment to participate in national and local politics. But this too varies across groups. Black and White Americans—members of groups that on average maintain strong political expressions of the honoring ancestors norm—are more likely to show changes in voting intention when confronted with these messages. In some cases, Asian Americans actually decrease their commitment to voting when they are reminded of the honoring ancestors norm. But these messages also show preliminary possibilities for shaping nonvoting activities among traditionally marginalized groups.

The compilation of evidence collected here establishes that the honoring ancestors and helping hands norms guide the political actions of many Americans. But they do so to varying degrees, informed by an individual's racial group membership and embeddedness. The likelihood that an individual feels compelled to vote or show up at a political rally is tied to how racial communities uniquely imagine the past and the poor. Racial identities, like all identities, have content, and in the United States today, beliefs about how best to honor the past and help those in need are part of what these identities entail. As members consider what is required of them, as they think about what is good and proper, they look to these norms for guidance. And when coupled with the promise of social rewards or psychological benefits, these norms can facilitate political participation, even in the face of uncertainty and tangible costs.

Norms of the Future

My findings throughout this book have primarily focused on defining and measuring group norms as they exist in the present moment. My goal has been to describe the status quo distribution of social norms related to political participation in American society and determine how this affects political involvement. But some findings in the previous chapters hint at something else: norms are not stagnant. They can be activated, manipulated, and even changed.

Part of this change, social psychologists suggest, is about perception. The fuzzy nature of norms means individuals must often speculate about normative standards, both the typical and the prescribed (Tankard and Paluck, 2015). This space between perception and reality leaves room for intervention. Individuals can learn about the average behavior of a group in ways that update their prior assumptions; social referents can change perceptions about the availability of social rewards for certain behaviors; and shifting the boundaries of groups can change which norms are prioritized (Goldstein, Cialdini, and Griskevicius, 2008; Gerber and Rogers, 2009; Paluck and Green, 2009; Paluck and Shepherd, 2012; Perkins, Craig, and Perkins, 2011). As a result, changing beliefs about what the past entails, updating concepts about who is in need, or altering the perceived boundaries of one's group can impact the content of participatory social norms and in turn, shape who engages in politics.

A History Told Twice

Let us consider an example of how this might work by telling two equally true stories about the history of Asian Americans and Latinos. We have learned that members of these two groups are less likely to couple the honoring ancestors norm to politics compared to White and Black Americans, especially when they are geographically or socially embedded in their in-group. I have suggested the on-average apolitical expression of an otherwise strong ancestors norm in these groups follows from two factors: the number of recent immigrants that comprise the group and the group's location on the *perceived foreignness* dimension of the American racial hierarchy (Lee, 2005; Zou and Cheryan, 2017).

While both these factors are likely to change as time progresses, perceived foreignness in particular is a dimension that may be responsive to norms interventions from either group elites or peer referents. We have learned that who our ancestors are and what we imagine they sacrificed for us shapes how we honor them. These stories are based on both reality and imaginings that bring salient people, events, and narratives to the fore.

Let me provide an example by telling two stories about Asian American and Latino group histories. In our first telling, we travel two centuries into the past. In the early 1800s, a booming southern economy and the nationalization of markets led Whites living in the American South to push further west, seeking new lands amenable to cotton production. Conflict over slavery and territory sparked a war between the nations of Mexico and the United States that ended over a decade later when the United States annexed what is now Texas, California, New Mexico, Arizona, and Nevada. Overnight, thousands of Mexicans living in these lands became American citizens and were promised the full rights accorded by the US Constitution (Flores, 2000; Rosales, 1997; Takaki, 2008). Around the same time, harsh economic conditions and the promise of gold in the American West sparked the first wave of Asian migrants from China, Japan, and later, the Philippines (Wong et al., 2011; Takaki, 2008). These migrants helped build the Transcontinental Railroad, opened businesses, and provided much-needed labor for farms and industries.

In the 170 years since the end of the Mexican-American War and the arrival of these first Asian migrants, Latinos and Asian Americans in the United States have fought against economic and political oppression applied by the American government. Denied citizenship and property rights, these minority communities have formed workers' unions, organized strikes, and filed court cases to challenge laws of exclusion and inequity. These efforts have provided the impetus for landmark policy changes in the areas of desegregation and labor. In 1938, a month-long strike of pecan workers in San Antonio laid the foundation for the Fair Labor Relations Act; decades of efforts among farmworkers in California led to the passage of a bill requiring collective bargaining; and nearly a decade before *Brown v. Board of Education*, the case of *Mendez v. Westminster School District of Orange County* set a legal prece-

dent declaring that segregation between Mexican and White school children violated of the Fourteenth Amendment (Tindall and Shi, 2004;
Takaki, 2008).

In this telling of Asian American and Latino group history, both
groups are deeply embedded in the American narrative. Asian and Latino ancestors helped to build a nation, comprised the early inhabitants,
and fought for democratic representation. Deemed unworthy of citizenship at various points in history, members of these groups—much like
Black Americans in the United States—have fought in the streets, the
courts, and the market for full inclusion in self-governance and economic prosperity (Takaki, 2008; Haney Lopez, 2006). When centered on
these referents, the ancestral history of Latinos and Asians in America
is old and long and includes the contested claiming of democratic power
along the way.

But there is an alternative history of Asians and Latinos in America that we can tell. This one begins much later, when shifting immigration policy and economic needs in the late twentieth century created
an influx of new American immigrants (Jiménez, 2010; Zong and Batalova, 2016; FitzGerald and Cook-Martin, 2015). After many years of restrictive immigration policy, a landmark bill was passed on the heels of
the Civil Rights Act, which reopened the nation's borders to Asian migrants (Masuoka and Junn, 2013). A rapid wave of immigration began,
exponentially increasing the Asian American population. Simultaneously, the destabilization of Central and South America led to a new influx of Latinos coming across the southern border of the United States
(Jiménez, 2010). In this telling, stories of lineage do not come from those
who forged the nation but are tied to the relatively recent ancestors who
crossed oceans and borders seeking the American dream.

These two concepts of the group—and parallel realities of the past—
exist simultaneously in the United States today. Asian Americans and
Latinos have long histories that stretch back to the early days of the nation. But they also have short histories, with life in America beginning
during a lived reality. My results suggest that the short history currently
dominates the narrative of ancestry for most Asian Americans and Latinos. The majority of Black and White Americans believe honoring the
past requires claiming the franchise—a concept built on the idea that
ancestors are uniquely American and deeply embedded in freedom
struggles—but less than half of Asian Americans and Latinos believe
the same. So while all minority groups face costs in terms of resource

and information constraints when considering whether to participate, Black Americans are more likely to confront powerful social and psychological rewards for voting than their Asian and Latino counterparts. These rewards offset the inherent costs of participating, lubricating collective action and increasing turnout.

This is the present condition of norms in the United States today, but it is not the only, or even inevitable, configuration. Individuals seeking to increase political participation among Asian Americans and Latinos may consider highlighting the long histories of both groups in the United States in ways that link recent immigration to parallel experiences in the past. Efforts that shift perceptions of who ancestors are and what they sacrificed, tying ancestral efforts to democratic inclusion and political involvement, may reforge the honoring ancestors norm in a way that more closely reflects average Black expressions.

Further, my results show that efforts to build panethnic group identity or increase American-based racial identities likely will also increase political participation through a reimagining of the honoring ancestors norm. Asian Americans and Latinos who are psychologically embedded in their group—that is, they feel close to other members of their American-based racial groups—are more likely to tie the honoring ancestors norm to political participation. This suggests that a strong American-based racial identity likely broadens perceptions of one's ancestors. Rather than imagining ancestors only as those recently arriving from foreign nations, Latinos and Asian Americans with strong panethnic identities also seem to encompass in their concepts of ancestors Americans from further into the past and see their sacrifices and stories as part of what honoring ancestors demands.

"Reality may refuse to go away," Thomas Rochon says, writing of social change, "but its meaning, and even whether we choose to give it any meaning at all, is a matter for the culture to decide" (Rochon, 1998, 15). Can new meanings be given to the honoring ancestors and helping hands norm among traditionally marginalized groups in America? I think that they can.

Imagining Norms as Community Assets

Most research on the political participation of American racial minorities focuses on what these communities currently lack, highlighting differences in resources, political socialization, and recruitment efforts.

My research suggests a complementary approach should be adopted for those who seek more equitable political participation and empowerment in traditionally marginalized communities in the United States: a reorientation to assessing what communities *have*. This is a concept I borrow from a tradition of strength-based interventions that proliferated beginning in the 1990s in the fields of social work, community development, and psychology (e.g., Kretzmann and McKnight, 1996; Mathie, Cameron, and Gibson, 2017). Collectively, this tradition attempts to solve problems by focusing on the assets already within communities that provide pathways for change. Assets are defined as the tangible or intangible "raw materials that community members can harness and build on . . . with the intention of using these resources as the basis for collective action" (Mathie, Cameron, and Gibson, 2017, 55). These resources can include a range of human, social, and cultural forms of capital (Benenson and Stagg, 2015).

In working to identify the strengths of a community, asset-based approaches attempt to shift the locus of power for change from outside needs providers to the hands of community members. In traditional community development work, organizers and specialists begin their process by mapping the deficiencies of communities identified as "at risk" or "underresourced," then identify how outside service providers can rectify these needs. In contrast, asset-based community development (ABCD) begins by mapping the assets of a community, then seeks to draw upon these reservoirs to build new services and economic opportunities (Kretzmann and McKnight, 1996). Through this approach, ABCD seeks to empower communities to see their "power to," "power within," and "power with" rather than simply others' "power over" (Cahill, 2008; Gaventa, 1982; Mathie, Cameron, and Gibson, 2017).

ABCD has faced criticism in recent years as some have argued that the approach is prone to neoliberal conclusions. In focusing on what a community already has rather than the structural disadvantages that often lead impoverished communities to their situations, heavy-handed interpreters may conclude that outside resources or structural interventions are unnecessarily for justice and equality (e.g., DeFilippis, Fisher, and Shragge, 2010; MacLeod and Emejulu, 2014). Placing agency in the hands of community members to enact change may lead to the conclusion that communities are also responsible for their challenges. Critics worry this victim-blaming interpretation of ABCD's principles leads to the withdrawal of resources from communities and the proliferation of political orientations that encourage "pick-yourself-up-by-your-bootstraps" policies instead of structural change (e.g., MacLeod and Emejulu, 2014). As a result, the very thing that makes asset-based approaches to community change so promising from a social justice perspective—that they empower communities with agency—is also their most dangerous component, leading to assigning blame to low-income or marginalized communities for their current socioeconomic status.

The most recent iterations of asset-based community development are careful to point out that their approach should be paired with, not replaced by, resources and services designed to address needs and solve structural inequalities in power and resources (Mathie, Cameron, and Gibson, 2017). These scholars argue that the needs- and asset-based approaches can exist in harmony. Asset-based approaches can seek to empower communities to find their voice, skills, and latent resources for the purposes of collective action targeted at policy change. Meanwhile, needs-based approaches can provide necessary short-term resources and identify the broader structural challenges that lead to inequities.

I take a similar attitude when proposing that organizers and community leaders think about the honoring ancestors and helping hands norms as two latent assets abundant in communities traditionally excluded from political representation and democratic governance. While pursuing solutions to structural inequalities through more inclusive recruitment by political parties and canvassers, redistribution of participatory resources, and the dismantling of barriers that increase costs disproportionately for the poor and racial minorities (García Bedolla and Michelson, 2012; Bentele and O'Brien, 2013; Ramírez, Solano, and Wilcox-Archuleta, 2018), academics and organizers should also consider the resources communities already have on hand that can be activated to increase mobilization and participation prior to or alongside these changes.

The honoring ancestors and helping hands norms are two such assets, sources of cultural capital within minority communities with latent political possibilities. This book has shown that these norms are widespread in communities across the United States and that the honoring ancestors norm is especially strong and abundant in communities of color. When these norms are coupled with political participation, they are potent motivators of political engagement. My results indicate that strong participatory interpretations of the honoring ancestors norm among Black Americans are precisely what enables this group to turn out at rates on par with White Americans. Organizing efforts that seek to connect these latent resources with politics may prove an avenue to increasing political participation in otherwise low-propensity communities.

White Racial Identity and the Past

Let's be clear, though: priming the past for the purposes of political engagement is not a universally rosy undertaking. Those who call upon the politically dominant cultures of the past will inevitably invoke a time when power was consolidated in the hands of White men. It is here that we confront an asymmetry in ancestral enterprises, again shaped at least in part by race: as racial minorities within the nation's borders fought for inclusion in the democratic process, the dominant group in the American racial hierarchy—White people—fought overwhelming to deny this access and retain power.

My analyses in chapter 4 suggested that many White Americans have strong ancestors norms that are tied to political participation. A growing literature on White racial identity suggests that these concepts of the past may be bundled for some into a quickly crystallizing White consciousness. Analyzing data from the late twentieth century, Wong and Cho (2005) concluded that White identity was widespread but not yet politically salient; more recent work shows how this identity is now deeply politicized. Potentially forming in response to the diversifying nation and related changes in status, White Americans are increasingly aware of their own race and conscious of their connection with other White people (e.g., Jardina, 2019; Sides, Tesler, and Vavreck, 2018; Weller and Junn, 2018). Distinct from but related to out-group prejudice, White racial identity has become a primary political predictor, shaping attitudes about everything from immigration to welfare policy to support for Donald Trump (Jardina, 2019).

Wong and Cho (2005) concluded in their prophetic article that "a demagogue could influence the salience of these [White] identities to promote negative outgroup attitudes, link racial identification more strongly to policy preferences, and exacerbate group conflict" (Wong and Cho, 2005, 716). Some pundits argue that this demagogue has arrived, citing Donald Trump's rapid rise to the American presidency. The businessman with no previous public service rose to political prominence when he repeatedly accused Barack Obama of not being an American citizen, demanding that he produce a valid birth certificate. In the years that followed, Trump's restrictive immigration and antitrade platform was headlined by the campaign slogan "Make America Great Again," arguably eliciting and idolizing a past when the privileges of citizenship, property, and political representation were assets available only to White Americans. In his powerful essay "The First White President," published in the *Atlantic* shortly after Trump secured the White House, Ta-Nehisi Coates (2017) explicitly links Trump's campaign to a concept of White ancestry. "Whereas his forebears carried whiteness like an ancestral talisman," Coates says of previous heads of state, "Trump cracked the glowing amulet open, releasing its eldritch energies" and "revealing just how much a demagogue can get away with."

My results suggest that as a White identity crystallizes and spreads, so too may the importance of the honoring ancestors norm as it relates to political participation. Not only will this change be consequential for policy and vote choice—the dominant thrust of the current literature— but also for turnout and mobilization. In drawing on not just White *identity* but White *ancestry*, the Trump campaign likely brought to the fore the sacrifices and struggles of a distinctly White American past and in doing so, mobilized voters to go to the polls to help usher him into the presidency.

Diversity and Obligation in America

Despite the linearity of history, it is difficult to tell a single chronicle of past events that encompasses the entirety of lived experience. Rather, the past is often truncated with some stories dominating our consciousness, while others fade away. Which chronicles of the past are worth remembering and the framing of those histories are constantly contested and change over time. As a result, a telling of history is just as much an act of human creation as was the process of writing this book.

But the histories we choose to tell, or the histories that are forced upon us by others, shape our perceptions of self, group, and morality. We have learned that our understandings of the past influence the social demands we face in the present but that both can change in the future. Participatory social norms are a powerful component of political participation in the United States. Elites can prime norms to increase turnout, boost investment in contentious political participation, and even get people interested in local politics. Peer-based social rewards further influence engagement, changing the incentive structure individuals face when deciding whether to engage. And when participatory norms are internalized, forming personal norms, they become among the strongest predictors of engagement, increasing political activity in everything from national elections to contentious protest movements.

However, the content and enforcement of social norms are inherently shaped by the context and history of groups. Because racial groups in the United States are segregated from each other, face distinct present-day challenges, and engender unique group-based histories, the form and content of social norms related to political participation are highly variable. Racial group membership and racial group embeddedness influence the internalization of participatory social norms and the likelihood of confronting peer-based rewards for engagement. Together, these shape large-scale, across-group trends in the likelihood of turning out and the pathways available for mobilization. In the mosaic that is America, obligation to one's community diverges by racial context. Collectively, these obligations shape political participation in the nation.

Acknowledgments

I was six when I told my grandmother I wanted to be a writer. We were waiting at a red light in her beige station wagon, and I was surrounded by my cousins. She turned around from her perch in the driver's seat to look right at me. "That's not practical," she explained. "Choose something else. If you like to write, find something that lets you do it as part of your job." This was the first piece of sage advice I received on the path to writing this book. Since then, many others have shared their invaluable wisdom, time, and resources.

I started this project with a set of foundational questions I was first exposed to as an undergraduate at the College of William and Mary. There, as a Sharpe Community Scholar, I was supplied with an incredible array of mentors who challenged me to think about scholarship in the context of community. I am grateful to Joel Schwartz, who convinced me at eighteen that political participation was worth studying; to Paul Manna, who taught me social science was a way to study it; to Monica Griffin for her fearless commitment to community-based research; and to Charles McGovern, who helped me see complexity in the story that is America. Throughout my time at William and Mary, the staff in the Office of Community Engagement and Scholarship helped me keep a foot in the communities I cared about and taught me the value of listening. I still often think of my experiences there when I imagine the kind of scholar I want to be.

When I arrived at Stanford for graduate school, I was lucky to find in my very first semester three scholars who thought my research questions were important: Gary Segura, Justin Grimmer, and Douglas McAdam. Together, Gary, Justin, and Doug helped this project grow from a first-year seminar paper into this book. Along the way, they provided me with not only intellectual support and resources but also their unending enthusiasm and kindness. I feel deeply grateful for their commitment to me and to my work.

Outside my core committee, I benefited from the financial, professional, and academic resources of a number of additional people and centers at Stanford. Paul Sniderman, Mike Tomz, and the members of the Laboratory for the Study of American Values helped me develop and field the earliest empirical tests in this book. Lauren Davenport and Dale Miller served as readers and provided feedback at various stages of the project's development. Tomás Jiménez taught the qualitative research methods class I enrolled in and provided a shining example of how interviews can generate new knowledge. The Office of the Vice Provost of Graduate Education at Stanford and its fearless leaders generously supported this work through grants and fellowship aid, and members of my graduate school cohort sat through many half-baked presentations of this research and its designs along the way. Panelists at the Midwest Political Science Association's annual meeting, the American Political Science Association's annual meeting, and other universities pushed me to clarify and tighten my findings in later stages of the project. I am thankful to this broad academic community both for improving the final product and for teaching me that scholarship is, if nothing else, a collaborative process.

I arrived at Vanderbilt in the fall of 2016 under the impression that this project was finished. My amazing colleagues made it clear that a dissertation is NOT a book and pushed me to see the full potential of this project. Since then, the data and scope of this book have more than doubled. I am especially grateful to Cindy Kam, Efrén Pérez, and Josh Clinton, who helped me design the final empirical tests in the arc of this project, read (many, many) drafts, and provided resources to finish it out the right way. In addition to these folks, I am quite certain I have found at Vanderbilt the most thoughtful and generous colleagues in this business and am deeply grateful for all the ways they have supported my transition from graduate school to life on the tenure track, making my job fun and rewarding even when it's so, so hard.

In January 2019, five scholars came to Nashville on Vandy's dime for a book conference: Kathy Cramer, Ryan Enos, Jane Junn, Jamila Michener, and Efrén Pérez. Reflecting the incredible collegiality and mentoring of my home department, many of my Vandy colleagues also attended the two-day conference. I circulated to this group a five-chapter manuscript that I felt very dissatisfied with. The final, eight-chapter book you have before you reflects the efforts of this group to improve the project in every dimension: accessibility, clarity, rigor, and theoretical reach, to name a few. These scholars helped me define the contribution of my research and exposed, sometimes with painful clarity, my biases and blind spots. I am incredibly grateful to these visiting scholars and my Vanderbilt colleagues for encouraging me to embrace the genre of *book*, freeing me to center my interview and descriptive data and helping me converge on a writing style that I think of as trying to teach instead of simply prove.

There are still others who contributed to this book. I am grateful to Drew Engelhardt and Alex Lawhorne for their work as research assistants; to the staff at the University of Chicago Press; to Adam Berinsky, who has guided me through the publishing process; to Nik Belanger, who read the manuscript in the final months before production to provide a nonacademic take on its accessibility and tone; and to the many interviewees, community partners, survey participants, and friends who shared with me their time and insights. I hope those who contributed to this book, along with the many communities it is meant to represent, will see in its findings evidence that I have listened.

Most importantly, I am grateful to my family—immediate and extended—for their patience and support throughout this process. I have worked many hours and faced many frustrations working on this research for nearly a decade. At every point, with every meltdown, they have shown me unending love and acceptance. I am grateful to my parents, who taught me early on that politics matters precisely because community and kindness matter and rooted in me strong ancestors and helping hands norms that I continue to fall back on in times of challenge. Their love and guidance has been the single most consistent force in my life. I am grateful to my sister, who listened with empathy across the many stages of this project, and to my mother-in-law, for the many hours of driving and unexpected days of babysitting she provided when a pandemic hit in the last months of editing this book. I am grateful to Andy, whose labor in our home over many years now has allowed me the space, sleep, and sustenance I needed for this research. I am grateful daily to be partnered with someone whose own beliefs about what makes for a virtuous life depart so radically from those commonly prescribed to his gender.

And last, but not least, I am grateful for Nina Valentine, whose obsession with Moana while I was writing the final chapters of this book helped me see the deep complexities of the honoring ancestors norm. Theo, too, deserves recognition. Arriving just in time to be included here, he contributed still by keeping me awake for many nighttime hours, during which I brainstormed a title for this book. For both of you, my wish is that whenever it is time to find home, you always know the way.

From Nashville,
Allison

Participatory Social Norms
Survey Instrumentation

The Participatory Social Norms Survey was conducted in March 2018. It was administered using the online platform GfK, which draws respondents from a preconstructed probability sample. To supplement the sample of Asian Americans available through that panel, an additional 601 Asian Americans were recruited by GfK through other survey platforms. The study was conducted in English and Spanish and resulted in 1,000 Latino, 1,000 White, 1,003 Black, and 1,020 Asian American respondents in total. All respondents were American citizens at least eighteen years of age.

This appendix provides question wording for items drawn from this survey that I analyze throughout this book. For the full Participatory Social Norms Survey instrument, as well as the Spanish-language version, please refer to the online appendix, where all supplementary materials are available: https://doi.org/10.7910/DVN/MWACHB.

Participatory Social Norms Survey Instrument

Let's begin with a few questions about the people who made it possible for you to be where you are today. This might include your parents, grandparents, leaders in your community, or historical figures. Tell us whether you agree or disagree with the next four statements. *Next four questions appear in random order.*

1. Honoring the struggles and traditions of my ancestors is a guiding principle in my life.
   (a) Strongly disagree
   (b) Somewhat disagree
   (c) Neither agree nor disagree
   (d) Somewhat agree
   (e) Strongly agree

2. I should respect the traditions and wishes of my family.
   (a) Strongly disagree
   (b) Somewhat disagree
   (c) Neither agree nor disagree
   (d) Somewhat agree
   (e) Strongly agree

3. Others made sacrifices so I could have the opportunities I do today.
   (a) Strongly disagree
   (b) Somewhat disagree
   (c) Neither agree nor disagree
   (d) Somewhat agree
   (e) Strongly agree

4. I feel a debt to those who paved the way for me.
   (a) Strongly disagree
   (b) Somewhat disagree
   (c) Neither agree nor disagree
   (d) Somewhat agree
   (e) Strongly agree

5. Think again about the people who made it possible for you to be where you are today. What do you think are the best ways to honor the legacy of these people? *Response options appear in random order, except for "Other" and "None," which are anchored at the end.*
   (a) Celebrate cultural or religious holidays
   (b) Continue traditional practices around food, clothing, music, or marriage
   (c) Speak a language other than English
   (d) Work hard to support my family
   (e) Pursue certain career opportunities
   (f) Pursue educational opportunities
   (g) Exercise my political rights
   (h) Vote in elections
   (i) Fight injustices when I see them

(j) Attend political rallies and protests

(k) Other [insert small text box][anchor]

(l) None of these [anchor]

Next, a few questions about those in need. This might include people who are struggling to get by or are experiencing hardship. Tell us whether you agree or disagree with the next four statements. *Next four questions appear in random order.*

6. Helping those in need is a guiding principle in my life.
   (a) Strongly disagree
   (b) Somewhat disagree
   (c) Neither agree nor disagree
   (d) Somewhat agree
   (e) Strongly agree
7. I should pursue what is best for me and my family even if it comes at the expense of people in need.
   (a) Strongly disagree
   (b) Somewhat disagree
   (c) Neither agree nor disagree
   (d) Somewhat agree
   (e) Strongly agree
8. I should make sacrifices of my own—time, money, or other things—to help people in need.
   (a) Strongly disagree
   (b) Somewhat disagree
   (c) Neither agree nor disagree
   (d) Somewhat agree
   (e) Strongly agree
9. I feel a moral duty to help those who are struggling.
   (a) Strongly disagree
   (b) Somewhat disagree
   (c) Neither agree nor disagree
   (d) Somewhat agree
   (e) Strongly agree
10. Think again about people who are in need. What do you think are the best ways to take care of these people? *Response options appear in random order, except for "Other" and "None," which are anchored at the end.*

(a) Give money to charitable causes

(b) Participate in charitable organizations

(c) Help strangers like the homeless and elderly when I run into them

(d) Give money to political causes

(e) Participate in political organizations

(f) Vote or engage in politics to change policy

(g) Pray for those in need

(h) Help those in need find religious communities

(i) Other [insert small text box][anchor]

(j) None of these [anchor]

11. Now, some questions about people you know. From time to time, most people discuss important matters with others. Looking back over the last six months, who are the people with whom you discussed matters important to you? List just the first names or initials of up to five people below. Please keep in mind that we are only asking for name or initials to reference them later in the survey.

(a) Person 1 [insert small text box]

(b) Person 2 [insert small text box]

(c) Person 3 [insert small text box]

(d) Person 4 [insert small text box]

(e) Person 5 [insert small text box]

12. What is the race/ethnicity of each person?

   Statements in row:

(a) (insert name provided for *Person 1*)

(b) (insert name provided for *Person 2*)

(c) (insert name provided for *Person 3*)

(d) (insert name provided for *Person 4*)

(e) (insert name provided for *Person 5*)

   Answers in column:

(a) White

(b) Black or African American

(c) Asian or Pacific Islander

(d) Latino or Hispanic

(e) Other

(f) Don't know

13. Now, something a bit different. Read the following message carefully. We will ask you some questions about it later.

   Imagine a respected community leader said to you: [insert DOV_treat]

(If DOV_treat=1, display:) "We must exercise. We all should take care of our body and mind."

(If DOV_treat=2, display:) "We must participate in politics. We all should seize the right to vote, attend political protests, even give money to political groups."

(If DOV_treat=3, display:) "We must honor the legacy of our ancestors. We all should claim the rights and opportunities those in the past fought so hard—even died—for us to have."

(If DOV_treat=4, display:) "We must participate in politics to honor the legacy of our ancestors. We all should seize the right to vote, attend political protests, even give money to political groups. These are rights and opportunities those in the past fought so hard—even died—for us to have."

14. It is difficult for people to find time to do everything they want to do, and most people have to make choices about what activities are most important to them. Considering the message you just read, please tell us how important it is to make time for each of the following activities. *Next four questions appear in random order.*

15. Find time to vote.
   (a) Not at all important
   (b) Slightly important
   (c) Moderately important
   (d) Very important
   (e) Extremely important
16. Find time to attend political protests for issues I care about.
   (a) Not at all important
   (b) Slightly important
   (c) Moderately important
   (d) Very important
   (e) Extremely important
17. Find time to take care of myself by exercising, eating well, and sleeping enough.
   (a) Not at all important
   (b) Slightly important
   (c) Moderately important
   (d) Very important
   (e) Extremely important

18. Find time to practice cultural traditions from my heritage.
    (a) Not at all important
    (b) Slightly important
    (c) Moderately important
    (d) Very important
    (e) Extremely important

19. Many local organizations are trying to get people more involved in politics. Would you like information at the end of this study about organizations in your area?
    (a) Yes
    (b) No

20. In the last two years, have you been contacted on behalf of any political candidates—whether it was by a letter in the mail, by telephone, or in person by a campaign worker?
    (a) Yes, in person
    (b) Yes, by telephone
    (c) Yes, by mail
    (d) Yes, some other way
    (e) No
    (f) I'm not sure

Finally, we'll end with some questions about groups you may identify with. These questions are about people who may be like you in their ideas, interests, and feelings about things.

21. Some groups of people you may feel close to, while others less so. How close do you feel to people in the United States who are . . .
    Statements in row (*appear in random order*):
    (a) White
    (b) Latino or Hispanic
    (c) Asian
    (d) Black
    Answers on column:
    (a) Not at all
    (b) Not very close
    (c) Somewhat close
    (d) Very close

Now, please tells us whether you agree or disagree with the following statements.

22. What happens generally to (*insert respondent's self-reported race*: White/ Black/Asian/Latino or Hispanic) people in this country will affect what happens to me.
    (a) Strongly disagree
    (b) Somewhat disagree
    (c) Neither agree nor disagree
    (d) Somewhat agree
    (e) Strongly agree
23. I don't think public officials care much about what people like me think.
    (a) Strongly disagree
    (b) Somewhat disagree
    (c) Neither agree nor disagree
    (d) Somewhat agree
    (e) Strongly agree
24. I consider myself well qualified to participate in politics.
    (a) Strongly disagree
    (b) Somewhat disagree
    (c) Neither agree nor disagree
    (d) Somewhat agree
    (e) Strongly agree

GfK Supplement

In addition to the questions I fielded as part of the PSNS, GfK also provided basic demographic information and standard political attitudes for the survey respondents. For most respondents, this information was collected through survey questions prior to the fielding of the PSNS and used for recruiting a representative sample. GfK then appended the answers to these questions to the PSNS for each respondent. However, for respondents that were recruited outside of GfK's usual panel, this demographic information was collected at the opening of the PSNS if it was needed to determine eligibility for the study and at the end if it was not.

1. Are you . . . ? Select one answer only.
    (a) Male
    (b) Female
2. How old are you? *Type in your age.* [PROMPT: Providing this information makes sure that answers from you help represent the entire US population.

Please remember that your individual responses are kept confidential. Thank you!]

(a) [Small text box] years old.

3. This is about your ethnicity. Are you Spanish, Hispanic, or Latino? *Select one answer only.*

   (a) No, I am not
   (b) Yes, Mexican, Mexican American, Chicano
   (c) Yes, Puerto Rican
   (d) Yes, Cuban, Cuban American
   (e) Yes, other Spanish, Hispanic, or Latino group (Please specify, for example Argentinean, Colombian, Dominican, Nicaraguan, Salvadoran, Spaniard, and so on) [small text box]

4. Please indicate what you consider your race to be. We greatly appreciate your effort to describe your background using these categories. While they may not fully describe you, they do match those used by the US Census Bureau.

   Please choose one or more race(s) that you consider yourself to be. *Select all answers that apply.* [PROMPT: We would like to have your answer to this question. Your individual responses will remain confidential.]

   (a) White
   (b) Black or African American
   (c) American Indian or Alaska Native
   (d) Asian
   (e) Native Hawaiian or other Pacific Islander
   (f) Some other race [small text box]

5. What is the highest level of school you have completed? *Select one answer only.*

   (a) Some high school or less—no diploma or GED
   (b) High school graduate—high school diploma or the equivalent (GED)
   (c) Some college, no degree
   (d) Associate degree
   (e) Bachelor's degree
   (f) Master's degree
   (g) Professional or doctorate degree

6. How much is the *combined income* of all members of YOUR HOUSEHOLD for the PAST TWELVE MONTHS?

   Please include your income PLUS the income of all members living in your household (including cohabiting partners and armed forces members living at home). Please count income BEFORE TAXES and from all sources (such as wages, salaries, tips, net income from a business, interest, dividends, child support, alimony, and Social Security, public assistance, pensions, or retirement benefits). *Select one answer only.* [PROMPT: We realize that this is personal information. We will ONLY ASK the range of your household income, NOT the exact amount.]

(a) Below $50,000
(b) $50,000 or more
(c) Don't know

7. *Shown only to respondents with household income below $50,000.* We would like to get a better estimate of your total HOUSEHOLD income in the past 12 months before taxes. Was it . . . *Select one answer only.*

(a) Less than $5,000
(b) $5,000 to $7,499
(c) $7,500 to $9,999
(d) $10,000 to $12,499
(e) $12,500 to $14,999
(f) $15,000 to $19,999
(g) $20,000 to $24,999
(h) $25,000 to $29,999
(i) $30,000 to $34,999
(j) $35,000 to $39,999
(k) $40,000 to $49,999

8. *Shown only to respondents with household income of $50,000 or more.* We would like to get a better estimate of your total HOUSEHOLD income in the past 12 months before taxes. Was it . . . *Select one answer only.*

(a) $50,000 to $59,999
(b) $60,000 to $74,999
(c) $75,000 to $84,999
(d) $85,000 to $99,999
(e) $100,000 to $124,999
(f) $125,000 to $149,999
(g) $150,000 to $174,999
(h) $175,000 to $199,999
(i) $200,000 to $249,999
(j) $250,000 or more

9. Were you born a United States citizen or are you a naturalized US citizen? *Select one answer only.*

(a) Born a US citizen
(b) Naturalized US citizen

10. Were both of your parents born in the US?
    (a) Both parents born in the US
    (b) One parent born in the US
    (c) Neither parent born in the US
    (d) Don't know

11. In general, how interested are you in politics and public affairs? *Select one answer only.*
    (a) Very interested
    (b) Somewhat interested
    (c) Slightly interested
    (d) Not at all interested

12. In talking to people about elections, we often find that a lot of people were not able to vote because they weren't registered, they were sick, or they just didn't have time.

    Did you happen to vote in the November 2016 elections for the US President or Congress? *Select one answer only.*
    (a) Yes
    (b) No

13. This question is about LOCAL elections, such as for mayor or a school board. Do you . . . ?
    (a) Never vote in local elections
    (b) Rarely vote in local elections
    (c) Sometimes vote in local elections
    (d) Always vote in local elections

14. Generally speaking, do you think of yourself as a . . .
    (a) Republican
    (b) Democrat
    (c) Independent
    (d) Another party, please specify: [small text box]
    (e) No preference

15. *Display to respondents who answer Republican.* Would you call yourself a . . .
    (a) Strong Republican
    (b) Not very strong Republican

16. *Display to respondents who answer Democrat.* Would you call yourself a . . .
    (a) Strong Democrat
    (b) Not very strong Democrat

17. *Display if respondent answers independent, another party, or no preference.* Do you think of yourself as closer to the . . .

(a) Republican Party
(b) Democratic Party
18. People may be involved in civic and political activities. In the past 12 months, have you . . . ? *Select all answers that apply.*
(a) Attended a political protest or rally
(b) Contacted a government official
(c) Volunteered or worked for a Presidential campaign
(d) Volunteered or worked for another political candidate, party, issue, or cause
(e) Served on a committee for a civic, non-profit or community organization
(f) Written a letter or email to a newspaper/magazine or called a live radio or TV show
(g) Commented about politics on a message board or internet site
(h) Shared your opinion about a town or community issue at a public meeting
(i) Held a publicly elected office
(j) Signed a petition
(k) None of these

Geographic Indicator Variables

GfK has the address of each survey participant on their panel, which can be used to produce geographic indicators such as census block. However, address—and even census block—reduce the anonymity of survey respondents considerably and introduce ethical complications for the researcher. To protect the identity of survey respondents, GfK did NOT provide me with addresses for any of the survey respondents, including those off-panel respondents for whom address data were collected at the start of the survey. Rather, GfK provided me with a census block indicator for respondents that was perturbed to help protect respondent identity. This is the company's standard practice when providing census block data, and they provided the following documentation regarding the process:

> In order to protect the confidentiality of our survey respondents, GfK has developed an algorithm to perturb the latitude and longitude of their addresses. This algorithm randomly shifts the geocoded latitude and longitude of each address in increments of 100 feet both in north or south and east or west di-

rections. Moreover, the extent of the shift depends on the population density of the corresponding Census Block Group within which a given respondent is located, with a more pronounced shift in areas with low population density where addresses are more dispersed. . . . Addresses in areas with a population density above the 75th percentile—those with the highest population density—are randomly perturbed from 100 to 500 feet; those in areas from the 50th to 75th percentile are randomly perturbed from 600 to 1,000 feet; those in the 25th to 50th percentile by 1,100 to 1,500 feet; and those in less than the 25th percentile—areas with the lowest population density—by 1,600 to 2,000 feet. For example, the latitude/longitude of the location of an individual who lives in a sparsely populated area could be randomly shifted 1,600 feet to the west and 1,800 feet to the north. Upon perturbation of the latitude and longitude of each address, the corresponding Census Block associated with the perturbed location will be identified and included with the final data files. (GfK, 2014)

Supplemental Material for Qualitative Interviews

Interview Procedure

Interviews for the qualitative portion of this project lasted between thirty-five minutes and one hour, twenty minutes, with an average length of one hour. The time it took to complete an interview was a function of both respondent availability and loquaciousness. I talked with some respondents during their lunch break, others on an evening or weekend. Some respondents had a lot to say and others much less. Those I recruited in early stages of this project—while I was still a graduate student at Stanford—agreed to volunteer their time. Later, after I started as an assistant professor at Vanderbilt and had a wider array of resources at my disposal, I paid respondents for their time with their choice of a ten-dollar gift card from either Target or Amazon.

All interviews were recorded and professionally transcribed. I used a two-step process to analyze the gathered data (Charmaz, 2014). First, in a round of initial exploration, the substance of early interviews was entirely coded, with no preconceived coding scheme in place. This process produced eighty-two codes applied to nearly five hundred excerpts. Based on these initial results, both I and a graduate research assistant independently coded the transcripts again, with a reduced, theoretically selected seventeen codes in mind.

My focus on norms in this study was hidden from respondents at the front end of interviews. In requests for interviews and in the consent documents, respondents were told that I hoped to talk with them about their experiences and beliefs about community and political engagement. When asked to extrapolate further, I deferred to the end of interviews. This seemed quite effective at preventing respondents from being primed to my interest in social norms or racial group dynamics. At the end of interviews, respondents would often ask me to tell them about the project, mentioning that even after answering questions for more than an hour, they did not know what the study was about.

The two samples of Black and Asian American respondents mirrored each other in terms of education and income but varied some with respect to age. Respondents' yearly household incomes ranged from \$12,000 to \$200,000 among Asian Americans and from \$8,400 to \$400,000 for Black Americans. For both groups, roughly half of the sample fell below the 2014 median household income of \$53,657 and the other half above (DeNavas-Walt and Proctor, 2015). With the exception of one Black respondent, all individuals in the sample had completed at least a high school degree. The age range of Black respondents was wider than that of Asian American respondents, and median ages of the two samples varied: twenty-six for Asian respondents, thirty-two for Black respondents. All but two Black respondents were born in the United States, and most did not provide an ethnicity on the additional demographic sheet I asked interviewees to complete at the end of our interview. Asian respondents, on the other hand, varied significantly in their ethnicity and nativity status. A table available in the online appendix (see appendix A) provides full demographic details for each respondent.

Throughout the book, I use pseudonyms for interviewees and change occupation details slightly to protect the identity of the respondents. When adding direct quotes from interviews to the book, I remove fill comments like "you know" and "like" that do not affect the meaning of the speaker's statement but do affect readability.

A Set of Example Questions

In line with the method of grounded theory, my question protocol for interviews was flexible. I primarily followed the conversation and cues of those I interviewed. My question protocol also evolved over time, reflecting the iterative approach of grounded theory development. I provide in the online appendix a combined list of questions used in early and later protocols, but below I outline a sample of commonly used questions that often yielded the most relevant content.

1. How would you describe yourself to someone who doesn't know you?
2. What are some things about yourself you are most proud of? (For young adults:) What do you think your parents are most proud of?
3. What are some of the things that brought you to this work/job/career?
4. One of the things I'm really interested in is how different people think about the meaning of their community. When you think about "your community," what do you think of? / Other people I've interviewed have talked a lot about "community." What do you think about when you think about "your community"?
5. Can you tell me about someone you know that stands out as a great community member?
6. What types of things does a good member of your community do?
7. (In your community,) What does it mean to be successful? What are the kinds of things someone who is successful does?

APPENDIX C

Supplemental Empirical Analyses

Chapter 1 Material

TABLE C.1 **Models of presidential year turnout**

	White	Black	Latino	Asian
2008				
(Intercept)	0.30 (0.01)*	0.50 (0.01)*	0.15 (0.02)*	0.18 (0.04)*
Education	0.07 (0.00)*	0.05 (0.00)*	0.08 (0.00)*	0.08 (0.01)*
Income	0.01 (0.00)*	0.01 (0.00)*	0.01 (0.00)*	0.01 (0.00)*
Foreign born	−0.09 (0.01)*	−0.10 (0.02)*	0.07 (0.01)*	−0.05 (0.02)*
N	57,341	6,550	5,599	2,432
2004				
(Intercept)	0.30 (0.01)*	0.39 (0.01)*	0.17 (0.02)*	0.29 (0.04)*
Education	0.07 (0.00)*	0.06 (0.00)*	0.08 (0.01)*	0.05 (0.01)*
Income	0.02 (0.00)*	0.01 (0.00)*	0.01 (0.00)*	0.00 (0.00)
Foreign born	−0.07 (0.01)*	−0.10 (0.02)*	0.08 (0.02)*	−0.04 (0.02)
N	62,326	7,036	4,972	2,055
2000				
(Intercept)	0.25 (0.01)*	0.31 (0.02)*	0.15 (0.02)*	0.29 (0.05)*
Education	0.07 (0.00)*	0.07 (0.01)*	0.07 (0.01)*	0.04 (0.01)*
Income	0.02 (0.00)*	0.01 (0.00)*	0.01 (0.00)*	0.00 (0.00)
Foreign born	−0.03 (0.02)*	0.01 (0.04)	0.08 (0.02)*	0.01 (0.03)
N	40,406	5,980	4,301	1,140

Notes: Analysis draws from the November Supplement of the Current Population Survey and is confined to citizens over the age of eighteen. CPS-provided population weights are applied to all calculations to ensure a representative sample. Education has six categories: less than high school, high school degree, some college but no degree, associate's or vocational degree, bachelor's degree, advanced degree. Income has sixteen categories ranging from under $5,000 a year to over $150,000 a year. Foreign born is a dichotomous variable that indicates whether the respondent was born abroad or not.

*$p < 0.05$.

Chapter 3 Material

TABLE C.2 **Within-group percentages for generational status in the United States**

Generation	Asian	Black	Latino	White
First	47.56	6.16	16.52	2.61
Second	41.97	6.99	40.07	5.73
Third or more	10.47	86.85	43.41	91.67

Notes: Estimates were calculated using pooled monthly data from the 2018 Current Population Survey (Flood et al., 2018). First generation indicates individuals who were born abroad and naturalized into American citizenship. Second generation indicates individuals for whom either or both parents were born abroad.

Chapter 4 Material

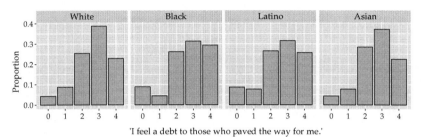

'I feel a debt to those who paved the way for me.'

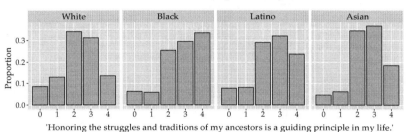

'Honoring the struggles and traditions of my ancestors is a guiding principle in my life.'

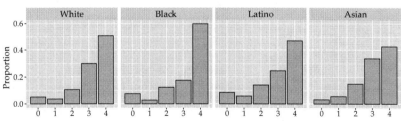

'Others made sacrifices so I could have the opportunities I do today.'

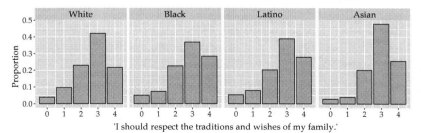

'I should respect the traditions and wishes of my family.'

FIGURE C.1 Distribution of items in the honoring ancestors scale

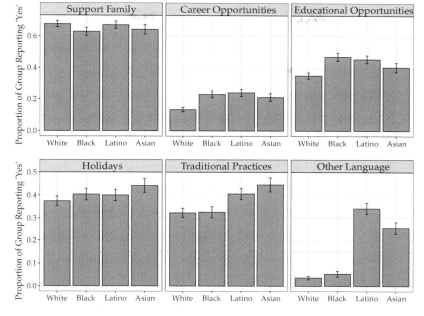

FIGURE C.2 Economic and cultural expression of honoring ancestors by group

TABLE C.3 **Racial embeddedness and the political ancestors index**

	Asian	Black	Latino	White
(Intercept)	0.26*	0.14*	0.25*	0.48*
	(0.09)	(0.06)	(0.08)	(0.10)
Coracial closeness	0.18*	0.28*	0.15*	0.12*
	(0.05)	(0.05)	(0.05)	(0.05)
Coracial network	−0.16*	0.06+	0.00	−0.02
	(0.03)	(0.03)	(0.03)	(0.05)
Coracial block	−0.13+	0.00	−0.08+	0.01
	(0.07)	(0.04)	(0.05)	(0.05)
Education (indiv.)	0.02+	0.03*	0.02*	0.01+
	(0.01)	(0.01)	(0.01)	(0.01)
Income (indiv.)	0.00	0.00	−0.01*	0.01
	(0.00)	(0.00)	(0.00)	(0.00)
2nd gen (indiv.)	0.01	−0.12*	0.00	0.05
	(0.04)	(0.04)	(0.03)	(0.05)
1st gen (indiv.)	0.04	−0.02	0.06+	−0.19*
	(0.04)	(0.05)	(0.03)	(0.07)
Education (tract)	−0.33*	−0.16	−0.16	−0.45*
	(0.16)	(0.13)	(0.15)	(0.13)
Income (tract)	0.00	0.00	0.00	−0.00*
	(0.00)	(0.00)	(0.00)	(0.00)
Nativity (tract)	0.14	0.05	0.12	−0.08
	(0.09)	(0.10)	(0.09)	(0.14)
R^2	0.10	0.10	0.05	0.04
Adj. R^2	0.08	0.08	0.04	0.03
N	597	803	802	822
RMSE	0.30	0.31	0.31	0.30

Notes: Entries show OLS regression coefficients with standard errors in parentheses. Outcome variable is the political ancestors index. Primary independent variables, scored from 0 to 1, are psychological embeddedness in racial group (i.e., strength of self-reported coracial group closeness); social embeddedness in racial group (i.e., proportion of close social network ties that are coracial); and geographic embeddedness (i.e., proportion of respondent's census block that is coracial). Control variables include individual level controls for education, household income, generational status (first or second compared to third generation or more) and geographic level controls including census tract median income, proportion of census tract older than twenty-five with at least a high school degree, and proportion of residents in census tract who are either naturalized or noncitizens.

*$p < 0.05$; +$p < 0.1$.

Chapter 5 Material

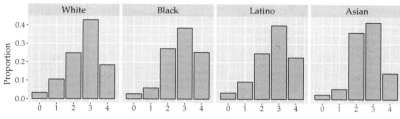

'I feel a moral duty to help those who are struggling.'

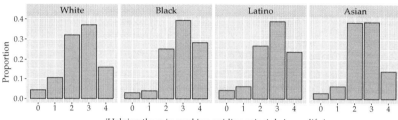

'Helping those in need is a guiding principle in my life.'

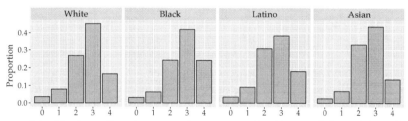

'I should make sacrifices of my own — time, money, or other things — to help people in need.'

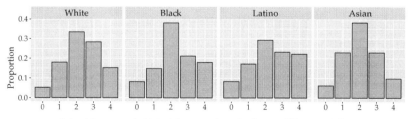

'I should pursue what is best for me and my family even if it comes at the expense of people in need.' (reverse coded)

FIGURE C.3 Distribution of items in the helping hands scale

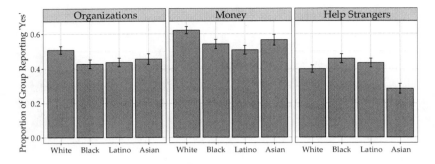

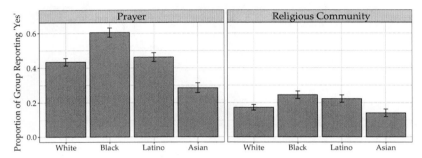

FIGURE C.4 Religious and charitable expression of helping hands by group

TABLE C.4 **Racial embeddedness and the political helping index**

	Asian	Black	Latino	White
(Intercept)	0.20*	0.11*	0.38*	0.30*
	(0.08)	(0.05)	(0.07)	(0.08)
Coracial closeness	0.10*	0.15*	0.02	0.03
	(0.04)	(0.03)	(0.04)	(0.04)
Coracial network	−0.08*	0.05+	−0.02	0.00
	(0.03)	(0.03)	(0.03)	(0.04)
Coracial block	−0.03	−0.07*	−0.07+	0.08+
	(0.06)	(0.03)	(0.04)	(0.04)
Education (indiv.)	0.01	0.02*	0.01*	−0.01
	(0.01)	(0.01)	(0.01)	(0.01)
Income (indiv.)	−0.01+	0.00	0.00	0.00
	(0.00)	(0.00)	(0.00)	(0.00)
2nd gen (indiv.)	0.05	−0.07*	−0.01	−0.01
	(0.03)	(0.03)	(0.02)	(0.04)
1st gen (indiv.)	0.05+	−0.02	−0.01	−0.14*
	(0.03)	(0.04)	(0.02)	(0.06)
Education (tract)	−0.49*	−0.18+	−0.48*	−0.50*
	(0.14)	(0.10)	(0.12)	(0.10)
Income (tract)	0.00	0.00	−0.00*	0.00
	(0.00)	(0.00)	(0.00)	(0.00)
Nativity (tract)	0.04	−0.05	0.09	0.12
	(0.08)	(0.07)	(0.07)	(0.11)
R^2	0.08	0.07	0.03	0.05
Adj. R^2	0.06	0.06	0.02	0.04
N	597	803	802	822
RMSE	0.25	0.23	0.25	0.25

Notes: Entries show OLS regression coefficients with standard errors in parentheses. Outcome variable is the political helping index. Primary independent variables, scored from 0 to 1, are psychological embeddedness in racial group (i.e., strength of self-reported coracial group closeness); social embeddedness in racial group (i.e., proportion of close social network ties that are coracial); and geographic embeddedness (i.e., proportion of respondent's census block that is coracial). Control variables include individual level controls for education, household income, generational status (first or second compared to third generation or more) and geographic level controls including census tract median income, proportion of census tract older than twenty-five with at least a high school degree, and proportion of residents in census tract who are either naturalized or noncitizens.

$^*p < 0.05$; $^+p < 0.1$.

Chapter 6 Material

TABLE C.5 **Predicting turnout with and without norms**

	Asian	Black	Latino	White
2016 turnout				
Base model				
(Intercept)	0.32 (0.03)*	0.61 (0.03)*	0.54 (0.04)*	0.70 (0.03)*
Income	0.00 (0.01)	0.00 (0.01)	0.00 (0.01)	0.00 (0.01)
Education	0.00 (0.01)	0.01 (0.01)	0.01 (0.01)	0.00 (0.01)
Naturalized	−0.05 (0.03)	−0.07 (0.07)	0.10 (0.04)*	0.11 (0.10)
N	1,012	967	945	970
Norms model				
(Intercept)	0.25 (0.04)*	0.43 (0.04)*	0.43 (0.04)*	0.56 (0.03)*
Income	0.00 (0.00)	0.00 (0.01)	0.00 (0.01)	0.00 (0.00)
Education	0.00 (0.01)	0.00 (0.01)	0.01 (0.01)	0.00 (0.01)
Naturalized	−0.05 (0.03)	−0.05 (0.06)	0.08 (0.03)*	0.18 (0.10)
Political ancestors	0.36 (0.05)*	0.45 (0.05)*	0.32 (0.06)*	0.32 (0.05)*
Political help	−0.07 (0.06)	0.06 (0.07)	0.09 (0.07)	0.17 (0.06)*
N	1,012	967	945	970
2014 turnout				
Base model				
(Intercept)	0.14 (0.03)*	0.49 (0.04)*	0.37 (0.04)*	0.57 (0.03)*
Income	0.01 (0.00)	−0.01 (0.01)	−0.01 (0.01)*	0.00 (0.01)
Education	0.01 (0.01)	0.03 (0.01)*	0.02 (0.01)*	0.00 (0.01)
Naturalized	−0.01 (0.02)	−0.14 (0.07)*	0.00 (0.03)	−0.04 (0.11)
N	1,002	954	909	959
Norms model				
(Intercept)	0.07 (0.03)*	0.31 (0.04)*	0.26 (0.04)*	0.45 (0.04)*
Income	0.01 (0.00)	−0.01 (0.01)	−0.01 (0.01)	0.00 (0.01)
Education	0.01 (0.01)	0.02 (0.01)	0.02 (0.01)*	−0.01 (0.01)
Naturalized	−0.02 (0.02)	−0.12 (0.07)	−0.02 (0.03)	0.03 (0.11)
Political ancestors	0.40 (0.04)*	0.38 (0.05)*	0.29 (0.06)*	0.27 (0.06)*
Political help	−0.12 (0.05)*	0.16 (0.07)*	0.10 (0.07)	0.14 (0.07)*
N	1,002	954	909	959

Notes: Entries show OLS regression coefficients with standard errors in parentheses. Data from the PSNS.
*$p < 0.05$.

TABLE C.6 **Conditions, neighbors experiment**

Category	Variables
Name	Louis, Anthony, Martin, David
Age	34, 35, 37, 38
Occupation	X-ray technician, high school teacher, physical therapist, legal assistant
Community activity	Votes in every presidential election, Annually attends political rallies, Annually attends neighborhood potluck dinners, Annually attends charitable events

Notes: The order of all values was randomly assigned except for the control condition, "Annually attends neighborhood potluck dinners," which appeared last for all respondents. Name, age, and occupation values were designed to be functionally equivalent. Names are gender consistent and were chosen to be racially ambiguous across Black, Latino, and White. I used the Nakao-Treas Prestige Score and the Hauser-Warren Socioeconomic Index to choose occupations considered generally equal in terms of socioeconomic status and gender distribution (Hauser and Warren, 1997). Furthermore, the assignment of each condition is randomized throughout the experiment, canceling out any unexpected effects.

TABLE C.7 **Testing for carryover effects, neighbors experiment**

	First appearance mean	Aggregate mean
Voting		
Likability	5.26	5.28
Respectability	5.48	5.44
Rally attendance		
Likability	4.90	4.97
Respectability	5.15	5.16

Notes: In all categories, the first appearance mean does not prove statistically different from the aggregate mean ($p < 0.05$) when tested using a two-sided t-test.

TABLE C.8 **Sample size for each subgroup, elite priming experiment**

	Low	Medium	High	Low	Medium	High
		Black sample			Asian sample	
Control	37	43	123	161	21	33
Traditional	42	58	131	163	24	46
Ancestors	42	44	132	163	23	50
Interaction	43	27	120	151	27	34
		Latino sample			White sample	
Control	47	55	81	37	29	143
Traditional	41	53	87	35	35	131
Ancestors	46	59	94	29	41	125
Interaction	60	48	99	42	46	140

Chapter 7 Material

TABLE C.9 **Predicting frequency of local vote, self-report**

	Asian	Black	Latino	White
(Intercept)	0.26 (0.10)*	0.18 (0.05)*	0.26 (0.05)*	0.21 (0.04)*
Political ancestors	0.21 (0.07)*	0.16 (0.05)*	0.08 (0.05)	0.08 (0.04)*
Political help	0.07 (0.07)	0.16 (0.05)*	0.11 (0.06)*	0.01 (0.04)
Recruitment	0.19 (0.04)*	0.17 (0.03)*	0.11 (0.03)*	0.14 (0.03)*
Interest politics	0.17 (0.06)*	0.08 (0.04)*	0.23 (0.04)*	0.23 (0.03)*
Linked fate	−0.05 (0.07)	0.08 (0.04)+	−0.02 (0.04)	−0.02 (0.04)
External efficacy	−0.05 (0.07)	0.07 (0.04)+	0.01 (0.04)	0.03 (0.03)
Internal efficacy	0.12 (0.07)+	0.00 (0.04)	0.11 (0.04)*	0.13 (0.04)*
Income	0.05 (0.05)	0.05 (0.03)	0.02 (0.03)	0.02 (0.03)
Education	−0.06 (0.05)	0.04 (0.03)	−0.02 (0.03)	−0.02 (0.02)
1st generation	0.03 (0.04)	0.05 (0.06)	0.02 (0.03)	0.01 (0.07)
2nd generation	−0.11 (0.06)+	−0.00 (0.04)	−0.01 (0.03)	−0.05 (0.04)
Age	0.40 (0.08)*	0.29 (0.04)*	0.20 (0.05)*	0.24 (0.04)*
Male	0.03 (0.04)	−0.02 (0.02)	−0.03 (0.02)	−0.01 (0.02)
Cultural ancestors	−0.10 (0.05)*	0.04 (0.04)	0.08 (0.04)*	0.02 (0.04)
Economic ancestors	−0.01 (0.06)	−0.01 (0.04)	0.02 (0.04)	0.08 (0.04)*
Charitable help	−0.02 (0.06)	−0.04 (0.04)	−0.03 (0.04)	−0.05 (0.03)
Religious help	−0.03 (0.06)	−0.01 (0.03)	−0.03 (0.03)	0.03 (0.03)
R^2	0.34	0.27	0.22	0.27
Adj. R^2	0.30	0.25	0.20	0.25
N	327	825	767	843
RMSE	0.34	0.30	0.32	0.27
SD of DV	0.37	0.37	0.39	0.34

Notes: Entries are OLS regression coefficients with standard errors in parentheses. All predicting variables are scaled from 0 to 1.

*$p < 0.05$; +$p < 0.1$.

TABLE C.10 **Predicting frequency of high-cost participation index, self-reported**

	Asian	Black	Latino	White
(Intercept)	−0.34 (0.22)	−0.11 (0.12)	−0.44 (0.11)*	−0.16 (0.12)
Political ancestors	0.63 (0.16)*	0.17 (0.11)	0.27 (0.12)*	0.28 (0.11)*
Political help	0.61 (0.17)*	0.67 (0.13)*	0.43 (0.13)*	1.08 (0.13)*
Recruitment	0.09 (0.09)	0.15 (0.07)*	0.09 (0.06)	0.12 (0.08)
Interest politics	0.57 (0.14)*	0.81 (0.09)*	0.94 (0.10)*	0.71 (0.10)*
Linked fate	0.12 (0.16)	−0.09 (0.10)	0.07 (0.09)	−0.11 (0.10)
External efficacy	0.10 (0.17)	−0.06 (0.10)	0.14 (0.10)	−0.17 (0.09)+
Internal efficacy	0.22 (0.15)	0.08 (0.10)	0.15 (0.09)	0.35 (0.10)*
Income	0.15 (0.11)	0.03 (0.08)	0.04 (0.08)	−0.04 (0.08)
Education	−0.22 (0.10)*	0.04 (0.06)	0.14 (0.07)*	−0.02 (0.07)
1st generation	0.05 (0.09)	−0.08 (0.14)	−0.17 (0.07)*	−0.26 (0.21)
2nd generation	0.15 (0.14)	−0.05 (0.10)	0.08 (0.07)	0.24 (0.11)*
Age	−0.04 (0.16)	−0.19 (0.11)+	0.06 (0.11)	−0.06 (0.11)
Male	−0.01 (0.08)	−0.02 (0.06)	−0.02 (0.06)	−0.11 (0.06)+
Cultural ancestors	−0.04 (0.11)	−0.17 (0.10)	−0.24 (0.09)*	−0.07 (0.11)
Economic ancestors	−0.49 (0.15)*	−0.10 (0.10)	0.11 (0.10)	0.06 (0.10)
Charitable help	0.12 (0.14)	−0.01 (0.10)	0.15 (0.09)	−0.06 (0.09)
Religious help	0.08 (0.12)	0.11 (0.08)	0.01 (0.08)	−0.05 (0.08)
R^2	0.34	0.24	0.30	0.33
Adj. R^2	0.30	0.23	0.29	0.31
N	351	862	833	883
RMSE	0.79	0.74	0.76	0.79
SD of DV	0.79	0.81	0.88	0.94

Notes: Entries are OLS regression coefficients with standard errors in parentheses. All predicting variables are scaled from 0 to 1.

*$p < 0.05$; +$p < 0.1$.

Notes

Chapter One

1. In contrast to US Census data (Wheaton, 2013), McDonald (2018) contends that this shift actually happened in 2008. He argues that coding of "no" responses in the Census Voter and Registration Report artificially increases the size of the denominator, altering turnout figures. But whether it first happened in 2008 or 2012, the point remains the same: a higher percentage of eligible Black Americans turned out than Whites.

2. Many others have made this claim, showing not just that resources do not explain cross-group differences (e.g., Danigelis, 1978; Fraga, 2018; Junn, 2015; Lien et al., 2001; Tam Cho, 1999) but also that income and education are weaker predictors of participation for all groups than originally thought (Ansolabehere and Hersh, 2013; Bernstein, Chadha, and Montjoy, 2001; Kam and Palmer, 2008; Silver, Anderson and Abramson, 1986).

3. The November Supplement of the Current Population Survey (CPS) is one of the rare data sets that includes both over-time data on turnout and large numbers of White, Black, Latino, and Asian American respondents. The CPS is administered jointly by the US Census Bureau and the US Bureau of Labor Statistics to approximately 60,000 households, resulting in roughly 110,000 to 135,000 respondents each cycle. The CPS's primary goal is to collect data on labor force statistics but in addition, the survey includes a biennial supplement on voting and voter registration. Furthermore, the bureaus occasionally field questions about civic and political engagement. While the CPS is not a validated voter supplement, its estimates more closely approximate confirmed turnout—perhaps because the official governmental nature of the study makes respondents less willing to inflate their answers.

4. Full regression results are available in appendix C, table C.1.

5. Throughout this book, I use pseudonyms for my interviewees and change details about their occupations slightly to protect their privacy.

6. Recent work on race has begun to take note that White people have a racial identity as well, one that increasingly seems to influence their orientation to politics separate and in addition to out-group prejudice (Jardina, 2019; Sides, Tesler and Vavreck, 2018; Weller and Junn, 2018), and a small literature examines racial animus among nonmajority racial group members (e.g., Gay, 2004; Kaufmann, 2003; Lopez and Pantoja, 2004).

7. It is of some irony that my own racial identity does not fit neatly into these four racial categories. According to census definitions, I am both White and Hispanic, but my dominant cultural and institutional experience is one of Whiteness—I think—and others seem to race me as White most of the time. This ambiguity in what exactly I am and the dissonance that comes when asked, "What is your race?" affects my interests, my experiences, my friendships, my psychology, my life. But all this complication is lost in my choice to simplify the data and define four separate racial categories, under which I would appear in the Hispanic/Latino set. This is in part a reflection of the constraints in my data collection: GfK, the survey platform I used, asks respondents about their race before I fielded the Participatory Social Norms Survey. But it is also a by-product of social science and statistics more generally: simplifications are made in the name of generalizability. However, if this is a topic that interests you, I suggest looking to any of the excellent treatises on mixed-race individuals, the crossing of ethnicity with race, and the creation of Latino/Hispanic as a category, including Davenport (2018), Smith (2014a), Waters (2009), Mora (2014), and Beltrán (2010). (I also write this note knowing that while its content will likely remain in perpetuity, my own racial identity is subject to change over time. Change is endemic in racial categorization precisely because it is a human construct—created by humans, contested by humans—but this is even more true for those currently "in-between" on the racial schema of the moment.)

8. This racial descriptive representation is important, as it allows representatives to better anticipate the needs of their constituents as new situations arise (Mansbridge, 1999) and empirically leads to more responsiveness from representatives (Broockman, 2013; Butler and Broockman, 2011).

9. In the words of Dr. Martin Luther King Jr. in his "Letter from Birmingham Jail," "Freedom is never voluntarily given by the oppressor; it must be demanded by the oppressed" (King, 1992).

10. A postsurvey weight was constructed and is applied for each racial group throughout to ensure the sample is roughly representative of the US population. The wording for questions analyzed appears in appendix A; the complete instrument, as well as the Spanish-language version, is in the online appendix (see appendix A for the URL). A total of 601 of the Asian respondents were drawn from an opt-in panel to supplement GfK's pool. For these respondents, the study was longer in length because I had to collect demographic data that were already on file for the other respondents.

11. Rarely are representative survey samples generated for the four largest racial groups in the United States on a single platform with respect to any
topic. Even the American National Election Studies, the most commonly used
data source among political scientists, rarely incorporates oversamples of Black
Americans and Latinos and has never produced a meaningful sample of Asian
Americans. One modern exception to this dearth of data is the Collaborative
Multiracial Post-Election Survey, a relatively new initiative that seeks to address
exactly this problem.

Chapter Two

1. Building off Downs (1957), Riker and Ordeshook (1968) formalize this
logic of voting with a simple equation: $R = (BP) - C$. Because costs of involvement (C) are ever-present and the likelihood that a citizen's vote decides the
electoral outcome (P) is quite small, the differential benefit for the individual
should their preferred candidate win (B) is overwhelmed. The result is predicted
nonparticipation; the utility for not voting outweighs the utility of voting ($-R$).
See Blais (2000) for a fuller treatise of this equation.

2. When visiting scholars gathered in Nashville to discuss a draft of my book,
I was told that my manuscript reeked of a "happy-all-the-time" mindset. Many
changes throughout now highlight, for instance, the ineffectiveness of participation and the pitfalls of evoking the past. Yet I remain ever inspired by people like
John Lewis and Alice Paul who tirelessly wielded political action to craft a better world.

3. For a critique of this theoretical lens, see Green and Shapiro (1996).

Chapter Three

1. My interviews lasted on average one hour, but completing each also involved significant coordination, preparation, and travel time, not to mention the
handful of cancellations and no-shows I experienced.

2. Appendix B provides a discussion of my interview collection process; a table available in the online appendix (see URL in appendix A) shows further demographic information about each respondent.

3. Appendix B provides a list of sample questions I used in my interviews; the
online appendix provides a complete list of questions included in the various iterations of my protocol.

4. While it is difficult to assess the exact number of Black Americans today
who had enslaved ancestors in the United States, an examination of immigration trends suggests the estimate would be a majority. Until the 2000s, it was esti-

mated that only 3% of the Black population was foreign born (Gambino, Trevelyan, and Fitzwater, 2014). Today, the number has grown to 9%. Furthermore, an estimated 7 million, or nearly one in five, Black citizens alive in 2014 were born before the passages of the 1964 Civil Rights Act, according to estimates based on data from the US Census Annual Estimates of the Resident Population by Sex, Age, Race, and Hispanic Origin for the United States: April 1, 2010, to July 1, 2014.

5. This reference to a civil rights leader is brief and appears in a nonpolitical context. But it serves to highlight how a legacy of the civil rights struggle is embedded in even the most basic decisions and descriptions by Black respondents. The owner of this statement, Royce, consciously wears a pair of glasses that make him look and feel like Malcolm X. These glasses are an enduring symbol of the antiestablishment civil rights leader, a symbol that scholar Carol Tulloch describes as the iconography of Malcolm X. She explains, "A solitary pair of horn-rimmed glasses initiates a ricochet of image references, teachings, and beliefs that *is* Malcolm X" (Tulloch, 2000, 306). Even Malcolm X recognized the importance of his glasses for his life and identity. In his autobiography, he describes his first purchases after being released from prison in 1952: "I remember well. I bought a better-looking pair of eyeglasses than the pair the prison had issued me; and I bought a suitcase and a wristwatch. I have thought since, that without fully knowing it, I was preparing for what my life was about to become. Because those are three things I've used more than anything else" (X and Haley, 1968, 289). This is a statement Royce is familiar with—he read it in Malcolm X's autobiography.

6. All names of interviewees are pseudonyms, and the details of occupations have been changed slightly to protect the identity of the respondents.

7. Immigrants from these four countries of origin, along with Vietnam and Korea, comprise 83% of the Asian American population in the United States today (*The Rise of Asian Americans*, 2012).

8. The connection between cultural activities and honoring the past was quite rare among Black Americans I talked with, but Dawson (2003) suggests that there have been times in the nation's history when this connection, especially to African heritage, was much more common.

9. In the face of these continued challenges and barriers, scholars remain conflicted about the extent to which Black America has moved toward financial parity with Whites (e.g., Dawson, 1994; Hochschild, Weaver, and Burch, 2012; Pettit, 2012; Wilson, 2011, 2012).

10. Martin and Royce were also the two most ideologically conservative Black respondents I talked with, both admitting to not having voted for Barack Obama in at least one presidential bid. This suggests that ideology, in addition to race, may shape the expression of the helping hands norm.

11. There does, however, exist wide variation in income and education by

country of origin, and a broader share of Asian Americans than non-Hispanic Whites live below the poverty line (*Immigrants in the United States*, 2018; Wong et al., 2011).

Chapter Four

1. I once had a conversation about ancestry with two friends. The first, a first-generation immigrant from Russia, explained that his Jewish ancestors had been chased across the globe for generations. The second, a multigenerational Black American, stated simply, "I wish I knew anything about my people's history before they were enslaved."

2. Estimates suggest that an additional 10.7 million Latinos are living in the Unites States undocumented (Passel and Cohn, 2018). These individuals do not appear in my survey data, which are constrained to citizens, and are largely excluded from my theorizing. This is not because understanding the potential political participation of these individuals is unimportant but because the avenues of participation and potential mechanisms of representation are significantly different for these individuals than for citizens.

3. An alternative statistical test—a confirmatory factor analysis—also demonstrates that these four items are unidimensional; they load together effectively and do so equally well for each of the four groups. The online appendix shows these results (see appendix A for the URL).

4. Using a bootstrap method to calculate skew (mean minus median), I find that the sample has a negative and statistically significant skew ($p < 0.05$).

5. For the distribution of each individual item in the ancestors scale, see appendix C, figure C.1.

6. The Pearson's correlation coefficient for selecting "none" and the honoring ancestors index is −0.22.

7. There are some differences between specific behaviors, though, as is evidenced in appendix C, figure C.2. Specifically, while all three non-White groups are statistically indistinguishable in the belief that supporting their families is a way to honor ancestors, minority Americans are more likely than Whites to tether "pursue career opportunities" and "pursue education opportunities" to the honoring ancestors norm.

8. Similar breakdowns for the cultural and economic response options are provided in appendix C, figure C.2.

9. These results are available in the online appendix.

10. Strength of partisanship is measured by combining a set of (up to three) branching questions designed to sort respondents into a spectrum of independents (0), partisan leaners (1), weak partisans (2), and strong partisans (3). Racial linked fate is measured by asking respondents to what degree they agree

with the statement "What happens generally to (White/Black/Asian/Latino or Hispanic) people in this country will affect what happens to me," with the racial category generated in the question matching the respondents' self-identification. Response options range from strongly disagree (0) to strongly agree (4). Political interest is measured by asking respondents how interested they are in politics and public affairs; respondents were provided with four response options ranging from not at all interested (0) to very interested (3). I purchased the political interest variable from the survey company GfK after the study was completed. This is one of its standard profile variables regularly collected for all on-panel respondents. Unfortunately, this meant that I did not collect political interest for the off-GfK panel Asian American respondents. As a result, any analyses that include political interest in this book are confined to the Asian Americans pulled from GfK's preconstructed panel of respondents.

11. As I was editing this chapter, the United States passed one hundred years since the ratification of the Nineteenth Amendment, which extended the franchise to (White) women. Celebrations around this milestone were widespread in Tennessee where I live, as the state was the thirty-sixth to ratify the amendment and thus solidify it as law. Friends, family, and colleagues alike sent me articles about women who imagine voting as a way to honor suffragettes and female trailblazers of the past.

12. The PSNS is not designed to provide representative samples of ethnic subgroups, but for the most prevalent ethnicities, it can provide to some degree a picture of within-group variation. I replicate my analyses for Mexican Americans, Chinese Americans, Indian Americans, and Filipino Americans separately in the online appendix for those who may be interested. These groups collectively make up about/at least half of their respective racial groups.

13. An alternative, empirical explanation is that the noneffect among Latinos and Asian Americans compared to Black and White Americans is a product of variation in the reference category. Census figures suggest that Black and White Americans included in the suppressed category largely consist of individuals whose ancestors have lived in the United States for more than three generations, but for Latinos and Asian Americans, the mode is likely third generation. Further analyses, however, show this is not the case. Changing the reference category from third to fourth generation and including an indicator for third generation (either all grandparents born abroad or at least one grandparent born abroad) shows no changes in the relationship between first- or second-generational status and the strength of the political ancestors index.

14. Material in the online appendix provides further information about these measures, including the distribution of each measure for each racial group and evidence that these measures are not interchangeable. Rather, the three measures are only weakly correlated with each other for each of the four groups.

15. Full regression results, including the relationship for control variables, are available in appendix C, table C.3.

Chapter Five

1. But see Lichter, Shanahan, and Gardner (2002), who suggest that one pro-social behavior in particular—volunteering—may be lower as a result of child-hood exposure to poverty.

2. A discussion and presentation of these analyses is available in the online appendix (see appendix A for the URL). Work on over-time trends has noted, however, that this orientation among Black Americans is declining (Hunt, 2007; Smith, 2014b).

3. The online appendix shows point estimates. Bobo and Kluegel (1997), Kinder and Kam (2010), and Peffley, Hurwitz, and Sniderman (1997) provide just a few examples of how this measure has been used elsewhere.

4. The Hart-Celler Immigration and Nationality Act, which took effect in 1968, opened up immigration from Asia for the first time in nearly a century and produced a wave of Asian immigrants who today comprise the majority of the group's members (Masuoka and Junn, 2013). The policy change built a clear selection bias into its priorities regarding who could gain legal permanent residency in the United States. Rather than quotas based on race and ethnicity as had been the case in the past, the new immigration system prioritized the entrance of highly skilled workers and those seeking family reunification. As a result, the vast majority of Asian migrants arriving in the United States over the past half century have been selected precisely because they are highly skilled and well educated (Junn, 2008; Masuoka and Junn, 2013).

5. Complete wording for the response items is available in appendix A. While the list of options is not designed to capture *all* the ways Americans might help those in need, an examination of the "none" and "other" response categories suggests it does capture most of the ways people act on this norm. Across the whole sample, 11% of respondents selected "none," and only 4% choose "other."

6. Similar breakdowns for the charitable and religious interpretations of the helping hands norm are available in appendix C, figure C.4.

7. Additional tests of within-group variation with respect to gender, age, socioeconomic resources, and generational status are available in the online appendix. These results show relatively little within-group variation with the exception of socioeconomic resources and age for Black Americans, gender for Latinos, and generational status for White Americans. I also break down the relationships for the largest within-race ethnic groups for Latinos and Asian

Americans in the online appendix. These groups collectively make up about/at least half of their respective racial group.

8. Strength of partisanship is measured by combining a set of (up to three) branching questions designed to sort respondents into a spectrum of independents (0), partisan leaners (1), weak partisans (2), and strong partisans (3). Political interest is measured by asking respondents how interested they are in politics and public affairs; respondents are provided with four response options ranging from not at all interested (0) to very interested (3). Because I purchased the political interest variable from the survey company GfK after the study was completed, the off-GfK panel Asian American respondents are excluded from this analysis. Finally, racial linked fate is measured by asking respondents to what degree they agree with the statement "What happens generally to (White/Black/Asian/Latino or Hispanic) people in this country will affect what happens to me," with the racial category generated in the question matching the respondents' self-identification. Response options range from strongly disagree (0) to strongly agree (4).

Chapter Six

1. As you'll recall, much of the empirical work presented in the previous two chapters confirms that these measures are valid, reliable, and statistically distinct from other known predictors of psychological investment in politics. You can return to "The Political Ancestors Index" (chapter 4) and "The Political Helping Index" (chapter 5) for further discussion of how each index is constructed.

2. Complete question wording for each measure is available in appendix A. Education, income, age, gender, and generational status were collected by GfK prior to the fielding of the PSNS for most respondents. For the 601 Asian Americans recruited off panel, these questions were asked at the beginning of the survey. Political interest was also collected prior to the fielding of the PSNS, but because I did not purchase this variable until after the PSNS was fielded (hindsight is twenty-twenty), I do not have it for the Asian Americans recruited off panel. As a result, the sample size for my analyses of this group is significantly reduced when political interest is included.

3. GfK provided within-group survey weights that are applied to each estimate, helping ensure that each racial sample reflects national group averages with respect to gender, age, education, census region, household income, home ownership, and metropolitan location.

4. This result also provides evidence that the indexes as developed are not simply picking up an endogenous relationship between norms and turnout. If it were the case that individuals who participate for some other reason simply

choose participatory behaviors when asked the best way to honor the past and help others, we would expect both norms to predict participation. But this is not the case.

5. One interesting anomaly appears in these analyses with respect to the helping hands norm: a charitable interpretation of the norm positively predicts turnout among Asian Americans. This result is unexpected. One possible explanation is that Asian Americans who connect the helping hands norm to charitable activity are also embedded in organizations that mobilize group members. For instance, Janelle Wong (2008) argues in her book *Democracy's Promise* that civic organizations are increasingly important for integrating immigrants into the American political system.

6. Complete results are available in the online appendix (see appendix A for the URL). Individuals who were not eligible to vote because of their age in 2012 and 2014 are dropped out of the analyses.

7. A careful observer will also notice that predicted turnout decreases for all four groups in the bottom two panels. This is to be expected: the honoring ancestors norm is heavily related to turnout and in this plot, we have effectively neutralized its contribution. In a hypothetical world where honoring ancestors is unconnected to politics for everyone, turnout is lower for all racial groups.

8. Readers can return to chapter 2 for a discussion of norm types and their relationship to groups. Cialdini and Trost (1998) also provide an excellent review.

9. Portions of these results appear in the article "What Makes a Good Neighbor? Race, Place and Norms of Political Participation" published in the *American Political Science Review* (Anoll, 2018). Due to resource constraints, the study was included on three omnibus surveys, fielded by either YouGov/Polimetrix or Latino Decisions. Together, the surveys produced sizable samples of White, Black, and Latino respondents but too few Asian Americans for any meaningful analyses.

10. See appendix C, table C.6, for full information about conditions and randomization.

11. The control is critical here, as it helps account for potential differences in item functioning. By including a nonpolitical control (potluck), I am able to account for any average sociability shifts that exist across groups. Furthermore, by including information about age, name, and occupation, I decrease the ability of respondents to guess the purpose of the study and possibly change their behavior as a result. Including this information also increases external validity by forcing respondents to consider multiple characteristics as they would a real human being. I use a within-subjects design in this study, which, in contrast to the counterfactual model (Holland, 1986; Rubin, 1974), draws from a tradition of crossover studies popular in medical trials (Chow and Liu, 1999) where each respondent views both the treatment and the control. One important assumption must hold true for within-subject crossover designs to properly identify treat-

ment effects: early treatment exposures must not affect the results of later ones. To rule out these potential carryover effects, I examined whether the means of the first appearance of each treatment were significantly different from the aggregate estimates. The results, presented in appendix C, table C.7, establish that there is no significant difference.

12. In contrast to the PSNS, data for this study were collected while I was a graduate student. As a result, resource constraints required that I work with other scholars in an omnibus setting to collect high-quality data for racial minorities, notoriously expensive populations to sample well. Thus, rather than using the ideal situation (a single survey with equal proportions of all three racial groups), I used three separate omnibus studies to construct a data set that eventually yielded a large and representative sample of each group.

13. YouGov/Polimetrix uses a combination of sampling and matching techniques to approximate the demographic composition of the United States.

14. To ensure the representativeness of my analysis, I constructed and applied a weight to the sample using Current Population Survey estimates.

15. Because I am now looking at heterogeneity within rather than across groups, I examine raw likability and respectability scores instead of those adjusted to the experimental potluck baseline.

16. Interestingly, the analyses of Latino respondents show the exact opposite relationship with respect to the proportion of a neighborhood that is foreign born. Moving from a zip code that is composed entirely of US-born citizens to a zip code composed completely of foreign-born residents (either naturalized or noncitizens) is correlated with a 23% increase in the social rewards distributed to voters. This finding warrants further exploration in future scholarship.

17. I have collected in the online appendix additional examples of this message being used in politics.

18. By including other activities in this battery in addition to the primary dependent variables (prioritization of voting), I decrease the likelihood of demand effects. Measurement of a system-challenging activity (protests) is also included as a dependent variable in the study. We'll discuss it in the next chapter.

19. The sample size for each of these subpopulations is available in appendix C, table C.8.

Chapter Seven

1. Camarillo (2007) notes that at the beginning of the twenty-first century, more than half of the one hundred largest cities in the United States were populated primarily by non-White residents.

2. The self-reported nature of these data suggests that these estimates are

likely inflated representations of the true values (Ansolabehere and Hersh, 2012; Christens, Speer, and Peterson, 2016).

3. Both measures were captured prior to the fielding of the PSNS by the survey company GfK, which helps to ensure that the measurement of the independent variables did not influence reports of the dependent variables. There is one exception to this: Asian Americans who were recruited off panel by GfK answered questions about their past political participation at the end of the study.

4. Full regression results are available in appendix C, table C.10. For those who may be curious about specific nonvoting acts, tables in the online appendix replicate analyses for each political act alone (see appendix A for the URL). Generally, the patterns that appear for the index measure hold, but there is some variability in the importance of each variable for each group depending on the specific participatory act under study.

5. Portions of these results also appear in the article "What Makes a Good Neighbor? Race, Place and Norms of Political Participation," published in the *American Political Science Review* (Anoll, 2018). These data were collected in 2014 prior to the fielding of the PSNS. Due to resource constraints, the study was included on three omnibus surveys, fielded by either YouGov/Polimetrix or Latino Decisions. Together, the surveys produced 1,254 White respondents, 1,229 Black respondents, and 748 Latino respondents, but too few Asian American respondents for any meaningful analyses.

6. For an in-depth discussion of the design of this experiment, see chapter 6. Additional information is also in appendix C, table C.6.

7. Although these outcome measures do not capture actual engagement in politics, they do measure *behavioral intention*. Extant meta-analyses suggest that intention is a key mediator in the process of manifesting actual behavioral outcomes, although measurement technique and the time interval between the measurement of intention and action can shape the strength of this relationship (Bagozzi, Baumgartner and Yi, 1989; Kim and Hunter, 1993a, 1993b; Randall and Wolff, 1994). A more complete discussion of the design of this experiment and its assets is available in chapter 6.

References

Aarts, Henk, and Ap Dijksterhuis. 2003. "The Silence of the Library: Environment, Situational Norm, and Social Behavior." *Journal of Personality and Social Psychology* 84(1): 18–28.

Abrajano, Marisa, and R. Michael Alvarez. 2010. *New Faces, New Voices: The Hispanic Electorate in America.* Princeton, NJ: Princeton University Press.

Abramson, Paul R. 1983. *Political Attitudes in America: Formation and Change.* San Francisco: Freeman.

Achen, Christopher H., and Larry M. Bartels. 2017. *Democracy for Realists: Why Elections Do Not Produce Responsive Government.* Princeton, NJ: Princeton University Press.

Ackerly, Brooke, Luis Cabrera, Fonna Forman, Genevieve Fuji Johnson, Chris Tenove, and Antje Wiener. 2018. "Grounded Normative Theory: Political Theorizing with Those Who Struggle." Working Paper.

Adorno, T. W. 1950. *The Authoritarian Personality.* New York: Harper and Row.

Alexander, Michelle. 2012. *The New Jim Crow: Mass Incarceration in the Age of Colorblindness.* New York: New Press.

"America's Foreign Born in the Last 50 Years." 2019. https://www.census.gov/programs-surveys/sis/resources/visualizations/foreign-born.html.

Anderson, Benedict. 2006. *Imagined Communities: Reflections on the Origin and Spread of Nationalism.* New York: Verso.

Anoll, Allison P. 2018. "What Makes a Good Neighbor? Race, Place, and Norms of Political Participation." *American Political Science Review* 112(3): 494–508.

Ansolabehere, Stephen, and Eitan Hersh. 2012. "Validation: What Big Data Reveal about Survey Misreporting and the Real Electorate." *Political Analysis* 20(4): 437–59.

———. 2013. "Gender, Race, Age, and Voting: A Research Note." *Politics and Governance* 1(2): 132–37.

Anzia, Sarah F. 2011. "Election Timing and the Electoral Influence of Interest Groups." *Journal of Politics* 73(2): 412–27.

Arceneaux, Kevin, and David W. Nickerson. 2009. "Who Is Mobilized to Vote? A Re-Analysis of 11 Field Experiments." *American Journal of Political Science* 53(1): 1–16.

Arendt, Hannah. 1963. *Eichmann in Jerusalem: A Report on the Banality of Evil.* New York: Viking.

Asch, Solomon E. 1955. "Opinions and Social Pressure." *Scientific American* 193(5): 31–35.

Avery, James M. 2015. "Does Who Votes Matter? Income Bias in Voter Turnout and Economic Inequality in the American States from 1980 to 2010." *Political Behavior* 37: 955–76.

Avery, James M., and Mark Peffley. 2005. "Voter Registration Requirements, Voter Turnout, and Welfare Eligibility Policy: Class Bias Matters." *State Politics and Policy Quarterly* 5(1): 47–67.

Bagozzi, Richard P., Johann Baumgartner, and Youjae Yi. 1989. "An Investigation into the Role of Intentions as Mediators of the Attitude-Behavior Relationship." *Journal of Economic Psychology* 10(1): 35–62.

Banks, Antoine J., and Heather M. Hicks. 2018. "The Effectiveness of a Racialized Counterstrategy." *American Journal of Political Science* 31(3): 157.

Barreto, Matt A., Sylvia Manzano, Ricardo Ramírez, and Kathy Rim. 2009. "Mobilization, Participation, and Solidaridad: Latino Participation in the 2006 Immigration Protest Rallies." *Urban Affairs Review* 44(5): 736–64.

Barreto, Matt A., and José A. Muñoz. 2003. "Reexamining the 'Politics of In-Between': Political Participation among Mexican Immigrants in the United States." *Hispanic Journal of Behavioral Sciences* 25(4): 427–47.

Barreto, Matt A., and Gary Segura. 2009. "Estimating the Effects of Traditional Predictors, Group Specific Forces, and Anti-Black Affect on 2008 Presidential Vote among Latinos and Non-Hispanic Whites." In *Papers Presented at the Mershon Conference on the Transformative Election of 2008.* Columbus, OH.

Bartels, Larry M. 2016. *Unequal Democracy: The Political Economy of the New Gilded Age.* Princeton, NJ: Princeton University Press.

Batson, C. Daniel. 1998. "Altruism and Prosocial Behavior." In *The Handbook of Social Psychology,* edited by Susan T Fiske, Daniel T Gilbert, and Lindzey Gardner, 282–316. Boston: McGraw-Hill.

Batson, C. Daniel, and Jay S. Coke. 1981. "Empathy: A Source of Altruistic Motivation for Helping." In *Altruism and Helping Behavior: Social, Personality, and Developmental Perspectives,* edited by J. Philippe Rushton and Richard M. Sorrentino, 167–87. Hillsdale, NJ: Erlbaum Associates.

Baum, W. M., P. J. Richerson, C. M. Efferson, and B. M. Paciotti. 2004. "Cul-

tural Evolution in Laboratory Microsocieties Including Traditions of Rule
Giving and Rule Following." *Evolution and Human Behavior* 25(5): 305–26.

Beltrán, Cristina. 2010. *The Trouble with Unity: Latino Politics and the Creation
of Identity.* Oxford: Oxford University Press.

Benenson, Jodi, and Allison Stagg. 2015. "An Asset-Based Approach to Volunteering." *Nonprofit and Voluntary Sector Quarterly* 45(1S): 131S–149S.

Bentele, Keith G., and Erin E. O'Brien. 2013. "Jim Crow 2.0? Why States Consider and Adopt Restrictive Voter Access Policies." *Perspectives on Politics*
11(4): 1088–1116.

Bernstein, Robert, Anita Chadha, and Robert Montjoy. 2001. "Overreporting
Voting: Why It Happens and Why It Matters." *Public Opinion Quarterly*
65(1): 22–44.

Betancourt, Hector. 1990. "An Attribution-Empathy Model of Helping Behavior: Behavioral Intentions and Judgements of Help-Giving." *Personality and
Social Psychology Bulletin* 16(3): 573–91.

Bhattacharya, Piyali. 2016. *Good Girls Marry Doctors: South Asian American
Daughters on Obedience and Rebellion.* San Francisco: Aunt Lute Books.

Bicchieri, Cristina. 2016. *Norms in the Wild: How to Diagnose, Measure, and
Change Social Norms.* Oxford: Oxford University Press.

Blais, André. 2000. *To Vote or Not to Vote? The Merits and Limits of Rational
Choice Theory.* Pittsburgh: University of Pittsburgh Press.

Blais, André, and Christopher H. Achen. 2019. "Civic Duty and Voter Turnout."
Political Behavior 41: 473–97.

Bobo, Lawrence, and Franklin D. Gilliam Jr. 1990. "Race, Sociopolitical Participation, and Black Empowerment." *American Political Science Review* 84(2):
377–93.

Bobo, Lawrence, and James R. Kluegel. 1993. "Opposition to Race-Targeting:
Self-Interest, Stratification Ideology, or Racial Attitudes?" *American Sociological Review* 58(4): 443–64.

———. 1997. "Status, Ideology, and Dimensions of Whites' Racial Beliefs and Attitudes: Progress and Stagnation." In *Racial Attitudes in the 1990s: Continu-
ity and Change,* edited by Steven A. Tuch and Jack K. Martin, 93–120. West-
port, CT: Praeger.

Bond, Robert M., Christopher J. Fariss, Jason J. Jones, Adam D. I. Kramer,
Cameron Marlow, Jaime E. Settle, and James H. Fowler. 2012. "A
61-Million-Person Experiment in Social Influence and Political Mobilization." *Nature* 489(7415): 295–98.

Bonilla-Silva, Eduardo. 2017. *Racism without Racists: Color-Blind Racism and
the Persistence of Racial Inequality in America.* Lanham, MD: Rowman and
Littlefield.

Bowler, Shaun, and Gary Segura. 2011. *The Future Is Ours: Minority Politics,*

Political Behavior, and the Multiracial Era of American Politics. Los Angeles: Sage.

Bradley, Gifford W. 1978. "Self-Serving Biases in the Attribution Process: A Re-examination of the Fact or Fiction Question." *Journal of Personality and Social Psychology* 36(1): 56.

Branton, Regina, Valerie Martinez-Ebers, Tony E. Carey Jr, and Tetsuya Matsubayahi. 2015. "Social Protest and Policy Attitudes: The Case of the 2006 Immigrant Rallies." *American Journal of Political Science* 59(2): 390–402.

Brickman, Philip, Vita Carulli Rabinowitz, Jurgis Karuza Jr., Dan Coates, Ellen Cohn, and Louise Kidder. 1982. "Models of Helping and Coping." *American Psychologist* 37(4): 368–84.

Broockman, David E. 2013. "Black Politicians Are More Intrinsically Motivated to Advance Blacks' Interests: A Field Experiment Manipulating Political Incentives." *American Journal of Political Science* 57(3): 521–36.

Burch, Traci. 2013. *Trading Democracy for Justice: Criminal Convictions and the Decline of Neighborhood Political Participation.* Chicago: University of Chicago Press.

Burns, Nancy, Kay Lehman Schlozman, and Sidney Verba. 2001. *The Private Roots of Public Action: Gender, Equality, and Political Participation.* Cambridge, MA: Harvard University Press.

Buss, David M., and Douglas T. Kenrick. 1998. "Evolutionary Social Psychology." In *The Handbook of Social Psychology,* edited by Daniel T. Gilbert, Susan T. Fiske, and Lindzey Gardner, 982–1026. New York: McGraw-Hill.

Butler, Daniel M., and David E. Broockman. 2011. "Do Politicians Racially Discriminate against Constituents? A Field Experiment on State Legislators." *American Journal of Political Science* 55(3): 463–77.

Byron, Kristin, and David C. Baldridge. 2007. "E-Mail Recipients' Impressions of Senders' Likability: The Interactive Effect of Nonverbal Cues and Recipients' Personality." *Journal of Business Communication* 44(2): 137–60.

Cahill, Amanda. 2008. "Power Over, Power To, Power With: Shifting Perceptions of Power for Local Economic Development in the Philippines." *Asia Pacific Viewpoint* 49(3): 294–304.

Camarillo, Albert M. 1990. *Chicanos in California: A History of Mexican Americans in California.* San Francisco: Boyd and Fraser.

———. 2007. "Cities of Color: The New Racial Frontier in California's Minority-Majority Cities." *Pacific Historical Review* 76(1): 1–28.

Campbell, Angus, Gerald Gurin, and Warren E. Miller. 1954. *The Voter Decides.* Evanston, IL: Row, Peterson.

Campbell, Donald T., and Donald W. Fiske. 1959. "Convergent and Discriminant Validation by the Multitrait-Multimethod Matrix." *Psychological Bulletin* 56(2): 81.

Carter, Niambi. 2019. *American while Black: African Americans, Immigration, and the Limits of Citizenship.* New York: Oxford University Press.

Chandra, Kanchan. 2006. "What Is Ethnic Identity and Does It Matter?" *Annual Review of Political Science* 9: 397–424.

Charmaz, Kathy. 2014. *Constructing Grounded Theory.* 2nd ed. Thousand Oaks, CA: Sage.

Chenoweth, Erica, and Jeremy Pressman. 2017. "This Is What We Learned by Counting the Women's Marches." *Washington Post*, Feb. 7, 2017. https://www.washingtonpost.com/news/monkey-cage/wp/2017/02/07/this-is-what-we-learned-by-counting-the-womens-marches/?utm_term=.259bf0832baa.

Chong, Dennis. 1991. *Collective Action and the Civil Rights Movement.* Chicago: University of Chicago Press.

———. 1994. "Tolerance and Social Adjustment to New Norms and Practices." *Political Behavior* 16(1): 21–53.

Chow, Shein-Chung, and Jen-Pei Liu. 1999. *Design and Analysis of Bioavailability and Bioequivalence Studies.* 2nd ed. New York: Marcel Dekker.

Christens, Brian D., Paul W. Speer, and N. Andrew Peterson. 2016. "Assessing Community Participation: Comparing Self-Reported Participation Data with Organizational Attendance Records." *American Journal of Community Psychology* 57(3–4): 415–25.

Cialdini, Robert B., Raymond R. Reno, and Carl A. Kallgren. 1990. "A Focus Theory of Normative Conduct: Recycling the Concept of Norms to Reduce Littering in Public Places." *Journal of Personality and Social Psychology* 58(6): 1015–26.

Cialdini, Robert B., and Melanie R. Trost. 1998. "Social Influence: Social Norms, Conformity, and Compliance." In *Handbook of Social Psychology*, edited by Daniel T. Gilbert, Susan T. Fiske, and Gardner Lindzey, 151–92. New York: McGraw-Hill.

Coates, Ta-Nehisi. 2017. "The First White President." *Atlantic*, October.

Coleman, James S. 1986. "Social Theory, Social Research, and a Theory of Action." *American Journal of Sociology* 91(6): 1309–35.

Conover, Pamela Johnston. 1988. "The Role of Social Groups in Political Thinking." *British Journal of Political Science* 18(1): 51–76.

Converse, Philip. 1964. "The Nature of Belief Systems in Mass Publics." *Critical Review* 18(1): 1–74.

Conway, M. Margaret. 2000. *Political Participation in the United States.* 3rd ed. Washington, DC: CQ Press.

Cost of 2018 Election to Surpass $5 Billion, CPR Projects. 2018. OpenSecrets.org, Center for Responsive Politics. http://www.opensecrets.org/news/2018/10/cost-of-2018-election.

Cramer, Katherine J. 2016. *The Politics of Resentment: Rural Consciousness in Wisconsin and the Rise of Scott Walker*. Chicago: University of Chicago Press.

Crandall, Christian C. 1988. "Social Contagion of Binge Eating." *Journal of Personality and Social Psychology* 55(4): 588–98.

Crenshaw, Kimberle. 1989. "Demarginalizing the Intersection of Race and Sex: A Black Feminist Critique of Antidiscrimination Doctrine, Feminist Theory and Antiracist Politics." *University of Chicago Legal Forum* (1): 139–67.

Cumming, Geoff, and Sue Finch. 2005. "Inference by Eye: Confidence Intervals and How to Read Pictures of Data." *American Psychologist* 60(2): 170–80.

Dahl, Robert A. 2005. *Who Governs? Democracy and Power in an American City*. New Haven, CT: Yale University Press.

Danigelis, Nicholas L. 1978. "Black Political Participation in the United States: Some Recent Evidence." *American Sociological Review* 43(5): 756–71.

Darley, John M., and C. Daniel Batson. 1973. "'From Jerusalem to Jericho': A Study of Situational and Dispositional Variables in Helping Behavior." *Journal of Personality and Social Psychology* 27(1): 100–108.

Davenport, Lauren D. 2018. *Politics beyond Black and White: Biracial Identity and Attitudes in America*. New York: Cambridge University Press.

———. 2020. "The Fluidity of Racial Classifications." *Annual Review of Political Science* 23(1): 221–40.

Dawkins, Richard. 1976. *The Selfish Gene*. New York: Oxford University Press.

Dawson, Michael C. 1994. *Behind the Mule: Race and Class in African-American Politics*. Princeton, NJ: Princeton University Press.

———. 2003. *Black Visions: The Roots of Contemporary African-American Political Ideologies*. Chicago: University of Chicago Press.

DeFilippis, James, Robert Fisher, and Eric Shragge. 2010. *Contesting Community: The Limits and Potential of Local Organizing*. New Brunswick, NJ: Rutgers University Press.

Delli Carpini, Michael X., and Scott Keeter. 1996. *What Americans Know about Politics and Why It Matters*. New Haven, CT: Yale University Press.

Delli Carpini, Michael X., Fay Lomax Cook, and Lawrence R. Jacobs. 2004. "Public Deliberations, Discursive Participation and Citizen Engagement: A Review of the Empirical Literature." *Annual Review of Political Science* 7: 315–44.

DeNavas-Walt, Carmen, and Bernadette Proctor. 2015. *Income and Poverty in the United States: 2014*. Current Population Reports P60-252. Washington, DC: US Census Bureau/US Government Printing Office.

Denny, Kevin, and Orla Doyle. 2009. "Does Voting History Matter? Analyzing Persistence in Turnout." *American Journal of Political Science* 53(1): 17–35.

DeSante, Christopher D., and Brittany N. Perry. 2016. "Bridging the Gap: How Geographic Context Affects Political Knowledge among Citizen and Non-Citizen Latinos." *American Politics Research* 3(44): 548–77.

de Tocqueville, Alexis. 2000. *Democracy in America*. Chicago: University of Chicago Press.

Devos, Thierry, and Mahzarin R. Banaji. 2005. "American = White?" *Journal of Personality and Social Psychology* 88(3): 447.

Diekman, Amanda B., and Emily K. Clark. 2015. "Beyond the Damsel in Distress: Gender Differences and Similarities in Enacting Prosocial Behavior." In *The Oxford Handbook of Prosocial Behavior*, edited by David A. Schroeder and William G. Graziano, 376–91. Oxford: Oxford University Press.

Dougherty, Kevin D. 2003. "How Monochromatic Is Church Membership? Racial-Ethnic Diversity in Religious Community." *Sociology of Religion* 64(1): 65–85.

Dovidio, John F. 1984. "Helping Behavior and Altruism: An Empirical and Conceptual Overview." In *Advances in Experimental Social Psychology*, vol. 17, edited by Leonard Berkowitz, 361–427. New York: Academic.

Downs, Anthony. 1957. *An Economic Theory of Democracy*. Boston: Addison Wesley.

Druckman, Jamie, and Dennis Chong. 2009. "Dynamics in Mass Communication Effects Research." In *The Sage Handbook of Political Communication*, edited by Holli Semetko and Maggie Scammell, 1–53. Thousand Oaks, CA: Sage.

Durkheim, Émile. 2014. *The Division of Labor in Society*. New York: Simon and Schuster.

Earl, Jennifer, Thomas V. Maher, and Thomas Elliott. 2017. "Youth, Activism, and Social Movements." *Sociology Compass* 11(4): 1–14.

Ellemers, Naomi, Russell Spears, and Bertjan Doosje. 2002. "Self and Social Identity." *Annual Review of Psychology* 53(1): 161–86.

Ellis, Christopher R., Joseph Daniel Ura, and Jenna Ashley-Robinson. 2006. "The Dynamic Consequences of Nonvoting in American National Elections." *Political Research Quarterly* 59(2): 227–233.

Elster, Jon. 1989. "Social Norms and Economic Theory." *Journal of Economic Perspectives* 3(4): 99–117.

Enos, Ryan D. 2017. *The Space between Us: Social Geography and Politics*. New York: Cambridge University Press.

Enos, Ryan D., Anthony Fowler, and Lynn Vavreck. 2014. "Increasing Inequality: The Effect of GOTV Mobilization on the Composition of the Electorate." *Journal of Politics* 76(1): 273–88.

Enos, Ryan D., Aaron Kaufman, and Melissa Sands. 2017. "Can Violent Protest Change Local Policy Support? Evidence from the Aftermath of the 1992 Los Angeles Riot." Presented at the Urban Political Economy Conference, Vanderbilt University.

Erie, Steven P. 1990. *Rainbow's End: Irish-Americans and the Dilemmas of Urban Machine Politics, 1840–1985*. Vol. 15. Berkeley: University of California Press.

Fellowes, Matthew C., and Gretchen Rowe. 2004. "Politics and the New American Welfare States." *American Journal of Political Science* 48(2): 362–73.

Festinger, Leon. 1954. "A Theory of Social Comparison Processes." *Human Relations* 7(2): 117–40.

———. 1957. *A Theory of Cognitive Dissonance*. Stanford, CA: Stanford University Press.

File, Thom. 2013. "The Diversifying Electorate—Voting Rates by Race and Hispanic Origin in 2012 (and Other Recent Elections)." US Census Bureau.

File, Thom, and Sarah Crissey. 2012. "Voting and Registration in the Election of November 2008." US Census Bureau.

Finkel, Steven E. 1985. "Reciprocal Effects of Participation and Political Efficacy: A Panel Analysis." *American Journal of Political Science* 29(4): 891–913.

———. 1987. "The Effects of Participation on Political Efficacy and Political Support: Evidence from a West German Panel." *Journal of Politics* 49(2): 441–64.

FitzGerald, David S., and David Cook-Martin. 2015. "The Geopolitical Origins of the U.S. Immigration Act of 1965." Migration Policy Institute. https://www.migrationpolicy.org/article/geopolitical-origins-us-immigration-act-1965.

Flood, Sarah, Miriam King, Renae Rodgers, Steven Ruggles, and J. Robert Warren. 2018. Integrated Public Use Microdata Series, Current Population Survey: Version 6.0 [data set]. Technical report, IPUMS. Minneapolis: IPUMS. https://doi.org/10.18128/D030.V6.0.

Flores, Richard R. 2000. "The Alamo: Myth, Public History, and the Politics of Inclusion." *Radical History Review* 77: 91–103.

Fontenot, Kayla, Jessica Semega, and Melissa Kollar. 2018. "Income and Poverty in the United States: 2017." US Census Bureau.

Foucault, Michel. 2012. *Discipline and Punish: The Birth of the Prison*. New York: Vintage.

Fowler, James H. 2006. "Habitual Voting and Behavioral Turnout." *Journal of Politics* 68(2): 335–44.

Fowler, James H., and Cindy D. Kam. 2007. "Beyond the Self: Social Identity, Altruism, and Political Participation." *Journal of Politics* 69(3): 813–27.

Fraga, Bernard L. 2018. *The Turnout Gap: Race, Ethnicity, and Political Inequality in a Diversifying America*. Cambridge: Cambridge University Press.

Franko, William W. 2013. "Political Inequality and State Policy Adoption: Predatory Lending, Children's Health Care, and Minimum Wage." *Poverty and Public Policy* 5(1): 88–114.

Gambino, Christine P., Edward N. Trevelyan, and John Thomas Fitzwater. 2014. "The Foreign-Born Population from Africa: 2008–2012." US Census Bureau.

Gans, Herbert J. 1979. "Symbolic Ethnicity: The Future of Ethnic Groups and Cultures in America." *Ethnic and Racial Studies* 2(1): 1–20.

——. 2012. "'Whitening' and the Changing American Racial Hierarchy." *Du Bois Review* 9(2): 267–79.

García Bedolla, Lisa. 2015. *Latino Politics.* New York: John Wiley and Sons.

——. 2019. "Epistemological Bias in the Study of Political Behavior in the United States." Technical report.

García Bedolla, Lisa, and Melissa R. Michelson. 2012. *Mobilizing Inclusion: Transforming the Electorate through Get-Out-the-Vote Campaigns.* New Haven, CT: Yale University Press.

Gaventa, John. 1982. *Power and Powerlessness: Quiescence and Rebellion in an Appalachian Valley.* Urbana: University of Illinois Press.

Gay, Claudine. 2004. "Putting Race in Context: Identifying the Environmental Determinants of Black Racial Attitudes." *American Political Science Review* 98(4): 547–62.

Gerber, Alan S., Donald P. Green, and Christopher W. Larimer. 2008. "Social Pressure and Voter Turnout: Evidence from a Large-Scale Field Experiment." *American Political Science Review* 102(1): 33–48.

Gerber, Alan S., Donald P. Green, and Ron Shachar. 2003. "Voting May Be Habit-Forming: Evidence from a Randomized Field Experiment." *American Journal of Political Science* 47(3): 540–50.

Gerber, Alan S., Gregory A. Huber, David Doherty, and Conor M. Dowling. 2016. "Why People Vote: Estimating the Social Returns to Voting." *British Journal of Political Science* 46(2): 241–64.

Gerber, Alan S., and Todd Rogers. 2009. "Descriptive Social Norms and Motivation to Vote: Everybody's Voting and So Should You." *Journal of Politics* 71(1): 178–91.

GfK. 2014. "Protecting Respondent Confidentiality by Perturbation of Location Identifiers." Sampling statistics document.

Gilens, Martin. 2005. "Inequality and Democratic Responsiveness." *Public Opinion Quarterly* 69(5): 778–96.

——. 2009. *Why Americans Hate Welfare: Race, Media, and the Politics of Antipoverty Policy.* Chicago: University of Chicago Press.

Gilligan, Carol. 1993. *In a Different Voice: Psychological Theory and Women's Development.* Cambridge, MA: Harvard University Press.

Gillion, Daniel Q. 2013. *The Political Power of Protest: Minority Activism and Shifts in Public Policy.* New York: Cambridge University Press.

Glaser, Barney G., and Anselm L. Strauss. 1967. *The Discovery of Grounded Theory: Strategies for Qualitative Research.* New York: Transaction.

Goldstein, Noah J., Robert B. Cialdini, and Vladas Griskevicius. 2008. "A Room with a Viewpoint: Using Social Norms to Motivate Environmental Conservation in Hotels." *Journal of Consumer Research* 35(3): 472–82.

Gomez, Brad T., Thomas G. Hansford, and George A. Krause. 2007. "The

Republicans Should Pray for Rain: Weather, Turnout, and Voting in U.S. Presidential Elections." *Journal of Politics* 69(3): 649–63.

Gonzalez-Barrera, Ana, and Mark Hugo Lopez. 2015. "Is Being Hispanic a Matter of Race, Ethnicity or Both?" Pew Research Center. http://www .pewresearch.org/fact-tank/2015/06/15/is-being-hispanic-a-matter-of-race -ethnicity-or-both/.

Graham, Jesse, Jonathan Haidt, Sena Koleva, Matt Motyl, Ravi Iyer, Sean P. Wojcik, and Peter H. Ditto. 2013. "Moral Foundations Theory: The Pragmatic Validity of Moral Pluralism." *Advances in Experimental Social Psychology* 47: 55–130.

Green, Donald P., Alan S. Gerber, and David W. Nickerson. 2003. "Getting Out the Vote in Local Elections: Results from Six Door-to-Door Canvassing Experiments." *Journal of Politics* 65(4): 1083–96.

Green, Donald P., and Ian Shapiro. 1996. *Pathologies of Rational Choice Theory: A Critique of Applications in Political Science.* New Haven, CT: Yale University Press.

Grieco, Elizabeth, Edward Trevelyan, Luke Larsen, Yesenia D. Acosta, Christine Gambino, Patricia de la Cruz, Tom Gryn, and Nathan Walters. 2012. "The Size, Place of Birth, and Geographic Distribution of the Foreign-Born Population in the United States: 1960–2010." Population Division Working Paper 96. Washington, DC: US Census Bureau. https://www.census.gov/ content/dam/Census/library/working-papers/2012/demo/POP-twps0096 .pdf.

Griffin, John D., and Michael Keane. 2006. "Descriptive Representation and the Composition of African American Turnout." *American Journal of Political Science* 50(4): 998–1012.

Griffin, John D., and Brian Newman. 2005. "Are Voters Better Represented?" *Journal of Politics* 67(4): 1206–27.

———. 2007. "The Unequal Representation of Latinos and Whites." *Journal of Politics* 69(4): 1032–46.

Grossmann, Matt. 2012. *The Not-So-Special Interests: Interest Groups, Public Representation, and American Governance.* Stanford, CA: Stanford University Press.

Guest, Greg, Arwen Bunce, and Laura Johnson. 2006. "How Many Interviews Are Enough? An Experiment with Data Saturation and Variability." *Field Methods* 18(1): 59–82.

Haidt, Jonathan. 2012. *The Righteous Mind: Why Good People Are Divided by Politics and Religion.* New York: Vintage.

Hajnal, Zoltan, and Jessica Trounstine. 2005. "Where Turnout Matters: The Consequences of Uneven Turnout in City Politics." *Journal of Politics* 67(2): 515–35.

Hamilton, David L., and Roger D. Fallot. 1974. "Information Salience as a

Weighting Factor in Impression Formation." *Journal of Personality and So-cial Psychology* 30(4): 444–48.

Haney Lopez, Ian. 2006. *White by Law: The Legal Construction of Race.* New York: New York University Press.

Harris, Frederick C., and Daniel Gillion. 2010. "Expanding the Possibilities: Reconceptualizing Political Participation as a Tool Box." In *Oxford Hand-book of American Elections and Political Behavior,* edited by Jan E. Leigh-ley, 144–61. Oxford: Oxford University Press.

Harris, Fredrick C., Valeria Sinclair-Chapman, and Brian D. McKenzie. 2005. "Macrodynamics of Black Political Participation in the Post–Civil Rights Era." *Journal of Politics* 67(4): 1143–63.

Harris-Lacewell, Melissa Victoria. 2010. *Barbershops, Bibles, and BET: Every-day Talk and Black Political Thought.* Princeton, NJ: Princeton University Press.

Haspel, Moshe, and H. Gibbs Knotts. 2005. "Location, Location, Location: Pre-cinct Placement and the Costs of Voting." *Journal of Politics* 67(2): 560–73.

Hauser, Robert M., and John Robert Warren. 1997. "Socioeconomic Indexes for Occupations: A Review, Update, and Critique." *Sociological Methodology* 27(1): 177–298.

Hefner, Philip. 1991. "Myth and Morality: The Love Command." *Zygon* 26(1): 115–36.

Hersh, Eitan D. 2015. *Hacking the Electorate: How Campaigns Perceive Voters.* New York: Cambridge University Press.

Hewstone, Miles. 1990. "The 'Ultimate Attribution Error'? A Review of the Lit-erature on Intergroup Causal Attribution." *European Journal of Social Psy-chology* 20(4): 311–35.

Highton, Benjamin, and Raymond E. Wolfinger. 2001a. "The First Seven Years of the Political Life Cycle." *American Journal of Political Science* 45(1): 202–9.

———. 2001b. "The Political Implications of Higher Turnout." *British Journal of Political Science* 31(1): 179–92.

Hill, Kim Quaile, and Jan E. Leighley. 1992. "The Policy Consequences of Class Bias in State Electorates." *American Journal of Political Science* 36(2): 351–65.

Hirschman, Charles. 2004. "The Origins and Demise of the Concept of Race." *Population and Development Review* 30(3): 385–415.

Hochschild, Jennifer L., and Maya Sen. 2018. "Americans' Attitudes on Individ-ual or Racially Inflected Genetic Inheritance." In *Reconsidering Race: Social Science Perspectives on Racial Categories in the Age of Genomics,* edited by Kazuko Suzuki and Diego A. Von Vacano, 32–49. New York: Oxford Univer-sity Press.

Hochschild, Jennifer L., Vesla M. Weaver, and Traci R. Burch. 2012. *Creating a New Racial Order: How Immigration, Multiracialism, Genomics, and the Young Can Remake Race in America*. Princeton, NJ: Princeton University Press.

Hogan, Wesley C. 2007. *Many Minds, One Heart: SNCC's Dream for a New America*. Chapel Hill: University of North Carolina Press.

Hogg, Michael A. 2003. "Intergroup Relations." In *Handbook of Social Psychology*, edited by John Delameter, 479–501. New York: Springer.

Hogg, Michael A., Deborah J. Terry, and Katherine M. White. 1995. "A Tale of Two Theories: A Critical Comparison of Identity Theory with Social Identity Theory." *Social Psychology Quarterly* 58(4): 255–69.

Holbrook, Allyson L., and Jon A. Krosnick. 2009. "Social Desirability Bias in Voter Turnout Reports: Tests Using the Item Count Technique." *Public Opinion Quarterly* 74(1): 37–67.

Holland, Paul W. 1986. "Statistics and Causal Inference." *Journal of the American Statistical Association* 81(396): 945–60.

Huddy, Leonie. 2013. "From Group Identity to Political Cohesion and Commitment." In *The Oxford Handbook of Political Psychology*, edited by Leonie Huddy, David Sears, and Jack S. Levy, 737–73. New York: Oxford University Press.

Hunt, Matthew O. 2007. "African American, Hispanic, and White Beliefs about Black/White Inequality, 1977–2004." *American Sociological Review* 72(3): 390–415.

Hutchings, Vincent L., and Nicholas A. Valentino. 2004. "The Centrality of Race in American Politics." *Annual Review of Political Science* 7: 383–408.

Iacoboni, Marco. 2009. "Imitation, Empathy, and Mirror Neurons." *Annual Review of Psychology* 60(1): 653–70.

Immigrants in the United States: A Profile of America's Foreign-Born Population. 2018. Center for Immigration Studies.

Iyengar, Shanto, Yphtach Lelkes, Matthew S. Levendusky, Neil Malhotra, and Sean J. Westwood. 2019. "The Origins and Consequences of Affective Polarization in the United States." *Annual Review of Political Science* 22: 7.1–7.18.

Janus, Alexander L. 2010. "The Influence of Social Desirability Pressures on Expressed Immigration Attitudes." *Social Science Quarterly* 91(4): 928–46.

Jardina, Ashley. 2019. *White Identity Politics*. Cambridge: Cambridge University Press.

Jargowsky, Paul A. 1996. "Take the Money and Run: Economic Segregation in US Metropolitan Areas." *American Sociological Review* 61(6): 984–98.

Jiménez, Tomás Roberto. 2010. *Replenished Ethnicity: Mexican Americans, Immigration, and Identity*. Berkeley: University of California Press.

Judis, John B., and Ruy Teixeira. 2004. *The Emerging Democratic Majority*. New York: Simon and Schuster.

Junn, Jane. 2008. "From Coolies to Model Minority: U.S. Immigration Policy and the Construction of Racial Identity." *Du Bois Review* 4(2): 42.

———. 2015. "On Participation: Individuals, Dynamic Categories, and the Context of Power." In *The Oxford Handbook of Americans Elections and Political Behavior*, edited by Jan E. Leighley. New York: Oxford University Press.

Kalla, Joshua L., and David E. Broockman. 2016. "Campaign Contributions Facilitate Access to Congressional Officials: A Randomized Field Experiment." *American Journal of Political Science* 60(3): 545–58.

Kam, Cindy D., and Carl L. Palmer. 2008. "Reconsidering the Effects of Education on Political Participation." *Journal of Politics* 70(3): 1–20.

Katz, Michael B. 2013. *The Underserving Poor: America's Enduring Confrontation with Poverty, Fully Updated and Revised*. Oxford: Oxford University Press.

Katznelson, Ira. 2006. *When Affirmative Action Was White: An Untold History of Racial Inequality in Twentieth-Century America*. New York: W. W. Norton.

Kaufmann, Karen M. 2003. "Cracks in the Rainbow: Group Commonality as a Basis for Latino and African-American Political Coalitions." *Political Research Quarterly* 56(2): 199–210.

Keyssar, Alexander. 2009. *The Right to Vote: The Contested History of Democracy in the United States*. New York: Basic Books.

Kibria, Nazli. 2002. *Becoming Asian American: Second-Generation Chinese and Korean American Identities*. Baltimore: Johns Hopkins University Press.

Kim, Min-Sun, and John E. Hunter. 1993a. "Attitude-Behavior Relations: A Meta-Analysis of Attitudinal Relevance and Topic." *Journal of Communication* 43(1): 101–42.

———. 1993b. "Relationships among Attitudes, Behavioral Intentions, and Behavior: A Meta-Analysis of Past Research, Part 2." *Communication Research* 20(3): 331–64.

Kinder, Donald R., and Cindy D. Kam. 2010. *Us against Them: Ethnocentric Foundations of American Opinion*. Chicago: University of Chicago Press.

Kinder, Donald R., and Lynn M. Sanders. 1996. *Divided by Color: Racial Politics and Democratic Ideals*. Chicago: University of Chicago Press.

King, Martin Luther, Jr. 1992. "Letter from Birmingham Jail." *UC Davis Law Review* 26: 835.

Kingdon, John W. 1984. *Agendas, Alternatives, and Public Policies*. Boston: Little, Brown.

Kirkland, Patricia A., and Alexander Coppock. 2018. "Candidate Choice without Party Labels: New Insights from Conjoint Survey Experiments." *Political Behavior* 40: 571–91.

Kirkpatrick, Lee A. 1999. "Toward an Evolutionary Psychology of Religion and Personality." *Journal of Personality* 67(6): 921–52.

Kochhar, Rakesh, and Richard Fry. 2014. "Wealth Inequality Has Widened along Racial, Ethnic Lines since End of Great Recession." *Pew Research Center* 12(104): 121–45.

Korpi, Walter. 2006. "Power Resources and Employer-Centered Approaches in Explanations of Welfare States and Varieties of Capitalism: Protagonists, Consenters, and Antagonists." *World Politics* 58(2): 167–206.

Kretzmann, John, and John P. McKnight. 1996. "Asset-Based Community Development." *National Civic Review* 85(4): 23–29.

Larson, Jennifer M., and Janet I. Lewis. 2017. "Ethnic Networks." *American Journal of Political Science* 61(2): 350–64.

Latane, Bibb, and John M. Darley. 1968. "Group Inhibition of Bystander Intervention in Emergencies." *Journal of Personality and Social Psychology* 10(3): 215.

Lawler, Edward, Cecilia Ridgeway, and Barry Markovsky. 1993. "Structural Social Psychology and the Micro-Macro Problem." *Sociological Theory* 11(3): 268–90.

Leal, David L. 2002. "Political Participation by Latino Non-Citizens in the United States." *British Journal of Political Science* 32(2): 353–70.

Lee, Taeku. 2005. "Bringing Class, Ethnicity, and Nation Back to Race: The Color Lines in 2015." *Perspectives on Politics* 3(3): 557–61.

Leighley, Jan E., and Jonathan Nagler. 2013. *Who Votes Now? Demographics, Issues, Inequality, and Turnout in the United States*. Princeton, NJ: Princeton University Press.

Leighley, Jan E., and Arnold Vedlitz. 1999. "Race, Ethnicity, and Political Participation: Competing Models and Contrasting Explanations." *Journal of Politics* 61(4): 1092–1114.

Lenz, Gabriel S. 2013. *Follow the Leader? How Voters Respond to Politicians' Policies and Performance*. Chicago: University of Chicago Press.

Lerman, Amy E., and Vesla M. Weaver. 2014. *Arresting Citizenship: The Democratic Consequences of American Crime Control*. Chicago: University of Chicago Press.

Lichter, Daniel T., Michael J. Shanahan, and Erica L. Gardner. 2002. "Helping Others? The Effects of Childhood Poverty and Family Instability on Prosocial Behavior." *Youth and Society* 34(1): 89–119.

Lien, Pei-te, Christian Collet, Janelle Wong, and S. Ramakrishnan. 2001. "Asian Pacific-American Public Opinion and Political Participation." *PS: Political Science and Politics* 34(3): 625–30.

Lofquist, Daphne, Terry Lugaila, Martin O'Connell, and Sarah Feliz. 2012. "Households and Families: 2010." US Census Bureau.

Logan, John R. 2011. "Separate and Unequal: The Neighborhood Gap for Blacks, Hispanics and Asians in Metropolitan America." US2010 Project.

Logan, John R., Jacob Stowell, and Deirdre Oakley. 2002. "Choosing Segre-

gation: Racial Imbalance in American Public Schools, 1990–2000." Lewis
Mumford Center for Comparative Urban and Regional Research, University
of Albany.

Logan, John R., and Brian J. Stults. 2011. "The Persistence of Segregation in the
Metropolis: New Findings from the 2010 Census." US2010 Project.

Lopez, Linda, and Adrian D. Pantoja. 2004. "Beyond Black and White: General
Support for Race-Conscious Policies among African Americans, Latinos,
Asian Americans and Whites." *Political Research Quarterly* 57(4): 633–42.

Lopez, Mark Hugo, Jeffrey S. Passel, and Molly Rohal. 2015. "Modern Immigration Wave Brings 59 Million to the U.S., Driving Population Growth and
Change through 2065." Pew Research Center.

Luria, Gil, Ram A. Cnaan, and Amnon Boehm. 2014. "National Culture and Prosocial Behaviors." *Nonprofit and Voluntary Sector Quarterly* 44(5): 1041–65.

MacLeod, Mary Anne, and Akwugo Emejulu. 2014. "Neoliberalism with a
Community Face? A Critical Analysis of Asset-Based Community Development in Scotland." *Journal of Community Practice* 22(4): 430–50.

Madison, James. (1787) 2004. *The Federalist Papers*. New York: Pocket Books.

Mahoney, J. 2006. "A Tale of Two Cultures: Contrasting Quantitative and Qualitative Research." *Political Analysis* 14(3): 227–49.

Mansbridge, Jane J., ed. 1990. *Beyond Self-Interest*. Chicago: University of Chicago Press.

———. 1999. "Should Blacks Represent Blacks and Women Represent Women?
A Contingent 'Yes.'" *Journal of Politics* 61(3): 628–57.

Manson, Steven, Jonathan Schroeder, David Van Riper, and Steven Ruggles.
2018. "IPUMS National Historical Geographic Information System: Version 13.0 [Database]." Minneapolis: University of Minnesota. http://doi.org/
10.18128/D050.V13.0.

Manza, Jeff, and Christopher Uggen. 2002. "Democratic Contradictions: Political Consequences of Felon Disenfranchisement in the United States." *American Sociological Review* 67(December): 777–803.

Marsden, Peter V. 1987. "Core Discussion Networks of Americans." *American
Sociological Review* 52(1): 122–31.

Maslow, Abraham H. 1943. "A Theory of Human Motivation." *Psychological
Review* 50(4): 370–96.

Massey, Douglas S., and Nancy A. Denton. 1993. *American Apartheid: Segregation and the Making of the Underclass*. Cambridge, MA: Harvard University Press.

Masuoka, Natalie. 2006. "Together They Become One: Examining the Predictors of Panethnic Group Consciousness among Asian Americans and Latinos." *Social Science Quarterly* 87(5): 993–1011.

———. 2008. "Defining the Group: Latino Identity and Political Participation."
American Politics Research 36(1): 33–61.

Masuoka, Natalie, and Jane Junn. 2013. *The Politics of Belonging: Race, Public Opinion, and Immigration*. Chicago: University of Chicago Press.

Mathie, Alison, Jenny Cameron, and Katherine Gibson. 2017. "Asset-Based and Citizen-Led Development: Using a Diffracted Power Lens to Analyze the Possibilities and Challenges." *Progress in Development Studies* 17(1): 54–66.

Mayhew, David. 1974. *Congress: The Electoral Connection*. New Haven, CT: Yale University Press.

McAdam, Doug. 1988. *Freedom Summer*. New York: Oxford University Press.

McAdam, Doug, and Yang Su. 2002. "The War at Home: Antiwar Protests and Congressional Voting, 1965 to 1973." *American Sociological Review* 67(5): 696–721.

McClain, Paula D., Jessica D. Johnson Carew, Eugene Walton Jr., and Candis Watts Smith. 2009. "Group Membership, Group Identity, and Group Consciousness: Measures of Racial Identity in American Politics?" *Annual Review of Political Science* 12(1): 471–85.

McClendon, Gwyneth H. 2014. "Social Esteem and Participation in Contentious Politics: A Field Experiment at an LGBT Pride Rally." *American Journal of Political Science* 58(2): 279–90.

———. 2018. *Envy in Politics*. Princeton, NJ: Princeton University Press.

McDonald, Michael. 2018. "National General Election VEP Turnout Rates, 1789–Present." US Elections Project. http://www.electproject.org/national-1789-present.

McKenzie, Brian. 2004. "Religious Social Networks, Indirect Mobilization, and African-American Political Participation." *Political Research Quarterly* 57(4): 621–32.

McMahon, Susan D., Jamie Wernsman, and Anna L. Parnes. 2006. "Understanding Prosocial Behavior: The Impact of Empathy and Gender among African American Adolescents." *Journal of Adolescent Health* 39(1): 135–37.

McPherson, Miller, Lynn Smith-Lovin, and Matthew E. Brashears. 2006. "Social Isolation in America: Changes in Core Discussion Networks over Two Decades." *American Sociological Review* 71(June): 353–75.

McPherson, Miller, Lynn Smith-Lovin, and James M. Cook. 2001. "Birds of a Feather: Homophily in Social Networks." *Annual Review of Sociology* 27: 415–44.

Meeussen, Loes, Ellen Delvaux, and Karen Phalet. 2014. "Becoming a Group: Value Convergence and Emergent Work Group Identities." *British Journal of Social Psychology* 53(2): 235–48.

Mendelberg, Tali. 2001. *The Race Card: Campaign Strategy, Implicit Messages, and the Norm of Equality*. Princeton, NJ: Princeton University Press.

Michelson, Melissa R. 2006. "Mobilizing the Latino Youth Vote: Some Experimental Results." *Social Science Quarterly* 87(5): 1188–1206.

Michelson, Melissa R., and Jessica L. Lavariega Monforti. 2018. "Back in the

Shadows, Back in the Streets." *PS: Political Science and Politics* 51(2): 282–87.

Michener, Jamila. 2018. *Fragmented Democracy: Medicaid, Federalism, and Unequal Politics.* New York: Cambridge University Press.

Milgram, Stanley. 1963. "Behavioral Study of Obedience." *Journal of Abnormal and Social Psychology* 67(4): 371.

Monroe, Kristen Renwick. 1994. "A Fat Lady in a Corset: Altruism and Social Theory." *American Journal of Political Science* 38(4): 861–93.

———. 2013. *The Hand of Compassion: Portraits of Moral Choice during the Holocaust.* Princeton, NJ: Princeton University Press.

Mora, G. Cristina. 2014. *Making Hispanics: How Activists, Bureaucrats, and Media Constructed a New American.* Chicago: University of Chicago Press.

Mori, Deanna, Shelly Chaiken, and Patricia Pliner. 1987. "'Eating Lightly' and the Self-Presentation of Femininity." *Journal of Personality and Social Psychology* 53(4): 693–702.

Morris, Michael W., Ying-yi Hong, Chi-yue Chiu, and Zhi Liu. 2015. "Normology: Integrating Insights about Social Norms to Understand Cultural Dynamics." *Organizational Behavior and Human Decision Processes* 129: 1–13.

Morrison, Kimberly Rios, and Dale T. Miller. 2008. "Distinguishing between Silent and Vocal Minorities: Not All Deviants Feel Marginal." *Journal of Personality and Social Psychology* 94(5): 871–82.

Most Children Younger Than Age 1 Are Minorities. 2012. US Census Bureau.

Nie, Norman H., G. Bingham Powell Jr., and Kenneth Prewitt. 1969. "Social Structure and Political Participation: Developmental Relationships, Part I." *American Political Science Review* 63(2): 361–78.

Niemi, Richard G., Harold W. Stanley, and C. Lawrence Evans. 1984. "Age and Turnout among the Newly Enfranchised: Life Cycle versus Experience Effects." *European Journal of Political Research* 12(4): 371–86.

Ogunwole, Stella, Malcolm Drewery Jr., and Merarys Rios-Vargas. 2012. "The Population with a Bachelor's Degree or Higher by Race and Hispanic Origin: 2006–2010," pp. 1–8. US Census Bureau.

Oliner, Samuel, and Pearl Oliner. 1988. *The Altruistic Personality: Rescuers of Jews in Nazi Europe.* New York: Free Press.

Oliver, J. Eric. 2010. *The Paradoxes of Integration: Race, Neighborhood, and Civic Life in Multiethnic America.* Chicago: University of Chicago Press.

Olson, Mancur. 1965. *The Logic of Collective Action: Public Goods and the Theory of Groups.* Cambridge, MA: Harvard University Press.

Omi, Michael, and Howard Winant. 2014. *Racial Formation in the United States.* 3rd ed. New York: Routledge.

Osajima, Keith. 2005. "Asian Americans as the Model Minority: An Analysis of the Popular Press Image in the 1960s And 1980s." *Companion to Asian American Studies* 1(1): 215–25.

Owens, Michael Leo. 2014. "Ex-Felons' Organization-Based Political Work for Carceral Reforms." *Annals of the American Academy of Political and Social Science* 651(1): 256–65.

Paek, Hye Jin, and Hemant Shah. 2003. "Racial Ideology, Model Minorities, and the 'Not-So-Silent Partner': Stereotyping of Asian Americans in U.S. Magazine Advertising." *Howard Journal of Communications* 14(4): 225–43.

Page, Benjamin I., and Martin Gilens. 2017. *Democracy in America? What Has Gone Wrong and What We Can Do about It*. Chicago: University of Chicago Press.

Pager, Devah. 2003. "The Mark of a Criminal Record." *American Journal of Sociology* 108(5): 937–75.

Pager, Devah, and Hana Shepherd. 2008. "The Sociology of Discrimination: Racial Discrimination in Employment, Housing, Credit, and Consumer Markets." *Annual Review of Sociology* 34(1): 181–209.

Paluck, Elizabeth Levy, and Donald P. Green. 2009. "Deference, Dissent, and Dispute Resolution: An Experimental Intervention Using Mass Media to Change Norms and Behavior in Rwanda." *American Political Science Review* 103(4): 622–44.

Paluck, Elizabeth Levy, and Hana Shepherd. 2012. "The Salience of Social Referents: A Field Experiment on Collective Norms and Harassment Behavior in a School Social Network." *Journal of Personality and Social Psychology* 103(6): 899–915.

Panagopoulos, Costas. 2010. "Affect, Social Pressure and Prosocial Motivation: Field Experimental Evidence of the Mobilizing Effects of Pride, Shame and Publicizing Voting Behavior." *Political Behavior* 32(3): 369–86.

Pantoja, Adrian D., Cecilia Menjívar, and Lisa Magaña. 2008. "The Spring Marches of 2006: Latinos, Immigration, and Political Mobilization in the 21st Century." *American Behavioral Scientist* 52(4): 499–506.

Pantoja, Adrian D., Ricardo Ramirez, and Gary M. Segura. 2001. "Citizens by Choice, Voters by Necessity: Patterns in Political Mobilization by Naturalized Latinos." *Political Research Quarterly* 54(4): 729–50.

Passel, Jeffrey S., and D'Vera Cohn. 2018. "U.S. Unauthorized Immigrant Total Dips to Lowest Level in Decade." Pew Research Center. https://www.pewhispanic.org/2018/11/27/u-s-unauthorized-immigrant-total-dips-to-lowest-level-in-a-decade/.

Pateman, Carole. 1970. *Participation and Democratic Theory*. New York: Cambridge University Press.

Peffley, Mark, Jon Hurwitz, and Paul M. Sniderman. 1997. "Racial Stereotypes and Whites' Political Views of Blacks in the Context of Welfare and Crime." *American Journal of Political Science* 41(1): 30–60.

Penner, Louis A., John F. Dovidio, Jane A. Piliavin, and David A. Schroeder.

2005. "Prosocial Behavior: Multilevel Perspectives." *Annual Review of Psychology* 56(1): 365–92.

Pérez, Efrén O., Maggie Deichert, and Andrew M. Engelhardt. 2019. "E Pluribus Unum? How Ethnic and National Identity Motivate Individual Reactions to a Political Ideal." *Journal of Politics* 81(4): 1420–33.

Perkins, Wesley H., David W. Craig, and Jessica M. Perkins. 2011. "Using Social Norms to Reduce Bullying: A Research Intervention among Adolescents in Five Middle Schools." *Group Processes and Intergroup Relations* 14(5): 703–22.

Petersen, Michael Bang. 2011. "Social Welfare as Small-Scale Help: Evolutionary Psychology and the Deservingness Heuristic." *American Journal of Political Science* 56(1): 1–16.

Pettigrew, Thomas F. 1979. "The Ultimate Attribution Error: Extending Allport's Cognitive Analysis of Prejudice." *Personality and Social Psychology Bulletin* 5(4): 461–76.

Pettit, Becky. 2012. *Invisible Men: Mass Incarceration and the Myth of Black Progress.* New York: Russell Sage Foundation.

Philpot, Tasha S., and Hanes Walton Jr. 2014. *African-American Political Participation.* Vol. 1 of *The Oxford Handbook of Racial and Ethnic Politics in the United States*, edited by David L. Leal, Taeku Lee, and Mark Q. Sawyer. Oxford: Oxford University Press.

Piff, Paul K., Michael W. Kraus, Stéphane Côté, Bonnie Hayden Cheng, and Dacher Keltner. 2010. "Having Less, Giving More: The Influence of Social Class on Prosocial Behavior." *Journal of Personality and Social Psychology* 99(5): 771–84.

Piston, Spencer. 2018. *Class Attitudes in America: Sympathy for the Poor, Resentment of the Rich, and Political Implications.* New York: Cambridge University Press.

Popkin, Samuel L. 1995. "Information Shortcuts and the Reasoning Voter." In *Information, Participation, and Choice: An Economic Theory of Democracy in Perspective*, edited by Bernard Grofman, 17–35. Ann Arbor: University of Michigan Press.

Poppendieck, Janet. 1999. *Sweet Charity? Emergency Food and the End of Entitlement.* New York: Penguin.

Portes, Alejandro, and Rubén G. Rumbaut. 2001. *Legacies: The Story of the Immigrant Second Generation.* Berkeley: University of California Press.

———. 2006. *Immigrant America: A Portrait.* Berkeley: University of California Press.

Prewitt, Kenneth. 2013. *What Is "Your" Race? The Census and Our Flawed Efforts to Classify Americans.* Princeton, NJ: Princeton University Press.

The Public, the Political System and American Democracy. 2018. Pew Research Center.

Ramírez, Ricardo. 2013. *Mobilizing Opportunities: The Evolving Latino Electorate and the Future of American Politics.* Charlottesville: University of Virginia Press.

Ramírez, Ricardo, Romelia Solano, and Bryan Wilcox-Archuleta. 2018. "Selective Recruitment or Voter Neglect? Race, Place, and Voter Mobilization in 2016." *Journal of Race, Ethnicity and Politics* 3(1): 156–84.

Randall, Donna M., and James A. Wolff. 1994. "The Time Interval in the Intention-Behaviour Relationship: Meta-Analysis." *British Journal of Social Psychology* 33(4): 405–18.

Reardon, Sean F., and Ann Owens. 2017. "60 Years after Brown: Trends and Consequences of School Segregation." *Annual Review of Sociology* 40: 199–218.

Reardon, Sean F., John T. Yun, and Tamela McNulty Eitle. 2000. "The Changing Structure of School Segregation: Measurement and Evidence of Multiracial Metropolitan-Area School Segregation, 1989–1995." *Demography* 37(3): 351–64.

Reist, Burton. 2013. 2010 Census Planning Memoranda Series. Technical Report 211.

Ridgeway, Cecilia L., and Shelley J. Cornell. 2006. "Consensus and the Creation of Status Beliefs." *Social Forces* 85(1): 431–53.

Riker, William, and Peter Ordeshook. 1968. "A Theory of the Calculus of Voting." *American Political Science Review* 62(1): 25–42.

The Rise of Asian Americans. 2012. Pew Research Center.

Rochon, Thomas R. 1998. *Culture Moves: Ideas, Activism, and Changing Values.* Princeton, NJ: Princeton University Press.

Rodriguez, Clara E. 2000. *Changing Race: Latinos, the Census, and the History of Ethnicity in the United States.* New York: New York University Press.

Rosales, F. Arturo. 1997. *Chicano! The History of the Mexican American Civil Rights Movement.* Houston: Arte Publico.

Rosenstone, Steven J., and John Hansen. 1993. *Mobilization, Participation, and Democracy in America.* New York: Macmillan.

Ross, Lee D. 1977. "The Intuitive Psychologist and His Shortcomings: Distortions in the Attribution Process." *Advances in Experimental Social Psychology* 10: 173–220.

Ross, Lee D., Teresa M. Amabile, and Julia L. Steinmetz. 1977. "Social Roles, Social Control, and Biases in Social-Perception Processes." *Journal of Personality and Social Psychology* 35(7): 485.

Ross, Lee D., Mark Lepper, and Andrew Ward. 2010. "History of Social Psychology: Insights, Challenges, and Contributions to Theory and Application." *Handbook of Social Psychology* 1: 3–50.

Rubin, Donald B. 1974. "Estimating Causal Effects of Treatments in Randomized and Nonrandomized Studies." *Journal of Educational Psychology* 66(5): 688–701.

Ryan, Camille L., and Kurt Bauman. 2016. "Educational Attainment in the United States: 2015." Technical Report P20-578, Current Population Reports. Washington, DC: US Census Bureau/US Government Printing Office.

Salisbury, Robert. 1969. "An Exchange Theory of Interest Groups." *Midwest Journal of Political Science* 13(1): 1–32.

Saperstein, Aliya, and Andrew M. Penner. 2012. "Racial Fluidity and Inequality in the United States." *American Journal of Sociology* 118(3): 676–727.

Scheffler, H. W., Robert F. Gray, Edmund Leach, and Leonard Plotnicov. 1966. "Ancestor Worship in Anthropology; or, Observations on Descent and Descent Groups [and Comments and Reply]." *Current Anthropology* 7(5): 541–51.

Schenker, Nathaniel, and Jane F. Gentleman. 2001. "On Judging the Significance of Differences by Examining the Overlap between Confidence Intervals." *American Statistician* 55(3): 182–86.

Schwartz, Shalom H. 1977. "Normative Influence on Altruism." *Advances in Experimental Social Psychology* 10: 221–79.

———. 1992. "Universals in the Content and Structure of Values: Theoretical Advances and Empirical Tests in 20 Countries." *Advances in Experimental Social Psychology* 25: 1–65.

Semega, Jessica, Melissa Kollar, John Creamer, and Abinash Mohanty. 2019. "Income and Poverty in the United States: 2018." Technical Report P60-266. Current Population Reports. Washington, DC: US Census Bureau/US Government Printing Office.

Sen, Maya, and Omar Wasow. 2016. "Race as a Bundle of Sticks: Designs That Estimate Effects of Seemingly Immutable Characteristics." *Annual Review of Political Science* 19: 499–522.

Sheils, Dean. 1975. "Toward a Unified Theory of Ancestor Worship: A Cross-Cultural Study." *Social Forces* 54(2): 427–40.

Sherif, Muzafer. 1936. *The Psychology of Social Norms.* London: Harper and Brothers Publishers.

Sidanius, Jim, and Felicia Pratto. 1999. *Social Dominance: An Intergroup Theory of Social Hierarchy and Oppression.* Cambridge: Cambridge University Press.

Sides, John, Eric Schickler, and Jack Citrin. 2008. "If Everyone Had Voted, Would Bubba and Dubya Have Won?" *Presidential Studies Quarterly* 38(3): 521–39.

Sides, John, Michael Tesler, and Lynn Vavreck. 2018. *Identity Crisis: The 2016 Presidential Campaign and the Battle for the Meaning of America.* Princeton, NJ: Princeton University Press.

Silver, Brian, Barbara Anderson, and Paul Abramson. 1986. "Who Overreports Voting?" *American Political Science Review* 80(2): 613–24.

Sinclair, Betsy. 2012. *The Social Citizen: Peer Networks and Political Behavior.* Chicago: University of Chicago Press.

Sirin, Cigdem V., Nicholas A. Valentino, and José D. Villalobos. 2016a. "Group Empathy Theory: The Effect of Group Empathy on US Intergroup Attitudes and Behavior in the Context of Immigration Threats." *Journal of Politics* 78(3): 893–908.

———. 2016b. "The Social Causes and Political Consequences of Group Empathy." *Political Psychology* 38(3): 427–48.

Smith, Candis Watts. 2014a. *Black Mosaic: The Politics of Black Pan-Ethnic Diversity.* New York: New York University Press.

———. 2014b. "Shifting from Structural to Individual Attributions of Black Disadvantage: Age, Period, and Cohort Effects on Black Explanations of Racial Disparities." *Journal of Black Studies* 45(5): 432–52.

Snowden, Lonnie, and Genevieve Graaf. 2019. "The 'Undeserving Poor,' Racial Bias, and Medicaid Coverage of African Americans." *Journal of Black Psychology* 45(3): 130–42.

Snyder, Mark, and Julie A. Haugen. 1994. "Why Does Behavioral Confirmation Occur? A Functional Perspective on the Role of the Perceiver." *Journal of Experimental Social Psychology* 30(3): 218–46.

Soss, Joe. 2002. *Unwanted Claims: The Politics of Participation in the US Welfare System.* Ann Arbor: University of Michigan Press.

Steadman, Lyle B., Craig T. Palmer, and Christopher F. Tilley. 1996. "The Universality of Ancestor Worship." *Ethnology* 35(1): 63–76.

Stephens, John D. 1979. *The Transition from Capitalism to Socialism.* London: Macmillan.

Tajfel, Henri, and John Turner. 1986. "The Social Identity Theory of Behavior." In *Psychology of Intergroup Relations*, edited by Stephen Worchel and William G. Austin, 7–24. Chicago: Nelson Hall.

Takaki, Ronald. 2008. *A Different Mirror: A History of Multicultural America.* Rev. ed. New York: Back Bay Books.

Tam Cho, Wendy K. 1999. "Naturalization, Socialization, Participation: Immigrants and (Non-)Voting." *Journal of Politics* 61(4): 1140–55.

Tankard, Margaret E., and Elizabeth Levy Paluck. 2015. "Norm Perception as a Vehicle for Social Change." *Social Issues and Policy Review* 10(1): 181–211.

Tavernise, Sabrina. 2012. "Whites Account for Under Half of Births in U.S." *New York Times*, May 17.

Tesler, Michael. 2013. "The Return of Old-Fashioned Racism to White Americans' Partisan Preferences in the Early Obama Era." *Journal of Politics* 75(1): 110–23.

Theiss-Morse, Elizabeth. 2009. *Who Counts as an American? The Boundaries of National Identity.* New York: Cambridge University Press.

Thøgersen, John. 2006. "Norms for Environmentally Responsible Behaviour: An Extended Taxonomy." *Journal of Environmental Psychology* 26(4): 247–61.

Tindall, George Brown, and David E. Shi. 2004. *America: A Narrative History.* New York: W. W. Norton.

Tolbert, Caroline, and Daniel Smith. 2005. "The Educative Effects of Ballot Initiatives on Voter Turnout." *American Politics Research* 33(2): 283–309.

Trounstine, Jessica. 2018. *Segregation by Design: Local Politics and Inequality in American Cities.* New York: Cambridge University Press.

Tuan, Mia. 1998. *Forever Foreigners or Honorary Whites? The Asian Ethnic Experience Today.* New Brunswick, NJ: Rutgers University Press.

Tulloch, Carol. 2000. "'My Man, Let Me Pull Your Coat to Something': Malcolm X." In *Fashion Cultures: Theories, Explorations and Analysis*, edited by Stella Bruzzi and Pamela Church Gibson, 298–314. New York: Routledge.

Uhlaner, Carole J. 1986. "Political Participation, Rational Actors, and Rationality: A New Approach." *Political Psychology* 7(3): 551–73.

Uhlaner, Carole J., Bruce E. Cain, and D. Roderick Kiewiet. 1989. "Political Participation of Ethnic Minorities in the 1980s." *Political Behavior* 11(3): 195–231.

US Census Bureau. 2012. "U.S. Census Bureau Projections Show a Slower Growing, Older, More Diverse Nation a Half Century from Now."

Velez, Yamil Ricardo, and Grace Wong. 2017. "Assessing Contextual Measurement Strategies." *Journal of Politics* 79(3): 1084–89.

Verba, Sidney, and Norman H. Nie. 1987. *Participation in America: Political Democracy and Social Equality.* Chicago: University of Chicago Press.

Verba, Sidney, Kay Lehman Schlozman, and Henry E. Brady. 1995. *Voice and Equality: Civic Voluntarism in American Politics.* Cambridge, MA: Harvard University Press.

Vollhardt, Johanna Ray. 2009. "Altruism Born of Suffering and Prosocial Behavior Following Adverse Life Events: A Review and Conceptualization." *Social Justice Research* 22(1): 53–97.

Walsh, Katherine Cramer. 2008. *Talking about Race: Community Dialogues and the Politics of Difference.* Chicago: University of Chicago Press.

Waters, Mary C. 1990. *Ethnic Options: Choosing Identities in America.* Berkeley: University of California Press.

———. 2009. *Black Identities: West Indian Immigrant Dreams and American Realities.* Cambridge, MA: Harvard University Press.

Waters, Mary C., and Philip Kasinitz. 2015. "The War on Crime and the War on Immigrants: Racial and Legal Exclusion in the Twenty-First-Century United States." In *Fear, Anxiety, and National Identity: Immigration and Belonging in North America and Western Europe*, edited by Nancy Foner and Patrick Simon, 115–43. New York: Russell Sage Foundation.

Waterston, Alisse. 2006. "Are Latinos Becoming 'White' Folk? And What That Still Says about Race in America." *Transforming Anthropology* 14(2): 133–50.

Weller, Nicholas, and Jane Junn. 2018. "Racial Identity and Voting: Conceptualizing White Identity in Spatial Terms." *Perspectives on Politics* 16(2): 436–48.

Western, Bruce. 2006. *Punishment and Inequality in America.* New York: Russell Sage Foundation.

Westfall, Jacob, Leaf Van Boven, John R. Chambers, and Charles M. Judd. 2015. "Perceiving Political Polarization in the United States." *Perspectives on Psychological Science* 10(2): 145–58.

Westphal, James D., and Michael K. Bednar. 2005. "Pluralistic Ignorance in Corporate Boards and Firms' Strategic Persistence in Response to Low Firm Performance." *Administrative Science Quarterly* 50(2): 262–98.

Wheaton, Sarah. 2013. "For First Time on Record, Black Voting Rate Outpaced Rate for Whites in 2012." *New York Times*, May 8.

White, Ismail K., and Chryl N. Laird. 2020. *Steadfast Democrats: How Social Forces Shape Black Political Behavior.* Princeton, NJ: Princeton University Press.

White, Ismail K., Chryl N. Laird, and Troy D. Allen. 2014. "Selling Out? The Politics of Navigating Conflicts between Racial Group Interest and Self-interest." *American Political Science Review* 108(4): 783–800.

Wilson, Edward O. 2000. *Sociobiology: The New Synthesis.* Cambridge, MA: Harvard University Press.

Wilson, William Julius. 2011. "The Declining Significance of Race: Revisited and Revised." *Daedalus* 140(2): 55–69.

———. 2012. *The Declining Significance of Race: Blacks and Changing American Institutions.* 3rd ed. Chicago: University of Chicago Press.

Wolfinger, Raymond E., and Steven J. Rosenstone. 1980. *Who Votes?* New Haven, CT: Yale University Press.

Wong, Cara J. 2010. *Boundaries of Obligation in American Politics: Geographic, National, and Racial Communities.* New York: Cambridge University Press.

Wong, Cara J., Jake Bowers, Tarah Williams, and Katherine Drake Simmons. 2012. "Bringing the Person Back In: Boundaries, Perceptions, and the Measurement of Racial Context." *Journal of Politics* 74(4): 1153–70.

Wong, Cara J., and Grace E. Cho. 2005. "Two-Headed Coins or Kandinskys: White Racial Identification." *Political Psychology* 26(5): 699–720.

Wong, Frieda, and Richard Halgin. 2006. "The 'Model Minority': Bane or Blessing for Asian Americans?" *Journal of Multicultural Counseling and Development* 34: 38–49.

Wong, Janelle S. 2008. *Democracy's Promise: Immigrants and American Civic Institutions*. Ann Arbor: University of Michigan Press.

Wong, Janelle S., S. Karthick Ramakrishnan, Taeku Lee, and Jane Junn. 2011. *Asian American Political Participation: Emerging Constituents and Their Political Identities*. New York: Russell Sage Foundation.

Wong, Paul, Chienping Faith Lai, Richard Nagasawa, and Tieming Lin. 1998. "Asian Americans as a Model Minority: Self-Perceptions and Perceptions by Other Racial Groups." *Sociological Perspectives* 41(1): 95–118.

Wright, Karen. 2001. "Generosity vs. Altruism: Philanthropy and Charity in the United States and United Kingdom." *Voluntas: International Journal of Voluntary and Nonprofit Organizations* 12(4): 399–416.

X, Malcolm, and Alex Haley. 1968. *The Autobiography of Malcolm X*. New York: Penguin.

Zimbardo, Philip G., Craig Haney, W. Curtis Banks, and David Jaffe. 1971. *Stanford Prison Experiment*. Stanford, CA: Zimbardo.

Zong, Jie, and Jeanne Batalova. 2016. "Asian Immigrants in the United States." Migration Policy Institute. https://www.migrationpolicy.org/article/asian -immigrants-united-states.

Zou, Linda X., and Sapna Cheryan. 2017. "Two Axes of Subordination: A New Model of Racial Position." *Journal of Personality and Social Psychology* 112(5): 696.

Zucker, Gail Sahar, and Bernard Weiner. 1993. "Conservatism and Perceptions of Poverty: An Attributional Analysis." *Journal of Applied Social Psychology* 23(12): 925–43.

Index

The letter *f* following a page number denotes a figure and the letter *t* denotes a table.

Made in the USA
Middletown, DE
26 April 2023

29500083R00148